THE POLITICS OF ARAB AUTHENTICITY

THE POLITICS OF ARAB AUTHENTICITY

CHALLENGES *to* POSTCOLONIAL THOUGHT

AHMAD AGBARIA

Columbia University Press
New York

Columbia University Press
Publishers Since 1893
New York   Chichester, West Sussex
cup.columbia.edu

Library of Congress Cataloging-in-Publication Data
Names: Agbaria, Ahmad, author.
Title: The politics of Arab authenticity : challenges to postcolonial thought / Ahmad Agbaria.
Description: New York : Columbia University Press, [2022] | Includes bibliographical references and index.
Identifiers: LCCN 2021053934 (print) | LCCN 2021053935 (ebook) | ISBN 9780231204941 (hardback) | ISBN 9780231204958 (trade paperback) | ISBN 9780231555760 (ebook)
Subjects: LCSH: Civilization, Arab—20th century. | Arab countries—Intellectual life—20th century.
Classification: LCC DS36.88 .A3845 2022 (print) | LCC DS36.88 (ebook) | DDC 909/.0974927—dc23/eng/20220314
LC record available at https://lccn.loc.gov/2021053934
LC ebook record available at https://lccn.loc.gov/2021053935

Cover design: Chang Jae Lee

CONTENTS

Preface and Acknowledgments *vii*

INTRODUCTION: VOICING THE PAST
1

I. FOUNDATIONS

1 THE EMERGENCE OF A NEW FIELD
31

2 THE GREAT CULTURAL WAR:
THE SOCIAL AND CONNECTED CRITICS
57

II. CURATORS

3 JABIRI AS A THINKER OF
(INTERNAL) DECOLONIZATION
89

4 RESTATING TURATH IN THE POSTCOLONIAL AGE
118

III. BACKLASH

5 THE MAKING OF A SOCIAL CRITIC: JURJ TARABISHI
147

6 A CRACK IN THE EDIFICE OF THE SOCIAL CRITIC: FROM THAWRAH TO NAHDA
183

CONCLUSION
209

Notes 221
Bibliography 247
Index 259

PREFACE AND ACKNOWLEDGMENTS

When I entered the historical guild in the fall of 2001, there were two pieces of prevailing wisdom about the Middle East and North Africa. The first assumption was that the so-called progressive world under the leadership of the United States faced looming attacks from Islamic groups based in the region. The second was that the Arabic-speaking world is held back by outdated traditions that impede its transition to democracy. The ambition to liberate these societies from the grip of past traditions soon became one of the most widely fostered articles of faith not only among scholars and foreign advisers but also among local intellectuals. While these assumptions did not hold up—at least not as they were supposed to—the arguments and debates they sparked increased my interest with regard to the intriguing ties that connect contemporary Arab peoples to their traditions and cultural inheritance.

The origins of this book lie in this curiosity about how and why some societies in the Global South—most notably Arab societies—find solutions to their current political paralysis and social fragmentation in their heritage. Though Arabs are not the only ex-colonized people whose past has captured the public imagination over the last few decades, they are, nevertheless, often singled out in the critique that blames them for letting past traditions guide them in the present. It is commonly argued that, instead of focusing on the future, Arab elites and intellectuals continue to take their cues and inspiration from the past—a focus that seems not only to derail but also to hamper all progress envisioned by local reformists and other future-looking individuals. No observer has given substance to this "politics of blame" better than Thomas Friedman, who has reiterated this line of reasoning on various occasions. "There are really two coalitions in the region today," he writes. "Those who want to let the future bury the past and those who want to let the past keep burying the future."[1]

As a Palestinian citizen who was born and raised in Israel, I have had to fend off similar taunts. If the Palestinian people would only get over their past, I have often been told, peace and amity between the two peoples would prevail. Alas, so long as the Palestinian people—like the rest of the Arab peoples in the Middle East and North Africa—hold on tightly to their traditions, the prospects for a new dawn in this part of the world are not promising. The disregard of the past and emphasis on the future is not unique to Israel, but has become a hallmark of the age we inhabit, a view that has informed the now ubiquitous perception that the past places a strain on the advancement and progress of humanity; as Andrew Sullivan writes, in America "the future is always more imperative than the past."[2] This contempt and indifference toward the past is what defines our modern age and sets us apart from our predecessors. Indeed, for the first time in the long evolution of human history, the past has gone from being regarded as a source of inspiration, a constant source of ideals, values, morals, and ethics, to a burden and a liability.

In many ex-colonized societies in the Global South, this negative conception of heritage as a burden resonated with a small yet significant group of anticolonial intellectuals and activists. The vast majority, however, continued to lead their lives according to traditions that gave meaning to their lives and endowed them with a deep sense of belonging. This discrepancy between the intellectual class that looked to the future with high expectations, on the one hand, and the rest of society that continued to adhere to past traditions, on the other, went along *almost* unnoticed. With the beginning of the postcolonial project in the

Middle East that came on the heels of the end of the colonial rule in 1945, the hostility toward the past and Arab heritage grew more pronounced. That project intended to achieve two major goals: first, to replace the old order, and, second, to create a new Arab subject who is free, autonomous, and liberated from the sway of the past. While the *rise* of this project forms one of the major axes through which Arab history was told, it is its *fall* that I am interested in exploring in this book. What comes in the wake of defeat and failure? How did the Arab intellectual conversation change in the wake of the collapse of the postcolonial project?

The ways in which defeats and failures inform human behavior and open up new avenues of thoughts are underrated within the historical guild. The tendency that unduly emphasizes how success and victories bring about change often almost overlooks the intellectual horizons and fresh thoughts that failures make possible. At the beginning of the 1970s, the defeat of the postcolonial project brought new thinking into being, informed by the desire for self-affirmation, for authentic living, along cultural norms bequeathed by earlier generations. With the implosion of postcolonial ambitions, everyone—young and old, urban and rural, educated and uneducated—appeared to rail against the emptiness of an age of materialism and social estrangement, and the promise of modernity heralded by the postcolonial project. In the Arabic-speaking world, these lamentations not only were articulated against the hypocrisy of the liberal-capitalist system; they also led to the realization that some modern ideas (e.g., secularism and individualism) and technologies had amplified the problems and challenges Arab societies faced rather than solved them.

In studying Arab political and intellectual debates over the last century, I have understood that I, too, was under the impression that the genuine ideas and tools provided by the modern age should be able to solve all of our problems, address our challenges, and ultimately save *us*. It never occurred to me that ideas that were invented in Europe and later exported to ex-colonial peoples would have a different effect. To acknowledge this implies that the same ideas that gave birth to European development and progress have similarly stunted development in other regions of the world. I owe this understanding to the recent scholarly contributions advanced by scholars including Wael Hallaq, Talal Asad, Saba Muhmood, Joan Scott, Pankaj Mishra, Samir Amin, Mahmood Mamdani, and David Scott. To read these authors' works is to rethink the ways in which history is told.

I am fortunate to have so many people to thank for their help and encouragement while I embarked on writing this work. It began with a dissertation at the University of Texas at Austin, where Yoav Di-Capua, Benjamin Brower, Tracie Matysik, and Mohammad Mohammad were my primary mentors. I thank Yoav Di-Capua for his comments, patience, and guidance over the years—not only for his persistence in reading and rereading my chapters but also for his spirit and humanity. Over the years I have come to know Yoav and his family, playing soccer with him every Saturday in Austin's sweltering heat. Yoav was both an academic adviser and a pleasant mentor and a friend whose indispensable help was essential to me in navigating the academic world.

I hope I have done justice to the insightful comments of Benjamin Brower, whose remarks and observations on earlier drafts of this work improved its arguments. Early on, Brower encouraged me to carry out research on Arab intellectuals, introducing me to the great tradition of European intellectual history. Lastly, I want to thank Mohammad Mohammad for teaching me how to be a Palestinian and a worldly scholar at the same time. To be close to him is to be close to the generation of the 1960s, who revolted against their parents, education, culture, and even religion.

I would also like to thank the following friends and scholars for their advice, conversation, and interest in my work: Seraj Assi, Lior Strenfield, Orit Bashkin, Mahmod El-Fkieki, Mardin Aminpour, Kamran Aghaie, Robert Cole, Hashem Alrifai, Mohammad Kabha, Javad Abedi, Kamran Asdar Ali, Mikiya Koyagi, Hina Azam, Dena Afrasiabi, and Itay Eisinger. The lengthy conversations on Arab intellectuals and political elites in the postcolonial world have forged enduring friendships and collaborations. It was through these little conversations that I began to rethink my ideas about the postcolonial project and its afterlives in the Arab world.

During these years, I was incredibly lucky to meet and interview Arab intellectuals and political activists in Amman, Paris, Jerusalem, and Princeton, New Jersey. Only a few months before he passed away, Jurj Tarabishi—one of the defeated heroes of this book—welcomed me into his apartment in Paris. The long walks and talks I had with him gave me a glimpse of the generation that he represented and defended. Sadiq Jalal al-Azm also was kind enough to share his thoughts, anxieties, and cultural concerns with me. I appreciate the time with these known and lesser-known Arab intellectuals and activists who fueled my passion and curiosity about the careers of intellectuals in the Global South.

This book has also benefited from a number of institutional scholarships and financial support. I'm thankful for the generous Fulbright fellowship that facilitated my postgraduate studies at UT-Austin, where the Department of History proved more generous and supportive than I could have expected. My special thanks go to Yoav Alon and the School of Historical Studies at Tel Aviv University that supported my research. Yoav Alon, a historian of Jordan, a great teacher, and a friend who guided me in my early career into the historical field, hosted me as a postdoctoral fellow during the two fruitful years 2019–2021.

At Tel Aviv University, I studied with Israel Gershoni, who was instrumental in clearing the way for my advancement. As a distinguished member in the field of Middle Eastern studies, Gershoni has influenced the way I came to think about local intellectuals and political activists in the Arabic-speaking world. Finally, I would like to thank my good fortune for providing me with pleasurable opportunity of working with Wendy K. Lochner and Lowell Frye at Columbia University Press. Wendy and Lowell stand out not only in their good judgment and efficiency but also in handling the process of publication in a proficient and always delightful manner.

Writing a book often times takes its toll on authors and their familial life. Over the past few years I have gained many intellectual capabilities but lost many others. The work in libraries and archives has eroded my social skills, turning me into a bad dancer. I want to thank my wife, Sundos Odeh, the one and only Sundos, who insists on teaching me how to dance. I want to thank my lovely children, Shafea, Rawd, and Amana, for believing in their dad and putting up with the time "wasted" on writing. Each time I look at you playing, I feel so proud to have you in my life—not only because you laugh at my jokes. This book is dedicated to you.

THE POLITICS OF ARAB AUTHENTICITY

INTRODUCTION

Voicing the Past

The grueling struggle of the Arab Writers Union in Syria to launch the journal *Majallat al-Turath al-Arabi* (Arab heritage) came to a fruitful end at long last when Syria's obstinate leader, President Hafiz al-Asad, finally relented and granted permission for its formation in 1979. The founding of this journal, the result of four years of sweat, determination, and perseverance, was surprising for a community of modernist writers that grew up denouncing its cultural heritage. It was hardly conceivable that a relatively progressive body of scholars that branded itself revolutionist and nationalist in character would establish a publication primarily focused on interrogating the Arab cultural inheritance. Hardly a decade had passed since the period during which the vast majority of Syrian intellectuals viewed the Arab past as a corpus of metaphysical thought rife with racial prejudices and thus not worth taking seriously.

The launching of such a publication would not only have been unthinkable during the 1950s and the "roaring 1960s," but the idea of *turath* (cultural heritage), which figured in the journal's title, also had little, if any, appeal at the time.[1] Few intellectuals entertained or courted this idea, much less explored its meaning. The extraordinary times of political activism, revolution, and decolonization that marked the early postindependence era (1945–1970s) turned attention away from turath and its concerns, focusing postcolonial writers' thought on the present and the future rather than the past. Yet, for Syrian writers in the late 1970s, political stalemate, social disintegration, and cultural crisis guaranteed a new look at turath. More than denoting a simple return to the past, turath formed an epistemological framework of reference linked to treatises on medieval Arab thought in the postcolonial era.[2] These include philosophy, Sufi literature and practices, law, grammar, linguistics, poetry, literature (*adab*), rhetoric (*balagha*), derivation (*ishtiqaq*), logic, medicine, mathematics and algebra, geometry, astronomy, music theory, geography, dialectics, psychology, politics, art, and ethics. This body of intellectual, political, cultural, and social texts frames the practices of contemporary Arab reasoning, providing cultural references and technologies of the self to act in the world. "It is from within this tradition of reasoning that claims are made and evaluated and are either rejected or accepted,"[3] as Samira Haj succinctly puts it. For many years, Syrian writers thought that the modern age offered a superior corpus of human knowledge that rendered these treatises obsolete. Yet that they came to reckon with these long-forgotten texts, deeming them a "repository of civilizational documents *and* . . . moral code," amounts to a radical shift in the way they came to see the world.[4]

For many years, the vast majority of Arab writers looked at Western civilization as the final form and norm of human existence. They came to stigmatize any engagement with their cultural heritage. "The West," as a fixed point relative to which others' histories developed, was deemed the only cultural referent to which many Arab intellectuals resorted. Indeed, in no other time had Arab nationalists, social critics, and revolutionaries' contempt and hostility toward turath been more salient than in the first three decades following World War II. In 1961, for instance, Adonis—a well-known Syrian poet and a progressive essayist—praised a colleague, Yusuf al-Khal, for successfully breaking the bonds imposed by previous frameworks, commending him as a writer who had "leapt over inherited boundaries, going beyond pastism."[5] This "eagerness to escape the constraints of history" was an imperative for many Arab writers and poets.[6] Like many other ex-colonized intellectuals in Asia and Africa, postcolonial Arab thinkers thought that their cultural heritage

80 percent of the Egyptian air force.[10] Fighting on three separate fronts against a tripartite Arab military coalition, Israel would dictate the terms of a cease-fire, ending the war. The key to Israel's success was a new military strategy that stressed speed, force, and surprise; Israel ripped through Arab armies' defenses by closely coordinating air power and mechanized ground forces. The war left millions of Arabs with a grim sense of shock and disbelief. How could a tiny nation score one of history's most stunning military victories at lightning speed? The mere thought of a meager three million Israelis overwhelming a forty-million-strong nation of Arabs sent a chilling message across the Arab world. Arab intellectuals and political activists could not help but question the very core principles and ideals that held their societies together.[11] This event marked the beginning of the end of the postcolonial project in the Middle East.

Ironically, in the intervening years between the end of World War II and 1967, the postcolonial world appeared to be a happy, optimistic, and dynamic place. Winds of political and social change blew in the streets and cafés of the Middle East, and a spirit of experimentation and revolution took hold of the intellectual imagination. Poets spoke of revolutionizing the structure of Arabic poetry, the last relic of Arab medievalism. Politicians inaugurated new political visions, which were reflected in the Non-Aligned Movement. A new generation promised to destroy the established order and give rise to the "new Arab subject." Arab leaders like Nasser of Egypt and Algeria's first president, Ahmed Ben Belleh, played a crucial role in the formation of the high dreams and expectations of a worldly generation in the Global South. A flurry of political, legal, and social activity marked this time of intellectual fermentation and creativity, translation and engagement with philosophical vogues. Political activists and social intellectuals pushed for a decolonization that aimed not only at reimagining their recently decolonized societies, but also to transform world politics altogether. As Adom Getachew writes, decolonization in the 1950s was not "limited to securing independence from the colonial master"; the decolonization movement overseen by the social intellectuals had a much larger agenda, to "overcome the background conditions of unequal integration and international hierarchy that facilitated domination."[12] Getachew goes so far as to consider decolonization "a project of reordering the world that sought to create a domination-free and egalitarian international order."[13]

The joyous mood that coursed through Arab cities in the 1950s and 1960s drew the attention of Europeans. Leftist European intellectuals, shell-shocked from the legacies of World War II, looked south for inspiration. Perched on the northern rim of the Mediterranean Sea, they were bemused and bewildered by the scale of changes washing over the ex-colonized world. The new societies that emerged in the wake of the war, administered by an activist generation, instigated a host of European philosophers—including Bertrand Russell, Albert Camus, Jean-Paul Sartre, and Simone de Beauvoir—to address the unfolding change in the Global South; they would establish close relations with their Arab interlocutors, write letters to Arab readers, answer inquiries, and even pay visits to the Arab world. Michel Foucault would spend a year in Tunisia. As one historian has recently written, "It would indeed be difficult to find another cross-cultural moment more intimate, intense, and hopeful than this one."[14]

By the 1970s, however, all of that was fading into memory. In the wake of the defeat in the Arab-Israeli War, Arab intellectuals' glee over the end of colonial rule proved ephemeral. The postcolonial state that emerged in the aftermath of World War II would soon encounter grave challenges and social quandaries that would sully its image in the eyes of its citizens and erode its legitimacy. Long before the devastating war in 1967, the postcolonial project had been faltering. Bloody coups, political setbacks, humiliating civil wars, and economic slowdown would derail its ambitions. Before long, newly decolonized Arab peoples would realize that their nation-states were subject to the same frailties, faults, and forces of gravity as any other country in the world.

More than the defeat—which soon took the name *naksa* (setback) in Arabic—had exposed the cracks running deep in the state as well as its mismanagement, revealing the simmering problems that derailed the Arab revolutionary agenda, which had informed the early years of the postcolonial era. The optimism, the totalizing agenda of social change, and the political expectations for reordering Arab society and redefining international relations were real but improbable ambitions. Arab activists' dream of reordering the world and remaking the Arab subject fell to pieces well before 1967. However, this defeat meant more than the end of Arabs' exuberance and hope.[15] It pronounced the beginning of a new chapter of decolonization marked by Arabs' quest for an authentic self in their lost history.

If the undeniable failure of the Arab armies to stave off the expansion of the Israeli army did not extinguish the extravagant hopes of revolutionary decolonization, one important event in the summer of 1965 signaled their end. In July 1965, a coup d'état in Algeria sent shock waves across the world, crushing the dreams of many revolutionists and social critics who had for long looked at this postcolonial state as the future of the world. For years Algeria's perseverance against the French colonial forces had been a source of inspiration to liberation movements, anarchists, European and American leftists, and revolutionaries in Latin America; no other country came as close as Algeria to giving form and meaning to the idea of Third Worldism in the context of the Cold War. As Jeffrey Byrne writes, "For those disillusioned with both the Western and Eastern examples, Algeria seemed set to fulfill the Third World's promise of a third way, a better way."[16] But that promise did not last long. On a sweltering July morning in 1965, the defense minister Houari Boumedienne staged a coup that deposed Algeria's revered president Ahmed Ben Bella, abruptly ending his political career and wrecking Algeria's reputation as a Third World project that had for so long provided hope and given "support and hospitality to a panoply of national liberation movements, guerrilla armies, and insurrectionary exiles."[17]

The Algerian coup did not extinguish the promise of the postcolonial project, but it did mark its frailty. And when it is viewed in line with other political coups in neighboring Arab countries, a new picture comes to the fore. As it were, the Algerian coup was pre-dated by bloodier coups and revolutions in Syria and Iraq in 1963 that forever soiled the agenda of political decolonization. The violent takeovers of "progressive" Baathists in Iraq (February 8, 1963) and soon after in Syria (March 8, 1963) were particularly brutal, leaving many young and radical activists bitter. In the wake of these convulsions, large numbers of eager intellectuals and political activists turned away from supporting the decolonized state, largely on account of what they saw as the new regimes' authoritarian slant. Still, nothing would be more shocking to a newly found class of concerned intellectuals and activists—the connected critics—as the realization that the postcolonial state followed the colonial state's policies, especially in its suspicion of local traditions.

The story of turath—the story of this book—begins with the defeat of the postcolonial project. It is born out of Arab states' policy of banishing and isolating local traditions, which would shake Arab intellectuals' fundamental faith in postcolonialism. Except for a dwindling group of Western-inspired fanatics, the consistent attempts to restrict and exclude past traditions in public life signaled to the swelling ranks of connected critics that the new state did not indeed depart from, but rather fell in line with, colonial policy. This loss of faith was constitutional to the cleavage among the ranks of Arab intellectuals. The connected critics, who initially believed that the act of political independence marked the end of colonialism, emerged misguided. Colonial legacy, they came to realize, was living on, shaping the minds of great many presumably decolonized thinkers. Nowhere was this profound sense of distress as vividly clear as in the 1970s, when talk about "neocolonialism" penetrated the cultural debate, a conversation that revealed not only the extend and scale of colonial legacy, but also, and most painfully, the cultural dependency and cultural imitation of the West. As Elizabeth Kassab writes, "The colonial legacy, the neocolonial constraints, and the disenchanting experience of postcolonial independent states compound greatly the complexities" of the question of human condition in the Arab world at this historical conjuncture.[18]

As this book aims to show, the disillusionment with the postcolonial project—which the new Arab state represented, with the support of elites, social intellectuals, and activists—propelled a significant contingent of connected critics to grapple with the question of turath, which signaled the early beginning of the age of authenticity. At the beginning of the 1970s, the connected critics began to comprehend the deeper dimension of their postcolonial ontology, which seemed to have dampened their revolutionary zeal. Belatedly, it dawned on them that while Arab states had achieved political independence, they had failed to fully decolonize the Arab subject from the authorities of Western culture, which exerted a great deal of power over him. These critics came to conclude that the postcolonial state that emerged in the aftermath of World War II and promised to usher in new social, economic, and political arrangements to end all injustices and correct the wrongs of colonialism left the Arab subject under the sway of Western culture. With the passing of Nasser in the fall of 1970, as the public passion for revolution began to subside, these connected critics began to grasp the ontological problem of cultural imitation and dependency that the postcolonial state left unaddressed. Central to this problem was the new realization that the state proved incapable of delivering the Arab subject from his enduring cultural servility and economic dependency on the West.

During the 1970s, the dependency theory, propagated by Egyptian economist Samir Amin and other ex-colonialist theorists from Latin America, captured the full scope of this reliance on outside powers. In a series of books that made their way to Arabic readers, Amin unmasked the myth that the decolonized Arab world would in due course achieve parity with the First World.[19] Focusing his analysis on the economy, his ideas of the center-periphery polarization, the globalization of capital, and underdevelopment struck a chord with connected critics in Morocco, Tunisia, and other places in the Arab world. Amin writes that "all peoples and nations of the peripheries have not only been subjected to the fierce economic exploitation of imperialist capital, they have also, consequently, been subjected just as much to cultural aggression. The dignity of their cultures, languages, customs, and history has been denied with the greatest contempt."[20] Local connected critics, struck by the fact that they had become imitators, would appropriate and deploy Amin's idiom and vocabulary and demonstrate that the ontological problem in the postcolonial Arab world stemmed from this embedded dependency on outside authority, which forced the ex-colonized to lead inauthentic lives.

Inauthenticity in one's culture, values, and traditions emerged as the result of this cultural reliance on the West. Soon the new emphasis on authenticity became an antidote to all the social and cultural ills that bedeviled the postcolonial project. Understood as a refusal to submit and surrender to external authority, authenticity assured the postcolonial subject an end to his dependency on the West. In *A Secular Age*, the late Charles Taylor defines authenticity in the simplest way, writing that "each one of us has his/her own way of realizing our humanity, and that it is important to find and live out one's own, as against surrendering to conformity with a model imposed on us from outside, by society, or the previous generation, or religious or political authority."[21] This definition, which pits authenticity against conformity and pushes back against the surrender to outside models, is essential to the new conversation about authenticity that took hold of the Arab imagination in the 1970s; it emphasizes insubordination to religious and political authorities and helps us decode and make meaning of these debates.

THE AGE OF AUTHENTICITY

As this book shows, the feeling that the Arab subject is cast adrift, alienated and unmoored from cultural anchorage, has been the experience of the ex-colonized Arab peoples as they entered the modern age. This remarkable yet vague idea of modernity made a strong claim to emancipate people from arbitrary culture and traditions, liberate the human from established authorities, and give the individual unfettered and autonomous choice. Yet the widespread erosion of traditions and the dissolution of cultural authority further subordinated the Arab world and intensely aggravated its ontological crisis. Put simply, the (forced) incorporation of modern ideas in the Arabic-speaking world have intensified the feeling of cultural estrangement, which began during the nineteenth century, when the Arab world was separated from its heritage in order to become modern. Colonial modernity, under the supervision of colonialist empires, assumed that religion should be marginalized and past traditions suppressed to prepare the ground before the colonized people to embrace modernity. If modernity is defined by the exclusions it authorizes, then one of its hallmarks in the colonial setting was the insistence on excluding the authority of the Arab past and turath. As many historians and anthropologists have demonstrated, during the nineteenth century much of the moral ecology, social relations, and intellectual habitus that for centuries supported the Arab subject simply broke down and disappeared. No historian has defined that collapse of the Islamic habitus better than Wael B. Hallaq, who writes that "there is little doubt that the century that stretched between 1826 and 1923 witnessed the major structural demolition of Islam's institutions. . . . In this period, all economic, social, religious, legal, and educational structures were either significantly or totally destroyed."[22] The structural devastation that Hallaq describes consisted of more than just the disappearance of guilds and Sufi brotherhoods. Essential to these profound changes is what Hallaq calls the "epistemic rupture" with past Islamic societies: "The wave of institutional destruction inaugurated by colonialism," he writes, "culminated in an epistemic rupture—the rupture that literally annihilated the forms of knowledge Islam had known for the twelve preceding centuries (from roughly 650 to 1850)."[23] The extinction of the diverse and various forms of medieval knowledge—which Hallaq refers to elsewhere as "structural genocide"—is caused by the logic of colonial modernity and by modernist Ottoman administrators and military officers who uncritically embraced European modernity. These reformists "embarked on a course of reform unparalleled in the entire legal and educational history of Islam. . . . In this flurry of reform, a spate of Islamic laws and customary practices were rapidly replaced by European codes implemented by new European-style institutions and modes of operation. . . . The effect of these 'reforms' was not merely to displace the Sharīʿa and the 'traditional' institutions of Islam, nor was it just to secularize them; it was to create a new subject, one who would see the world through the lens of the modern state and the nation."[24]

The creation of the "new subject" who conceives "the world through the lens of the modern state" came fully into being only in the wake of the rise of the modern Arab state. The establishment of the sovereign Arab state entailed not only a sharp break with the past, but also the repudiation of turath. This rejection and suppression of the cultural heritage of turath—an epistemological framework of reference that for a long time undergirded the Muslim community and gave meaning to Islamic rules and governance—was the second constitutive act that fragmented the colonized subject and created what Kassab identifies as a "damaged self," an Arab subject who is "caught between a colonial past and a neocolonial present, between an external dependency and an internal social and political oppression."[25] This is how the new Arab state and the old policy of colonial modernity forged a modern Arab subject who was a rootless, alienated imitator—or, in a word, inauthentic.

As Hallaq, Talal Asad, and others have shown, colonial modernity had created a split self in the colonies. The very prescription of colonial modernity for the Arab subject to disown his past in order to be modern created the conditions of inauthenticity. Yet, as the colonized subject felt deprived of his cultural moorings, stripped of his heritage, he came to rethink his connections to his lost cultural inheritance as turath. Formerly, he did not need a past, nor did he think of turath as a separate category, "for the rhyme of life since [Prophet] Muhammad until the beginning of the last [i.e., nineteenth] century was symmetrical and analogical," as Mohammad Abed al-Jabiri writes. "There was no need to raise the question: how do we address turath? There had been no incidents in the life of the Arab-Muslim subject that forced him to feel that he is separated from 'turath.' His present was an extension to his past."[26] The tragic events of the nineteenth century, however, which had cruelly removed the Arab subject from his past, forcefully snatching him away from his cultural anchorage, created the context in which the colonized Arab subject came to refer to his suppressed heritage as *turath*.

The introduction of turath as a category of Arab thought during the nineteenth century to refer to cultural heritage did not turn it immediately into a flash point; on the contrary, it rarely drew adequate intellectual attention before the 1970s. This indifference toward turath, however, incited the rage of early twentieth-century scholars. In "Our Ancient Turath," the eminent essayist and editor Ahmad Amin (1886–1954) expresses his disbelief and surprise at the way his intellectual peers "mocked and despised old Arabic books." Amin published a series of articles in the respected Egyptian journal *al-Risalah* in which he marveled at the different ways Arab writers disclaimed turath; mystified, he wondered how these intellectuals could be more acquainted with the latest European theories while remaining completely uninformed of their turath. For Amin, the fact that Arab intellectuals "crave European books more than Arabic literature and Islamic philosophy" was abnormal.[27] Amin's articles fell almost on deaf ears; except for a few colleagues, his pleas with Arab intellectuals gained little attention. To his dismay, Arab intellectuals were more at home with modern dictionaries than with medieval ones, more comfortable reading Western literature than medieval adab. Yet Amin's call would not go unnoticed: the politics of despair, the defeated postcolonial project, the neocolonial reality, and the yearning for authentic sources of the self conspired together to redeem his call in the 1970s, when revolutionary decolonization emerged as incapable of guaranteeing true sovereignty and dignity to the Arab people.

The failure of the postcolonial project in the Third World is central to the making of the age of authenticity. It would deprive the newfound Arab nation-state of much of its remaining moral prestige. That phenomenon had allowed Arabs to make unprecedented strides; in its name they nationalized foreign companies, built bridges and dams, opened schools and universities, and established a social safety net for all citizens. It also provided the framework to order the new state. Within this framework new bureaucracy emerged, sporting facilities and national teams appeared, and new medicine was introduced to curb long-standing diseases that had for ages ravaged the Middle East. Not since or before the postcolonial era had Arab leaders been more assertive, respected, and venerated on the world stage. When Egyptian leader Gamal Abed al-Nasser spoke to his people, not only Egyptians crowded around radio sets, but political pundits, advisors, and officials in the White House and the Kremlin also listened attentively.

However, none of these achievements would withstand the cultural backlash of the 1970s. The search and hunger for one's own authentic self emerged as a new cultural need. All at once the legacy of political decolonization of the 1960s seemed to offer little guidance to intellectuals, who felt estranged from the new state and its apparatus. The postcolonial leaders who took power in the 1970s turned out to be as exploitative and corrupt as their colonial predecessors. They feigned democratic elections and concocted constitutions they never intended to follow. As Albert Memmi writes, "There has been a change of masters, but, like new leeches, the new ruling classes are often greedier than the old."[28] With intellectuals and activists losing faith in their revolution, the appeal of alternative modes of decolonization grew stronger.

The need for authenticity would not have been so strong if the early political decolonization model had been more accommodating to people's traditions, values, and culture. Unfortunately, the revolutionary agenda in the postcolonial project required a radical rupture with earlier styles of being and a complete break with past traditions. It showed little tolerance toward gradual change and reform. As Getachew argues, "Anticolonial nationalists refigured decolonization as a radical rupture-one that required a wholesale transformation of the colonized and a reconstitution of the international order."[29] But the insistence on a clean break with the past, which emerged in the wake of the epistemological rupture during the nineteenth century, amplified the search for authentic technologies of the self. The predominant feeling of the loss of cultural anchors made the ex-colonized vulnerable to external authority and established Europe as the model and all others as imitators. With this new diagnosis, which the defeat of the postcolonial project had so powerfully revealed, Arab intellectuals turned to their cultural heritage, believing authenticity to be the most probable solution to their ontological problem.

THE GREAT CULTURAL WAR: THE LONG STRUGGLE FOR THE ARAB'S SOUL

The primary goal of this book is to understand the nature of the intellectual conversation in the Arab world in the wake of the defeat of the postcolonial project. The book argues that the failure of this project gave birth to a fascinating engagement with turath, which in turn instigated a cultural war that restructured the Arab intellectual landascape. Why would Arab intellectuals resort to their turath in late modernity? Drawing on past historical experiences is all too human. As Hallaq writes,

> Just as the modern West drew and continues to draw on its last five centuries of experiences and traditions, on its Renaissance, Enlightenment, and liberal thought, Muslims nowadays are challenging this traditional narrative and are increasingly developing their own history—as a discursive moral practice—in such a way as to provide a source of their own . . . [it] mean(s) that Muslims still find in their history—just as the West finds in the Enlightenment—a resource on which they can capitalize while facing the challenges of the modern project, a project that has proved incapable of solving even those problems of its own making.[30]

In this quote Hallaq provides an essential point of entry to the study of turath and the ensuing cultural war. He rightly insists on the undeniable cultural demand of postcolonial Arabic speakers to restore their "own history," which could "provide a [moral] source of their own." It remains unclear, however, why Hallaq limits this yearning for "history" and "moral sources" to the Sharia, which constitutes merely one aspect—albeit a significant one—of the broader cultural repertoire of turath. Despite this reductive emphasis on the Sharia, which he conceives as the "central domain" in Islamic history, Hallaq's ideas are crucial to my arguments about turath. Hallaq calls upon students of this region to heed new investments in past traditions against the growing failures of the nation-state and modern epistemologies. That investment and reckoning with turath, I argue, led to the great cultural war among Arab writers and intellectuals, which is central to any understanding of the intellectual and public conversation in the Arabic-speaking world today.

When and where did this cultural war start? Long before the new guard of local intellectuals picked up on Amin's call and entertained the possibility that ideas from turath might still be available for critical appropriation in the present, tensions among Arab intellectuals had been brewing. The swift political changes in Lebanon (Lebanese Civil War,

1975–1989) and Egypt (the installation of a new president favored by Islamists) amplified these frictions, destabilizing Cairo and Beirut, where the most established class of Arab social critics and anticolonial nationalists took refuge. The fall of the social critics who clustered in Cairo and Beirut is a very important part of the cultural war; raised on historicism, these critics were extreme contextualists who believed that any idea taken from the distant past suffered the stigma of illegitimacy, since "any idea that is displaced from the unique context of its initial articulation can no longer be considered the same idea at all."[31] But the political events that swept through the Arab world demonstrated the tenuousness and vulnerability of these insights and intellectual presumptions. As we will see in chapter 1, the civil war that began in Beirut in 1975 chipped away at the class of social critics, substantially diminishing their visibility and symbolic capital. In their place a group of intellectuals would arise—the connected critics—by questioning the cultural assumptions of their predecessors. The emerging guard of connected critics like Jabiri would establish their intellectual careers and legitimacy by asking whether Arab nations were well served by embracing universal principles and teachings that stripped them of their authenticity. How could the postcolonial subject be authentic if he followed the European/modern prescription and cut ties with his past? The cultural dilemma of the question of turath that connected critics like Jabiri imposed on Arab readers made everyone aware of the dark side of modernity, which social critics and anticolonial nationalists in Cairo and Beirut heralded as a transformative catalyst for progress.

Yet propagating turath as the solution for the postcolonial condition provoked a backlash. Intellectuals in Cairo and Beirut, whose cultural capital had shrunk but not disappeared altogether, responded with significant questions: How could Arabs be modern if they ditched European prescriptions and drew only on their turath? Should the modern-day Arab subject choose to honor it and lock himself into deadening habits or routines? Rejecting the notion of turath as a binding framework of reference in modernity, they deemed it a hurdle on the road to true decolonization. Nowhere on the Arab intellectual horizon was there a solution to this problem. Indeed, many of the intellectual arrangements in the contemporary Arab world have been the result of a foundational question: Should turath as such ground modern Arab peoples, as it did individuals and cultures long ago, or are Arab peoples better off cutting ties with the past in order to make room for modernity? The three-decades-long exchange between the connected critic Mohammad Abed al-Jabiri and and the social critic Jurj Tarabishi captures this cultural war in its fullness.

MOHAMMAD ABED AL-JABIRI

In June 1970, Morocco celebrated the graduation of the first student in the country's history ever to be granted a PhD in the humanities. Mohammad Abed al-Jabiri (Moḥammad ʿĀbid al-Jābirī) was thirty-four years old when he defended his work in front of a committee of five professors. With his doctorate in philosophy, Jabiri would soon rise to national prominence in a postcolonial state longing for national pride, in a country that had for a long time suffered from French colonialism, afflicted with a legacy of cultural inferiority. Though a limited number of Moroccan students had previously attained doctoral degrees in France, Jabiri was different. Defying established protocols, he insisted on writing his dissertation in Arabic, signaling the rise of a generation eager to explore its lost, unwritten history. Jabiri surely gave evidence of that unspoken cultural ambition when he chose to write on Ibn Khaldun, an eminent medieval Arab philosopher of North African origins.[32]

Jabiri's dissertation would not have stirred much intellectual commotion had it not foreshadowed the profound change underway in Arab thought. It gave early expression to a growing emphasis that the rising generation of intellectuals placed on turath. Over the course of his lifetime, Jabiri positioned turath as an antidote to the agonies of colonialism. For Jabiri, only by connecting (*rabt*) the Arab self to an Arab heritage could one assure a sense of continuity. Connectivity, per Jabiri, amounts to an indispensable condition for nurturing a unified, authentic, and free Arab subject.

No book marked the beginning of the cultural war on turath as intensely as Jabiri's 1980 *Naḥnu wal-Turath* (The heritage and us). What set this work apart was Jabiri's appreciation of turath as a "primal" point of origin that affords enough leverage to call into question many of the givens of the present. In the small world of the Arab intellectual scene, where ideas like revolution, anti-imperialism, cultural change, Third Worldism, and political sovereignty dominated the landscape, Jabiri's writings on turath as a destabilizer of the status quo were abrupt and startling. Many postcolonial Arab nationalists and social critics hitherto believed that cultural change and social progress unfolded solely by following European prescriptions, and that the postcolonial world could catch up and achieve parity with Europe by imitating it. The mere possibility that changes could proceed from looking back to turath, rather than by copying Europe, was simply unimaginable.

In the discourse of Arab nationalists, turath was described in terms of darkness, confusion, and deception, a repository of thought that those aspiring to effect social and cultural change should abandon. Jabiri turned this entrenched understanding upside down: he proposed dispensing with the interpretation of turath as a source of social stagnation and conformity, religious prejudice, and ethnic antagonism. With the publication of *Naḥnu wal-Turath*, Jabiri placed the problem of turath front and center, giving rise to the scholarly persona of the connected critic—one who superseded historical rupture with historical continuity. The remarkable reception of this book, which inspired debate, dissent, and outrage, signaled the beginning of a new age in Arab thought.[33] It was thanks to Jabiri's many critics that he gained so much fame and prestige. Among them, no one stood out in his original insights and analytical depth more than Jurj Tarabishi.

JURJ TARABISHI

The other protagonist of this book is the social critic Jurj Tarabishi (Jūrj Ṭarābīshī), who spent the best part of his remarkable career pushing back against connected critics like Jabiri. A longtime liberal from Aleppo and a leftist in the mold of Salama Musa, Tarabishi launched his career at the early age of eighteen, writing articles and translating Western literature. He believed that Europe provides the model for other societies to follow, and that change unfolds through revolutions, not reforms. More interestingly, for young and radical social critics like Tarabishi, the postcolonial condition required the reading of Western theorists, since no revolution could proceed without a theoretical foundation and framework.[34] Assuming Europe to be the only source of theories, Tarabishi writes that "we were fully aware that we own no theory. The only available theory was the socialist theory." Like many of his progressive leftist colleagues, he thought that "the only possible revolutionary theory today is Marxism."[35]

In his writing and commentaries, Tarabishi epitomized the career of the social critic of the 1960s. He dismissed social hierarchies, mocked old traditions, rejected the social order, and despised religious beliefs. He drew only on Western epistemologies and avidly read the works of European philosophers. His theoretical world held no place for the past or turath. One of his guiding assumptions was that what had perished ought simply to be buried and forgotten; no value existed in exhuming traditions that had lost their bearing on the modern world. The intellectual class to which Tarabishi belonged thought it had to destroy the social order to create a new society. Indeed, Tarabishi admitted that Marxism was a great theory because it "has taught us how to destroy."[36] Ever since the defeat of the postcolonial project, Tarabishi adopted a grim view of the Arab world, and he would develop one of the most compelling narratives to unify its crumbling class of social critics and anticolonial nationalists. In his narrative, which historicized the descent of the Arab world and the retreat of an entire region from history to amnesia, he described a trajectory of a world derailed into insanity. Indeed, reading post-1970s Tarabishi is akin to reading a dreary story punctuated by fatal choices, like viewing a world in the midst of a free fall.

No other book has come as close to capturing Tarabishi's wrath as his unsubmitted dissertation, "Arab intellectuals and turath," which he finished writing in early 1988. Like Jabiri's dissertation, it was extraordinary. But instead of celebrating turath as containing important traditions that carry with them a repertoire of critical concepts that have been occluded, suppressed, or simply forgotten, Tarabishi's dissertation reviled turath, in the most condemning terms. His rejection of Arab intellectuals' obsession with it accelerated the cultural war that he had encouraged with his very writings. In the late 1990s, Tarabishi would go out of his way to salvage what remained from the class of social critics and establish the Arab Rationalist Association in Paris, the first anti-turath movement in Arab history. The founding of this association did not intend simply to bring Jabiri and other connected critics under fire, but also to assert that the solutions for much of the social and cultural woes of the postcolonial Arab societies lay in modernity, not in turath.

HISTORIOGRAPHY

Three historiographical issues stand at the center of this book: the cultural war between the social and connected critics, the advent of North Africa as a center of new Arab thought, and the discovery of turath that reimagined the role of the Arab intellectual.

The utter novelty of the cultural war—sparked by the question of turath—is too easily dismissed. It marked the birth of the connected critic: a scholarly persona that affords new analytical possibilities in the current historiography. In this sense, Jabiri's most important contribution was, in fact, that he formulated this new positionality, most remarkably in *Naḥnu wal-Turath* (The heritage and us). In this work Jabiri furnished new insights that ran counter to cultural conventions that unified postcolonial intellectuals. This can be seen from his title, which boldly posed a challenge to the prevailing intellectual assumptions and cultural expectations of the social critic, who thought ill of turath and past traditions. Previously, it was Constantin Zuriq's notable work *Naḥnu wal-Tārīkh* (The history and us), published in 1959, that captured the intellectual mood of the 1950s–1960s. Zuriq, a secular Syrian nationalist, articulated his generation's enchantment with modernity, nationalism, and reason, which he defined by its hostility toward turath. For Zuriq's generation, which was raised on the principles of "colonial humanism" expounded by writers like Taha Hussain and Salama Musa, the Arab version of modernity found its meaning in its contradistinction from and antagonism to turath. In *Naḥnu wal-Tārīkh*, Zuriq offered a firm expression of that mutual understanding as he grimly warned against making recourse to the past: "The most perilous undertaking [today] is to rely solely on the past [*naktafī bil-māḍī*], to succumb to its vestiges, to inherit its deformed characteristics like tribal solidarity [*ʿaṣabiya*] and quarrels."[37] At the beginning of 1970s, however, it was clear that Zuriq's cultural approach had grown outdated. The transition from the cultural assumptions and intellectual consensus represented by Zuriq to those of Jabiri lies at the center of this book.

Jabiri's ascent reflected a more pervasive and far-reaching trend than discrediting Zuriq's: the rise of the Maghreb. For years Mashreqi scholars like Zuriq and Tarabishi have been given the biggest platforms for interpreting culture. For many decades, the hubs of Arab thought were in the Mashreq (eastern Mediterranean), specifically in cities like Beirut, Cairo, Alexandria, Aleppo, and Damascus, where great intellectuals and award-winning writers clustered.[38] In practice this meant that the spaces in peer-reviewed journals, universities, translation movements, free poetry movements, and publishing industries where predominant ideas, debates, and national mythologies had been formulated were largely taken up by Mashreqi scholars. Rarely had Morocco's writers and intellectuals been seen as vital players in shaping the architecture of Arab intellectual thought. The same applied to other North African states like Algeria and Libya; Tunisia was exceptional in this regard. The Maghreb was persistently deemed by domineering Arab nationalists and social critics the intellectual backwater of the Arab world. Even when North African writers made substantial contributions to the making of the nineteenth century *nahda* (Arab awakening) literature, these contributions were made public via Cairo and Beirut. Indeed, it was in the Mashreq, rather than the Maghreb, where the literary ferment took place during the late nineteenth and the better part of the twentieth centuries.[39]

Leading historian Albert Hourani's classic work *Arab Thought in the Liberal Age* exemplified these trends. Hourani was early among those to authorize this division of Arab intellectual labor when he drew the first and most durable outline mapping major intellectual themes and questions that preoccupied Arab intellectuals. Hourni's focus on Mashreqi intellectuals was justified, since it reflected the spirit of the time. When he embarked on this work at the beginning of the 1960s, the intellectual disparity between the Mashreq and Maghreb was unmistakably pronounced. In the humming cities of the Mashreq, Arabic journals, new poetry, philosophies, and public and private presses appeared, while Morocco and other North African countries played only a marginal role in its making. As one Arab writer points out, "In 1965, the population of the Arab world was 110 million, which constituted %3.3 of the world population. In that same year, the entire Arab world produced close to 5000 books. Egypt, Syria and Lebanon [i.e., the Mashreq] produced 4186." The Maghreb produced way less, with "Morocco 180, Algeria 131, Tunisia 200."[40]

These distinctive historical trends are breathtaking, not because they exonerate Hournai's working assumptions, but because those assumptions no longer hold. In the wake of the 1970s, the Maghreb would catch up with and sometimes rival the Mashreq. North African intellectuals, either following Jabiri's lead or in opposition to him, gave rise to a new intellectual landscape that featured new interpretative approaches, cultural concerns, and intellectual questions that the Mashreq had excluded and made almost unthinkable. One of those questions was the long-standing question of turath.[41] But whenever the occasion forced Mashreqi intellectuals to address this question, they gave it short shrift, treating it as secondary and often parasitic to their main preoccupation with Western epistemologies.[42] Therefore, adhering to the scholarly norms that Hourani endorsed and consecrated—norms that for so long excluded North African scholars—rendered many new and genuine Arab voices silent.

This unconscious geography of the Arab intellectual landscape since the nahda, endorsed and authorized by the current historiography, was disrupted for the first time in the 1970s with the rise of a stratum of connected critics from the margins, especially Morocco.[43] The crucial role connected critics like Jabiri played in articulating the new intellectual concerns warrants a revision of the current historiography. The rise of the connected critic had not only moved the center of intellectual gravity westward toward Morocco, but also rendered this historiography that ignored the question of turath quite obsolete.

The failure to account for the debates that turath spurred in the post-1970s era had given rise to what I call the "stagnation model." According to this model, the Arab world is stagnant, and the Arab national-secular movement is dead, or, at best, on the rocks. Triumphant a half-century ago, when national regimes appeared to have prevailed definitively over the conservative and austere Islamists, the Arab national-secular movement is now under siege from within and from without. Plenty of works on contemporary Arab thought align, in one way or another, with this pessimistic model. Its logic lies in dividing twentieth-century Arab history into two major periods, each with its own distinctive ideologies and dominant epistemologies. In the first half of the twentieth century, a nationalist ideology dominated the intellectual field and shaped the public imagination. Islamic ideology, meanwhile, superseded it in the second half of the century.[44]

The historiography of the stagnation model views the war of 1967 as a tipping point where one ideology (leftist secular nationalism) gave way to another (Islamism or political Islam).[45] Many social, political, and cultural manifestations presumably affirmed its accuracy. The Islamist Revolution in Iran 1979 was seen as a "superevent" that this model seemed to have prophesied. Public piety, reflected in the increasing numbers of young Arab men growing beards and women covering their heads (hijab, niqab) and bodies, Islamic parties and charitable organizations, as well as the substantial increase in the number of mosques—all were seen as definitive marks of the stagnation model. The emphasis on Islam and on Islamists and their careers in the postcolonial condition, however, relegated the intense debates on turath to the background.[46] The mounting commentaries were haphazardly placed under the Islamic umbrella, viewed as no more than an interpretation of the Islamic corpus, one that flies under the radar of the stagnation model and its underlining assumption of the "return" to Islam.[47]

This stagnation model that centralizes modern secular logic is problematic. It accounts for all social or cultural phenomena as either religious or secular, while neglecting the large spaces—the unmarked domain—between these two poles. This secular-oriented scholarship unduly emphasizes the increase of veiled women in the Arab world, a phenomenon that is interpreted uncritically as a return to Islam. The veil, for example, was rarely referred to as a cultural symbol or an expression of Arab authenticity; that wearing it could represent the return to turath, or an expression of a society in search for authenticity, was almost unthinkable. Religious symbols in Europe were narrated differently. When the Grand Chamber of the European Court of Human Rights "ruled in 2001 . . . that the crucifix was a *cultural symbol* that represented the identity of 'Italian civilization' and its 'value system of liberty, equality, human dignity and religious toleration,'" very few asked why the veil continued to signal the return to Islam.[48] The Supreme Administrative Court in Italy, which took the case first, argued that "the crucifix did not have any religious connotation in Italy. Instead, it symbolized Italy's historical and cultural value, which may have had religious origins in the past but did not anymore."[49]

CHAPTERS OUTLINE

This book unfolds in three parts, each consisting of two chapters. At its heart lies a careful reconstruction of the intense rivalry between the Moroccan philosopher Mohammad Abed al-Jabiri and the Syrian critic Jurj Tarabishi. Since the beginning of the 1970s, few intellectuals have been more influential in shaping the Arab intellectual conversation on heritage and cultural inheritance than these two.

Chapter 1 explores the historical circumstances that gave rise to the angst around cultural heritage starting in the late 1960s and addresses a set of fundamental questions: Where did this conversation begin? What are the intellectual and social conditions that underlay (and fueled) a renewed preoccupation with cultural heritage? Who were its standard-bearers and major propagators? This chapter recounts three major moments that accelerated the trend toward turath: the mid-century rediscovery boom of the medieval Islamic canon in the fields of law, philosophy, poetry, and literature; the creation of the Center for Arab Unity Studies, which galvanized the rising strata of connected critics and presided over the conferences that endorsed turath as a central issue in the postcolonial condition; and the political context of the 1970s (most remarkably the civil war in Beirut), which ate away at the status of the intellectual guard that dominated Arab debates in the early postcolonial period. The conflation of these three episodes demonstrates how a coherent community of anticolonial nationalists was broken into pieces, giving way to the rise of a new class of scholars from the margins of the Arab world.

Chapter 2 reconstructs the ways that divergent cultural sensibilities informed the social and connected critics in their engagement with the turath in late modernity. Though these personae are idealistic types, they allow for a new understanding of how social critics and their rising opponents (connected critics) uphold disparate views, not only with regard to the shape of the past, but also to the challenges modern knowledge presents in non-Western spaces. This theoretical exercise charts a new trajectory in the making of the Arab intellectual, raising the question of what remains when we dispense with the modernist terminology of secular versus religious, left versus right, and traditional versus progressive. How have these dualities prevented us from seeing the full scope of the Arab intellectual conversation? Steering away from these binaries, this chapter examines two actors who offer distinctly different representations of turath. While the social critic borrows from Western frameworks, the connected critic takes his cues from Arab cultural heritage. These divergent perspectives led to the great cultural war in the Arabic-speaking world, a war that defines intellectual habitus, public sensibilities, and policy.

If every age has its defining major and minor characters, little doubt exists that the connected critic Mohammad Abed al-Jabiri counts among those intellectuals who crafted a new cultural positionality and articulated questions crucial to defining the boundaries of Arab heritage. Chapter 3 offers a comprehensive intellectual biography of Jabiri, examining his upbringing in a small and destitute town in southeast Morocco, his enrollment in the national movement, his education in national schools, and his early publications. Though Jabiri has been increasingly subjected to academic commentary in recent years, this chapter expands on this body of work by analyzing his "new vision" and examining the disruptive effect of his early work on Arab Marxists and other social critics in Beirut and Cairo. As an intellectual who was accused of being "modern," Jabiri emerges here more complex, and his writings are more nuanced, than previous scholarship has suggested. This chapter concludes by demonstrating that social and cultural change emerges from the introduction of new categories and taxonomies. Jabiri's famous taxonomy, though debatable, reintroduced cultural heritage as a field of research that affords a new cultural positionality from which to undercut the liberal order.

Chapter 4 centers around Jabiri's trenchant critique of Arab intellectuals for failing to acknowledge the influential power of past traditions and demonstrates how crises expose long-festering social problems and make starkly visible social hierarchies that had previously gone unseen. It is argued here that the defeat of the postcolonial project invited intellectuals not only to rethink the shortcomings of the postcolonial state, but also to assert the need for reclaiming a forgotten intellectual tradition. No Arab intellectual has been more willing to take on, question, and attack the social critic than Jabiri. Recounting how Jabiri deconstructed the project of the social critic, who dominated the intellectual field for a half-century, this chapter demonstrates how he advocated for the reactivation of the rationality of the forgotten Andalusian school and called on Arab scholars to de-Orientalize their Islamic philosophy. Ultimately, these two chapters establish Jabiri as a founder of the discourse on Arab cultural heritage.

Chapter 5 excavates the cultural and political conditions that went into the making of the social critic Jurj Tarabishi. It starts with a historical description of the political tumult in Syria, specifically in its early years after independence, which moved a previously apolitical young adult to develop nationalist and revolutionary views. Recounting the historical progression of Tarabishi's making from a family setting in Aleppo to an ideological education in Damascus and finally to cultural production in Beirut provides the intellectual trajectory of mid-century social critics like Tarabishi who took the national, existential, and ultimately Marxist path. Very few contemporary Arab intellectuals could rival Tarabishi's commitment to Western theories or his visceral disdain for Arab heritage.

Chapter 6 reconstructs the intellectual strategies Tarabishi and other social critics deployed to counter the rising star of connected critics like Jabiri. Starting with the radical displacements incurred by the Lebanese Civil War, the historical analysis presented here shows how Tarabishi's early writings held the transient promise to surpass the framework of the nineteenth-century Arab awakening, or nahda. Yet, as they began losing ground in the cultural war on heritage from the 1970s onward, they increasingly assumed a nahdawi agenda. This chapter recounts how Tarabishi stood up to his adversaries by demonstrating the merits of the nahda, the shortcomings of turath, and the collapse of the progressive Arab intelligentsia. Central to his counterassaults against the connected critics are the ways in which Tarabishi showed how Arab intellectuals yielded before the past. In his unique style of analysis, Tarabishi demonstrated how progressive Arab writers had retreated from their earlier commitment to secularism, democracy, and equality for women all in the name of a faked authenticity.

In sum, this book narrates the great, brutal culling of the defeat in 1967 and the ensuing loss and cultural disorientation that rippled through the postcolonial Arab world. Its primary aim is to explore the long process through which the preoccupation with cultural heritage took hold of the Arab intellectual and public imagination during the 1970s and the 1980s. The breakdown in norms and set of rules that for a long time had provided the frameworks through which Arab writers addressed social and cultural challenges ushered the Arab world into the age of authenticity.

I

FOUNDATIONS

1

THE EMERGENCE OF A NEW FIELD

Very few Arab authors could capture the shifting grounds in the Arab intellectual landscape as Zaki Najib Mahmud (1902–1993), Egyptian positivist and author of many philosophical works in Arabic. In 1971, Mahmud published his best-known work, *Tajdid al-Fikr al-Arabi* (Renewal of Arab thought), a book that combined biographical anecdotes with an expansive, structural interrogation of the status quo. Mahmud prefaced this work with a candidate note, writing in the third person singular:

> The author of these pages had no chance over the preceding years of his life to carefully read works from Arab *turath*. He is one among thousands of Arab intellectuals, who opened their eyes on European thought -classic and modern alike- that instilled the belief that it is the only possible human thought. This author upheld this attitude too and for many years: I studied European thought as a student, I taught European thought as a professor, I read European thought for fun in free time. The *turath*'s philosophers [*a'lām*] and schools of thought [*mathāhib*] did not come to me but as fragments and sporadic echoes, like leery ghosts popping up on my pages.[1]

Known for his eloquence and lucid style, Mahmud encapsulated in very few lines the main "absence" in the dominant modes of Arab thought before the 1970s. He professed that literature associated with turath went unrecognized by "thousands of Arab intellectuals" for many years. The same spirit of revelation, and perhaps shock, was reflected in searing testimony by Syrian writer and social critic Jurj Tarabishi (1939–2016), whose first foray in the study of turath came in the form of a personal confession. Tarabishi wrote, "I belong to a revolutionary generation that was preceded by two generations of the *nahḍa*, where we lived in a complete break with *al-turath*. Our mental structure [*dhihniya*] and thought were all directed toward modern Western ideologies, which [we] turned into sacred books-whether [these works were] Marxist, Nationalist, Socialist, or Unionist. We lived an absolute break [*qaṭīʿa kāmila*] with *al-turath* and viewed it [with disdain] as no more than *yellow* [cheap and unworthy] books."[2] The sense Mahmud and Tarabishi conveys is unmistakable: it captures a belated awareness of a new dimension of Arab reality that had previously escaped notice. Prior to the 1970s, many generations felt as if they had missed the opportunity to study their cultural heritage while investing only in European ideologies and theories. But the testimonies of these two authors communicates something broader than their choices and intellectual tastes and indexes what this book is trying to establish: the shift in cultural concerns that upended the intellectual hierarchy that had ordered Arab thought for many decades.

Interestingly, Mahmud and Tarabishi share the same intellectual sensibilities that animated Arab intellectuals for the best part of the twentieth century. They grew up within the relatively unified cultural climate of the Mashreq, which placed added value on the translation and adaptation of Western ideas. Like many Mashreqis, they firmly believed in the diffusion model that was dominant in the colonial period, certain that once the Arab adopted European ideas they would catch up with the West. Even if they belonged to different generations, young Tarabishi deemed Mahmud his teacher, and a sense of inexorable continuity structured the relations between the two.

As protagonists of the diffusion model, they gained notoriety for their translations of classic European literature and for being avid readers of Western thought. Mahmud translated important works such as Bertrand Russell's *History of Western Philosophy* in 1954 and John Dewey's *Logic:*

A Theory of Research in 1959. In collaboration with other late nahdawi scholars like Ahmad Amin (1886–1954), Mahmud was initiated into the intellectual field during the 1930s "liberal moment"of Egypt's history,[3] when Ahmad Amin and Ahmad Hassan al-Zayat—two luminaries of the Egyptian cultural milieu where Taha Hussain wrote his myth-shattering works—invited him to write monthly articles on modern philosophy and social theories in their journal, *Al-Risālah*. Later on, when Amin and Zayat established yet another important journal, *Al-Thaqāfa*, Mahmud was called upon to serve on its editorial board.

In 1967, the year the Arab armies melted down, Mahmud was working on a translation of Henry Taylor's *The Classical Heritage of The Middle Ages*.[4] This was an interesting juncture in Mahmud's life, after which he was no longer willing to translate. Abandoning translation meant, among other things, that he had come to a conclusion that the diffusion model has its limits.[5] In other words, expounding European philosophy to Arab readers, exposing the Arab readership community to new ideas, did not stir a social change as expected. This realization marked a profound turnover in Mahmud's career, especially when compared with the previous two decades, in which he had rendered to Arabic close to twenty philosophical works, including *The Myth of Metaphysics* (1953), *Theory of Knowledge* (1956), *Toward a Scientific Philosophy* (1959), and an intellectual biography of David Hume. Before the publication of *Tajdid al-Fikr al-Arabi* in 1971, Mahmud could not think except through Western theories, idioms, and vocabularies; even when he endeavored to write literary fiction, he would fall back on Western philosophical traditions, as a long list of his early novels attest: *Shakespeare* (1943), *The Paradise of the Fool* (1947), and *Sunshine from the West* (1950). The last work Mahmud translated in 1967 augured a new phase in his life, one marked by a disillusionment with the power of Western ideas to spark a progressive social movement in the East. Mahmud's new interests in turath literature, though personal and conditional, throws some light on the broader shifts and changes that stirred the ensuing generation.

Tarabishi trekked a parallel path. He launched his intellectual career as a political activist and translator of French philosophers like Jean-Paul Sartre and Albert Camus. In 1961, at the age of twenty-one, he completed his first translation of Simone de Beauvoir's *The Makings of an Intellectual Woman*. Tarabishi's translations were so well known that he was credited with introducing the Arab reader with many works by Marcuse, Hegel and Freud. Some Arab scholars estimated that Tarabishi had translated over one hundred books to Arabic in thirty years.[6] Not since the nahda has there been an Arab writer so fundamentally shaped by Western scholarship—in his life, perspectives, and outlook—as Jurj Tarabishi. Like Mahmud before him, Tarabishi was an ardent reader of Western literature, and "one of the most prolific and powerful thinkers of the second half of the twentieth century."[7] A recent Arab reader has argued that Tarabishi should not be seen as a regular reader and commentator of Western philosophy, but a "gallant defender" of Western epistemology in Arabic.[8]

Tarabishi was not only a preeminent translator of French and German authors, but also an intellectual who made some of Europe' authors and philosophers household names in Arabic. Yet, by the late 1980s, and against all expectations, Tarabishi would change direction and dip into turath studies, dedicating the rest of his career to reading treatises on the subject. In 1989, Tarabishi also decided to stop translating Western works, dedicating his time to the study of turath instead. Though he deemed the current penchant toward turath that "abdicated Arab thought from its original [nahdawi] track" as irrational, Tarabishi's writings nonetheless attest to the power of the new paradigm of Arab thought in the postcolonial age.[9]

Since the 1970s, Arab intellectuals and political activists have changed the way they appropriate and deploy their cultural repertoire, turath. Once seen in a negative light in these circles turath has increasingly gained in positive associations over the years. The negative connotations of turath, in its earliest usages, testify to its placement within national-centered discourses. If, before the 1970s, turath had been subsumed within national discourse as its antithesis, now the tables had turned: the national discourse became the negative "other" of turath. This chapter addresses the question of why turath was invisible for so many years. How does one explain the salience and (re)discovery of turath among a growing number of Arab intellectuals such as Mahmud and Tarabishi?

As the writings of Mahmud and Tarabishi amply demonstrate, Arab intellectuals and activists had begun organizing themselves around a new set of cultural themes and questions. Mahmud's revelation illustrates a moment in which these figures began bracing themselves to address new problematics that were inconceivable a mere decade earlier. The new intellectual groups that formed around and against the question of turath suggest that the declarations of a lethargic Arab intellectual scene were premature and unsubstantiated.[10] The unmapped polemics explored here for the first time provide yet more compelling evidence for revisiting the normative story of contemporary Arab thought; they point to an extraordinary, dynamic conversation among the progressive forces that, if fully investigated, defy these significations. In this I follow the "bold claim" made by historian Carool Kristen that "the most interesting developments are taking place on the progressive side of the spectrum, where thinkers contextualize the relevance of Islam's intellectual legacy for Muslims today through postmodern and postcolonial lenses."[11]

Admittedly, very few intellectual changes have been as groundbreaking in the field of contemporary Arab thought as the rediscovery of turath. Whether it was manifested as the epic collection of Arab historical books in law, theology, jurisdiction, literature and poems; collective and oral memory, old practices that seeped into the routines and rituals of modern Arab peoples; or a tradition of discursive styles of thinking reflected in the compendiums of Islamic history, the fascination with turath became a marked feature of the new intellectual and public debates in the last three decades of the twentieth century.[12] Almost instantly the cultural tide toward turath conferred a new identity on the Arab intellectual landscape. However, the fact that turath studies become so prominent a problem is not nearly as obvious; the decline of Marxism and the relative eclipse of nationalism and Arab socialism in the 1970s could in themselves have given rise to a variety of new intellectual fashions.

Where did this discussion begin? Who were its standard-bearers and major propagators? What are the intellectual and social conditions that underlay—and fueled—a renewed preoccupation with turath? How did turath come to bear on questions of politics, society, and even modernity? These questions entail a rather expansive look at the formulation of different events and figures who contributed in various ways in construing turath as either a problem or a solution in the postcolonial era. In what follows I examine the intellectual and social contexts in which turath gained traction and popularity.

THE SHIFT IN CULTURAL ATTITUDES

Historically speaking, the engagement with turath is not utterly new. The term *turath* appeared in the writings of the late nineteenth-century nahda writers, whose new editions and printings of classic Arabic manuscripts launched a new interest in Arabic classical writings.[13] The tense encounter with Europe—or what is now referred to as the Arab "rediscovery of Europe" during the nineteenth century—prompted Arab intellectuals to look into their cultural heritage.[14] While it is acceptable to think that during that period many medieval manuscripts and documents of turath slowly began to see the light for the first time, the vast majority of these manuscripts remained buried well into the twentieth century.[15] Interestingly, Western Orientalists played a crucial yet unacknowledged role that enacted a process by which Arab intellectuals discovered their own turath.[16] Not only did Orientalists take an active part in unearthing priceless scripts that made Arab history legible, but they also helped define the main contours of Arab history.[17] It was not until the late 1960s, however, that turath took on a new form and meaning, transforming from a mere intellectual *ihtimām* (interest) to a problem-space in the 1970s that bears on political and cultural problematics (*Ishkāliyya Thaqāfiyyah-Siyasiyyah*). How did this happen?

For a long time, the exclusive domain of the religious and quasi-religious scholars (*ʿulama*), turath was conceived primarily as a source for scholars of Arabic grammar, synthetics, poetry, and, above all, Islamic jurisprudence. Islamic institutes were seen by everyone—Islamists and nationalists alike—as the primary and natural sites for poring over the study of turath. Secular and nationalist intellectuals, on the other hand, rebuffed any engagement with it, viewing it as a hindrance on the secular path, or, as Mahmud succinctly put it, "a sign of backwardness."[18] The gap between secularists/ nationalists and religious men was almost unbridgeable, each focusing on his own territory, rarely sharing a common intellectual platform or agenda. Commenting on a specific case study in Saudi Arabia, Stéphane Lacroix observes that "'ulama and intellectuals simply were not speaking the same language. While the former dealt with medieval treatises on theology and law, the latter were promoting concepts such as 'modernity' (*hadatha*) and 'development' (*tanmiya*) unknown to their counterparts. As a result, no debate between the two groups was possible."[19]

Indeed, before the beginning of the 1970s, secularists/nationalists brushed turath aside, finding their calling in translating Western thought into Arabic. Yet translation entailed, as Marwa Elshakry demonstrates, a return—indeed a renewed interest—in turath. The translators of the first half of the twentieth century engaged in a "process of literally grafting new terms onto older ones."[20] But this interest in turath was limited in scope, especially when compared with the massive writings on the subject in the wake of the 1970s. Intellectuals in the first half of the twentieth century almost always kept turath only secondary, even subsidiary, to translation. Their vision was directed instead toward questions of modernity, or hadatha: how to assimilate modernity and instill modern ways into Arab societies.

In the early postcolonial era, this trend continued unabated. Postcolonial writers would attack their own newfound governments during the 1950s and 1960s—not on the grounds that these governments did not abide by past traditions, but for falling short of adopting modern and revolutionary ways of being.[21] The decades that followed World War II in the Arab world were, as Samir Amin observes, marked by modernity, an ideology that implied their investment in the *present* rather than the past: "Modernity is based on the principle that human beings, individually and collectively, make their own history, and to do that, they have the right to innovate and not respect tradition."[22] If national positivists and social critics made random incursion into examining their turath, they did so "without seeing the past as the necessary support of the present in any but a symbolic sense," writes Aziz al-Azmeh. "[They] tended to see historical continuities and the appeal to past glories as rather a burden upon the present, one from whose effects one needed to emancipate oneself—the past here is a substantive burden, and a [mere] symbolic incentive."[23] The most consequential question was not how to establish a continuity with Arab heritage, but how to eliminate and minimize the influences of past traditions. In this vein literature was conscripted in this effort to undermine the authority of the past in order to establish the political present. For political presentism to proceed, it seemed, one had to disavow his past. This postcolonial emphasis on what Tarabishi called an "epistemological break" with past traditions was understood by Arab writers as a universal principle, a necessary condition for all societies to emerge. It is unfortunate that so many Arab writers thought of the suppression of turath and other past traditions as a universal rather than "a particular relationship that the west developed with itself and with its own past."[24]

It is quite striking that the first postcolonial generation (1950–1970) assumed that the only avenue to achieve social progress, emergence, and revolution was through ignoring turath and its order altogether.[25] This is surprising, since earlier generations of the nahda thought to accommodate modern norms in (traditional) Arab societies. Late nahdawis like Taha Hussain, Abbas al-Aqad, and Tawfiq al-Hakim, among others, were in many ways genuine "modernists," yet less hostile toward turath; they did not precondition social progress and growth on the subjugation of traditions. In fact, at different stages in their careers, these late nahdawis willingly incorporated themes from turath in their writing.[26] Scholars like Butrus al-Bustani (1819–1883) turned to different chapters in the cultural history of Arab rationalist learning in the Abbasid Empire to substantiate his arguments with regard to the universality of rational thinking in the nineteenth century.[27] The postcolonial writers, on the other hand, rejected turath and subjected their elders to harsh critique for trying to wed together modern norms and traditional values. Samir Amin, for instance, argues that "the Nahda did not understand the modernity that made Europe powerful." He even critiques the early generation of Nahdawis for their failure to make the necessary break with the past: "The Nahda did not implement the necessary ruptures with tradition that define modernity."[28]

Was this hostile attitude the direct result of a century of socialization and cultural training—the spirit the nahda fostered and privileged? Or was it a departure from the nahda's core principles? It is hard to tell, because the nahda had given birth to both modernist and traditional paths that could substantiate either argument. Be that as it may, there is little doubt that the early postcolonial generation proved impatient with turath, fully adopting Western ideologies that articulated it negatively. This negative association came to a head after World War II, when turath came to signify a dark past that must be forgotten, old and entrenched habits that inhibit modern citizenry, superficial and timeworn styles of thinking, and metaphysical Islamic thoughts that prevented Arab societies from fully embracing new models of socialization. For the dominant class of social critics in the 1950s, turath made sectarian tensions pronounced and religious distinctions more visible. Turath, they argued, worked against the very idea of nationhood that strove to cancel out linguistic and ethnic differences among citizens; in its place, they wanted Western revolutionary ideologies to remake the "corrupted" social order. During the early years after independence (1945–1970), almost all the theories that commanded epistemological authority among Arab intellectuals and political activists—positivism, existentialism, Marxism, nationalism and socialism—called to dispense with turath and past traditions. These modern philosophies and ideologies helped to define a prevalent attitude toward turath, one that was particularly condescending. Put differently, these philosophies propounded the misguided assumption that modernity amounts to an autonomy that requires the shedding of any internal guardship. Since turath was conceived as a past authority that continued to exert power over people in the twentieth century, the cultural demand was to do away with it. National Arab intellectuals' resolution to steer clear of turath was not a diktat, but a common understanding of modernity that reflected the spirit of the time.

EMBRACING TURATH

In light of this aversion to turath, one might not expect many nationalists to come to terms with it. Yet this is precisely what transpired in the course of the 1970s, and even more intensely after the 1980s, when an increasing number of nationalists embraced the subject with original research questions and the development of full-fledged projects. This singular shift in themes and tropes signaled a rupture in Arab intellectual landscape that was marked by a substantial expansion of the field.

Many works published during the 1970s attest to this dramatic transition. The eminent Syrian poet Adonis, whose work engaged poetry from turath, is perhaps the best known, but by no means the only case in the Levant. Adonis's 1973 dissertation, *al-Thābit wal-Mutaḥaūil* (Continuity and change), was a bewildering tract in light of his previously celebrated radical writings, which rebelled against turath. Formerly, Adonis was part of the Shiʿr group, which took its clues from French poets like Charles Baudelaire. Translating Baudelaire to Arabic, Adonis took up many of the assumptions that guided the poet, who is notorious for disseminating radical modernist sensibilities, especially with regard to the new and novel. For the new to gain ground and footing, Baudelaire famously argued, the old and the outworn had to be swept away. As one historian points out, "In the nineteenth century such an attitude often implied outright destruction of the past. Especially in 'progressive' circles in Europe, demolition was the preferred mode of dealing with outdated survivals."[29] As Adonis translated Baudelaire to Arabic, his excitement about the values of the new and novel, on the one hand, and his wish to destroy the old, on the other, were clearly reflected in each of his pursuits. "Culture," Adonis writes, "symbolizes the rejection of what we have inherited and what has come down to us, and what has been written for us and about us."[30]

Yet that Adonis takes a detour into turath seems inconsistent, even incommensurate, with his revolutionary record, which he famously established in his radical journal, *Mawāqif*, started by him in 1968. This work perhaps rises to Freud's notion of a "literary event" that presaged a shift in the dynamics and tastes of Arab intellectuals. In *al-Thābit wal-Mutaḥaūil*, Adonis indeed resorts back to turath, subjecting to analysis the formative centuries of Islam to distill what he termed the "ethos" that governs poetic tastes in classic Arab culture. Though he concludes that turath valorizes an ethos of conformity and emphasizes continuity over creativity, his turn to turath was not expected.[31] Never before had Adonis been so interested in Arab heritage, especially in the light of his frequent calls to disrupt the social order.

In the same year in which Adonis published his work, Egyptian writer and committed materialist Ghali Shukri addressed the question of turath in his book *al-Turath wal-Thaūra* (Turath and revolution). With this title, once oxymoronical, even paradoxical, ideas of turath and revolution became compatible within mainstream intellectual discourse, and many Marxists and anticolonial nationalists followed suit, enhancing the same trend. Lebanese Marxist Husayn Muruwah was an exception, as he was among the first to engage turath from a Marxist-materialist perspective. As early as 1957 he published a book entitled *Kayfa Nafhamu al-Turath* (How to make sense of turath), which was remarkable in its exceptionalism. The title conveys how turath was conceived of as foreign to modern Arab peoples. When the vast majority of Arab intellectuals were obsessed with translated literature, Muruwah's work was an outlier.[32] Yet, in the 1970s, Muruwah would publish his major work on turath by seizing on materialist tools in his analysis of the formation of the first Islamic community. Three years before Muruwah's seminal 1978 work *Al-Nuzʿāt Al-Māddīyah Fī Al-Falsafah Al-ʿArabīyah Al-Islāmīyah*, preeminent Syrian Marxist Tayyib Tizini published his first volume (of twelve) in 1976, offering a materialist reading of turath.

Not only Marxists wrote on turath, but also avid liberals like Egyptian Naser Hamid Abu Zaid, as well as a long list of scholars.[33] The change in literary tastes and intellectual frameworks had never been more obvious.

With the beginning of the 1980s, the trend toward turath continued relentlessly, with genuine projects grappling with this problem of the past in the postcolonial age.[34] One Arab intellectual, Al-Hashimi Bashir, took note of the fact that Arab thought had been swept up by the question of turath. In the paper "On the Arab Book Market in the 1970s," he revised the newly installed intellectual trends, which he defined as "both lamentable and worrisome." The publication in the 1970s, he remarked, reflected a substantial "decline in creativity" (*hubūṭ al-Qīmah al-Ibdāʿiyyah*) that plagued Arab publications during this decade, as Beirut replaced Cairo as the epicenter of Arab scholarly publication. Hashimi maintained that "most of the books and publications during the seventies do not reflect new or substantial additions in terms of general cultural [knowledge]. But a digression on previously extant literature in one way or another. One can possibly argue," he concluded, "that even highly significant books and publications of this time are tied to *old themes* and expressed *past time conditions*."[35]

Hashimi viewed the new writings on turath as a dangerous "degradation" in the quality of Arab thought. Undoubtedly, this assessment is defined by a modernist metric and the fear that the past drowns out the future. The mere fact that Arab intellectuals launched a new interest in turath is denounced as digression. This modernist assumption, based on the misguided idea that if we fail to escape the past we are condemned to repeat it, has it that Arab writers should have cut their ties with the past rather than build new bridges to link to it. While baffled by the new intellectual trends of the 1970s, Hashimi's bewilderment rarely led him to offer an explanation beyond condemning the emerging Arab intellectual landscape. The question of why so many secular and anticolonial nationalists who previously denounced turath and antagonized any treatment of its literary corpuses wound up embracing it barely finds its resolution. Yet Hashimi's observations on the new trends in Arab thought remain valid and significant.

UNDEAD PAST: THE REDISCOVERY OF TURATH

It is commonly accepted that Arab intellectuals' recourse to turath came as an answer to a new reality of increased theology and piety. Many of them wanted to claim turath for their own "non-Islamist" projects. Less than a decade after the defeat in 1967, turath began to emerge as the new battleground for intellectuals both religious and nonreligious. Aziz al-Azmeh has argued recently that turath has become increasingly Islamic: "Having been previously characterised as Arab with Islamic elements . . . a shift of emphasis is perceptible from occupation with Arab traditions in literature, philosophy, and profane knowledge, to strikingly inexpert burrowing into works of Muslim exegesis, theology, and jurisprudence."[36] Indeed, the Islamization of Arab society triggered Arab intellectuals to study turath to redeem the Arab past from the hands of Islamic scholars. The new commitment to this study, however, after a long period of disregard, came to satisfy other needs, one of them being the understanding of the impossibility of making social progress without first dealing with turath. Another need is that the study of turath must not only signal the end of religious scholars' hold on the field, but also the formation of a new way of seeing the past. Simply put, this turn toward turath effected a genuine earthquake in the intellectual order and cultural hierarchy in the Arab world. With the creation of this field, new research possibilities came into being, not the least of which were the emergence of new conceptualizations of rationality and secularism, and, ultimately, the rise of new types of intellectuals, not only in the centers of Arab culture, but "from the historically marginalized regions of the Arab world."[37]

The (re)turn to turath did not only occur at the discursive level. Many social developments helped to sustain the cultural trend. To understand how Arab intellectuals grappled with the question of turath and how it gained currency and new urgency, I examine a constellation of political, social, and institutional considerations that galvanized the trend since the 1970s. Three developments in particular have combined to assert turath as a major framework that secularist/nationalist intellectuals could no longer afford to ignore: 1) the archival breakthrough, an intellectual enterprise that was taken up most earnestly by Egyptian writer Abed al-Rahman Badawi; 2) the institutional breakthrough, the rise of a publishing industry concerned with ideas of unity, nationalism, and authenticity that led to the emergence of a new stratum of intellectuals; and 3), the Lebanese Civil War, which led to the eclipse of the most bustling cultural hub of intellectual thought in the Arab world. The conflation of all these factors set the course for the advent of cultural dynamics that made the restitution of turath all but inevitable.

THE ARCHIVAL BREAKTHROUGH

Against all odds, it was progressive intellectuals rather than Islamist scholars who gave rise to turath as a field of study. Islamists continued to adhere to primarily one aspect of turath, *fiqh* (jurisprudence), while mindfully disregarding other significant aspects that seem to have impugned on fiqh's authority. Islamists wanted to recreate the past and failed to think of turath as a framework of reference. This insistence on rewinding the clock kept the field of turath limited and underdeveloped. The Egyptian publishing industry addressed this and played a vital role in establishing turath front and center. The new publications on turath have helped diversify the writings and outlook on otherwise little-known traditions and cultural practices. In particular, many credited eminent Egyptian writer Abed al-Ruhman Badawi (1917–2002) for overseeing a national project that aimed at editing and publishing different manuscripts. In *Naqd al-Turath*, Moroccan writer Abed al-Ilah Balqaziz attributes the inauguration of turath to the Egyptian philosopher Badawi, "one figure who stood out above all of his generation in bringing turath to the fore." In a highly dense and elaborative work, Balqaziz salutes Badawi for setting the course to the beginning of the formation of a field: "One man worked meticulously to match the work of an entire institution."[38]

Balqaziz offers one of the most comprehensive accounts yet of the emergence of and the growing engagement with turath in contemporary Arab thought. Although, he argues, turath as a "subject" appeared in the late nineteenth century, at the start of the 1960s turath studies began to establish itself as a "theme."[39] Even if writing on turath reaches back to the previous century, Balqaziz asserts, it was yet "unthinkable". Egyptian writer Badawi, whom Balqaziz singles out as a founder of the field, was a mid-century student of philosophy, an eminent graduate of Cairo University at a time when most of its faculty consisted of classical Orientalists. Badawi's two main professors were Taha Hussain and Ali Abed al-Raziq, the only two Arab faculty members in the early twentieth century.[40] Badawi dedicated his career to bring to light as many archival manuscripts as humanly possible. His editions bestowed on him much respect and popularity.[41]

Badawi applied a philological method to his research on turath that helped him in the editing, proofreading, and publishing of great texts hitherto unknown to many Arab writers. "Badawi was working like an Arab orientalist," Balqaziz writes. What Badawi indeed achieved was to demonstrate that only when one goes knee-deep in the manuscripts of turath, one begins to appreciate the effect of the lost, forgotten heritage of the Arab people. By mid-century, thanks to Egyptian publishers and Badawi's teams, it became increasingly clear that nineteenth-century knowledge of turath texts had been dwarfed by the greater discoveries of manuscripts unknown to previous generations. By mid-century, massive stores of still-buried material awaited the advent of scholars like Badawi. Not only did he bring to light unknown works by al-Ghazali, Ibn al-Nadim, and other significant writers from the Arab past, but he also wrote on topics no one dared to broach before him, such as his well-known work *The History of Atheism in Islam*. The number of classic books in Sufism, Kalam, medieval science, and Islamic arts excavated by Badawi are essential to the constitution of turath as both a framework of reference and a problem in the postcolonial era. Comparing Badawi's work with those of other eminent Egyptian scholars of the previous generation, Balqaziz gives the impression that turath as a field of study was "impossible" before the multiple volumes that Badawi helped edit and print.[42]

Historian Ahmad Khan, in examining the editing, printing, and publishing of medieval texts in the modern Islamic world, argues that "the rise of a new professional class of scholars-cum-editors had important implications for the reception of classical tradition in the modern world. Printing press, publishing houses and editors became embroiled in debates over the production of the premodern textual tradition."[43] Tunisian historian Abed al-Majid al-Sharafi affirms this conclusion in his book *Taḥdīth al-Fikr al-Islamī*: "The last thirty years has seen the publication of a significant number of primary sources, so that the reassessment process of the old jurisprudence became feasible only now."[44] Sharafi references many essential works that saw the light only in the second half of the twentieth century without which it would be almost impossible to understand turath; in particular, Sharafi points to "*al-Muʿtamad fi ʻUsūl al-fiqh for the Motazilite Abi Husayn al-Basri, ʻUsūl al-Sarkhasi, al Burhan* by Jouini, *al-Mankhul* by Ghazali, *Ahkam al-Fusul* by Baji, *Mizan al-ʻUsual* by Samarkundi, *al-Mahsul* by Razi, *al-Hasil wal-Mahsul* by Armaui, *al-Tamhid* by Kalwadhani, and probably the last source to be published was *al-Ibhaj fi sharh al-manahij* by Sabki. This list is by no means comprehensive."[45] These new publications of texts previously unaccessible to readers brought fresh insights of past Islamic traditions and cultural history that increased turath's symbolic value.

Badawi's outstanding work of exhuming, rescripting, and editing valuable turath texts (for which he wrote introductions) was not without flaws. One must keep in mind that, despite his herculean efforts, Badawi did not go beyond a preliminary survey and mapping of old texts. In his account, Balqaziz refrains from taking a critical approach toward Badawi by demonstrating how the process of printing of these texts was fraught with moral and ethical judgments. More important, Badawi doctored many of these turath texts, redacting, censoring, and selecting certain works over others. His editions were not immune to his "modernist" positionality and "ethical judgments," which oftentimes forced him to omit unbecoming texts that include "sexual contents" that he and his team deemed inappropriate or morally corrupt.[46]

Yet, the scale and magnitude of these texts forced a set of questions: What are to be done with these traditions that constitute part of the Arab self? Is it possible to continue to overlook these important breakthroughs in the field of turath? How do these newly explored textualities comport with the European texts that many Arab translators thought the only norm of the human condition in late modernity?

THE CENTER FOR ARAB UNITY STUDIES

The making of turath into a pressing cultural question began to loom large in the wake of the proliferation of new cultural institutions invested in seeking Arab authenticity and unity. At the forefront stands the Center for Arab Unity Studies (Markiz Dirasat al-Wihda al-ʿArabiyya), one of the most important cultural institutions the modern Arab world has ever known. The center was exceedingly important in propagating the urgency of the question of turath, defining it the "mother of all Arab affairs."[47] Presiding over dozens of conferences in the last three decades, a home to hundreds of intellectuals, the center has turned in the last few years into a dominant powerhouse for intellectual debates and intellectual exchanges.[48] It convened the first conference on turath in 1984, and, according to one scholar who has studied the intellectual and political impact of the center, "it is impossible to carry out any research on the Arab world today without resorting to the body of texts the center has produced over the past few years."[49]

With its establishment in March 1975, the political and economic landscape did not look very auspicious for its survival. Indeed, very few could have appreciated that the center (turned publishing house in 1981) would sway the intellectual conversation in the Arab world in new ways. Conceived during a precarious time of political tumult, pessimism, and loss of faith among Arab writers and intellectuals, it came into existence only a couple of months prior to the outbreak of the Lebanese Civil War, when sectarian tensions reached the point of explosion. Because many publishing houses shut their doors during the war while others had to cut down on the number of publications, hardly anyone could have estimated that the center would carry any cultural weight, much less to forge ahead in new directions. Yet the center's first feat was to survive amid turbulent times.

As its name implies, the Center for Arab Unity Studies was an immediate response to the fading idea of Pan-Arab nationalism. Instituted by nationalist intellectuals and publishers who came together to repel the onslaught on their ideology, the center's doctrines and principles were articulated against the death of Nasser, who held the banner of Arab nationalism for almost two decades. At its core the center was an intellectual endeavor to resuscitate the idea of Arab unity against the unfolding reality of increasing division and fragmentation among Arab states.[50] None of its founders, however, could have predicted that this institution would so grow in import as to bend Arab thought in the direction of turath. When the thirty-two authors, writers, publishers and translators convened in Beirut to declare its foundation, what they had in mind was to assert the vitality of Arab unity to fend off the political trends that had begun to override it. Bashir al-Daouk, the founder of Dar al-Taliah, was among the signatories. Suhayl Idris, the owner and founder of Dar al-Adab publishing house, also played a fundamental role in the logistics of creating the center. Yet these two publishers, who preferred "translated literature," were dominated by the members of the board, most prominently the two cofounders of the center: Khair al-Din Hasib and Saadun Hamadi. Indeed, Hamadi and Hasib were much more invested in the study of Arab history. Though they had an extensive working history with Dar al-Taliah and Dar al-Adab reaching back to the early 1950s, Hamadi made it clear that the center would primarily prioritize works on turath written by Arab scholars.

Within a few years of its establishment, especially after 1983, the center had become instrumental in steering debates toward turath. Though the idea of turath did not figure in its "outline and principles of the declaration," the center nevertheless took up turath due to the underlying ideology of its members. From its inception, the center was amenable to bringing to life the now-waning idea of Arab unity. Pioneered by what Shibley Talhami calls "new Arabism," which differs from Nasser's "Arabism of the 1950s and 1960s," this group focused on questions that transcended state boundaries and anchored Arabism in a shared cultural past.[51] Guided by this principle, the center gave priority to "original writing [read: authentic] over translations [read: Western ideas], and non-controversial issues over more sharply contentious issues."[52] This agenda, which pandered to the most basic common denominator, predestined the center's orientation toward turath.

Regardless of the fact that it has been overlooked by scholars, the creation of the center marks a highly important development in contemporary Arab thought. It published 770 books between 1981 and 2010—a staggering number in the market of Arabic books. With these publications, the center's epistemic influence over the new Arab intellectuals became palpable, especially in determining whose stories should be honored and disseminated and whose stories should be silent. Until 1975, only extraordinary writers steeped in theoretical knowledge were allowed to speak—specifically, knowledge of foreign languages and expertise in Western theories were the unspoken preconditions for gaining access to intellectual circles, or getting published by Dar al-Taliah and Dar al-Adab. The center challenged these unspoken rules, pushing back against the class of scholars who dominated the field of Arab thought (see chapter 2). In so doing, the center democratized the Arab intellectual field by diversifying the intellectual guard—hinting at a broader problem with the themes and intellectual tastes at hand. In other words, it is almost impossible to understand the ways in which the turath discourse was constituted without accounting for the institutions that undergirded this discourse.

Starting in 1979, the center held conferences that emphasized a curious change in the national identity of the attendees. The center's rank and file was increasingly staffed by a new type of intellectual who oriented this institution's publications toward their intellectual tastes. One of the most salient figures was Mohammad Abed al-Jabiri, who, to the center, became a cultural icon in the Arabic-speaking world, and whose original research on turath cannot be separated from the center—though Jabiri published his early work with Dar al-Taliah in Beirut, he soon republished all his works with the center—and the possibilities it opened up for him. The center's ambition to democratize the list of invitees to include speakers from the Arab Gulf and North Africa meant reversing the traditional Mashreq-centric tradition and including perspectives that had previously been excluded. Between 1979 and 2010, the center held

51 conferences and more than 130 seminars. To emphasize democratization and diversity, the center adopted a policy to convene these conferences in different Arab countries, partly to enact the principle of equality, inclusivity, and equal access for all, and partly to engage other cities that for long were overlooked as potential sites for intellectual debates. However, this policy was oftentimes undermined due to the refusal of certain Arab countries to host the annual conferences—notably, Syria. In 1983, for example, no Arab country was willing to host the conference on "The Crisis of Democracy in the Arab World." The organizers did not yield to this rejection, but carried their plans through and held the conference in Limassol, Cyprus.

The rise of the center affords a rare window through which to examine the ways in which turath percolated in Arab intellectual debates. By ideologically privileging authentic ideas over translated and "imported" ones, the center was poised to look back into Arab history for ideas that could be grafted into the new conditions of postcoloniality to sustain its march toward cultural renewal—an orientation that positioned the center to revive and invigorate the discourse around turath. Though the center was born with no particular identity outside of its concern with Arab unity and the angst over the faltering project of postcolonialism, its emphasis on turath gave it its true identity. In immersing itself in turath, the center gave rise to the coinage of new words: *Māḍawī* (pastness,) *al-la Tarikhiya* (ahistory), *al-laturathiya* (anti-heritage,) *al-Talfiqiyya* (communsurability), *al-Asrawiya* (contemporaneity,) *al-Wuthuqiyya* (certitude,) and *al-Taḥyidiya* (marginalization).[53]

In the fall of 1984, the center convened ninety-seven writers in Cairo for a three-day conference to discuss turath entitled "Heritage and the Challenges of the Age in the Arab Homeland."[54] Sayyid Yasin, the director of the Al-Ahram Center for Strategic Studies, launched the proceedings by emphasizing how turath grew to the most important question in the Arab world. "There is no doubt," Yasin told his audience, that turath "stands at the agenda's top end of the major concerns which preoccupy the thought of Arab intellectuals and ordinary people alike."[55] This conference was the first of its sort in which turath was consecrated as a major problem to reckon with beside democracy, Arab women and social justice, and political corruption. Still, what is striking about this conference in particular was its participants. There is little doubt that representation matters, because representation invokes questions such as who shapes the current narrative in the Arab world, and whether or not that narrative is neutral. With the new diversity emphasized by the center, the old guard of Mashreqi intellectuals saw their lot contracting.

Admitting new intellectual voices to the privileged circle of writers was a laudable act, many critics claimed, except that it took the form of a backlash against Mashreqi writers. For critical writers like Georges Corm, the center emphasized a "regressive inward turn towards Islamic identity as a means to better respond to external challenges."[56] Of the ninety-seven participants, the presence of Moroccan scholars was conspicuous. Remarkably, only four Syrians were invited: Tayyib Tizini, Aziz al-Azmeh, Riyad al-Rayis, and Mutaa Safadi. Only the first writer lived in Syria while the rest resided outside of Syria. Worse, of the fifteen conferences the center convened in its first eight years, none was held in Syria. In Arab politics, these numbers are not trifling matters.

THE LEBANESE CIVIL WAR

For many years Beirut was the unparalleled intellectual hub in the Arab world. No historian of modern Arab thought could afford ignoring this city and its entrenched intellectual class, press, and translation and poetry movements. The city of Beirut was not only a place, but a cultural sensibility. For emerging writers who wished to gain entry to its extensive publishing industry, Beirut was the place to start a career. Only with the beginning of the Lebanese Civil War in 1975, the structure and sensibility that Beirut had maintained for over a century began to crack, the repercussions of which went well beyond Lebanese politics, affecting the entire Arab world, as we shall see. The decline of Beirut, beginning in the mid-1970s, set a ripple effect that chipped away at the city's intellectual supremacy and, to some extent, opened up the intellectual field for the emergence of new voices.

The war had begun at a moment of growing consolidation and homogenization in Beirut's publishing industry. No one had anticipated the Lebanese Civil War to start, much less to persist for fifteen years. At the beginning of 1970, Philip Hitti celebrated the vigorous stability of his country of origin, comparing it to the inherently unstable Syria, which had "experienced no less than thirteen coups" since independence in 1943. Hitti wrote that "of all the Arab republics of the area, Lebanon has been the most stable."[57] Like many others, the outbreak of the civil war proved him swiftly wrong.

The war almost reached a conclusion as early as May 1976, one year after its outbreak, in April 1975, when the allied Palestinian-Leftist party gained the upper hand against "conservative" Christian parties. But that outcome went against the vested interests of an array of regional powers, not least of which was Syria, setting the stage for the fighting to resume.[58] Foreign countries attempted to mediate a ceasefire, to no avail. With the Arab League failing to contain the fighting parties in late 1976, the meddling of both the United States and France proved no more fruitful and may even have been devastating. In a historical perspective, the resignation of foreign countries left Lebanon all alone to face its predicament; the so-called open window of the Middle East slammed shut. Exhausted but determined, sectarian parties—Christians, Sunnis, Shiʿis, Druze, and Palestinians—proved impervious to international pressure. The unraveling of the state of Lebanon seemed all but inevitable as violence spun out of control. In the summer of 1984, nine years into the raging war, Lebanon took a dangerous turn, forcing many intellectuals to flee the Arab world for the first time in their lives. For many intellectuals who had found refuge and asylum in Beirut, the descent of Lebanon into medieval-style massacres was inconceivable. Beirut, the crown of Arab cities, the "Paris of the East," and the long-time commercial and educational nexus of Arabs, Jews, Armenians, Turks, and Iranians,[59] was practically carved up into "private fiefdoms."[60] The mounting violence dared many ordinary Lebanese to risk their families' lives as they set to cross the 138 miles that separated Beirut from Cyprus, the closest island off Lebanon's shores. When the civil war finally came to an end in 1989, with an estimated 120,000 fatalities, it left festering wounds.[61]

After the war, Lebanon showed little signs of resilience, and Beirut has never fully recovered. A fifteen-year period of pillaging, looting, and mutual killing took a toll on pluralist Lebanon that eventually led the country to surrender to sectarianism. The war shattered the hope for a better future for which this small country stood, wreaking havoc on the fragile business and intellectual class that set it apart in the region. Economically, the war dissuaded wealthy oil-producing Gulf states to continue bankrolling the national infrastructure projects already underway. The withdrawal of financial investment sent waves through Lebanon's shaky banking system, erasing Lebanon's economic edge as its stock tumbled. With Lebanon's global trade quickly deteriorating, its slowing economy sapped the intellectual infrastructure and institutions. As the war unfolded, many poets, journalists, academics, artists, sculptors, and scholars fled, further diminishing the already-reduced middle class. Lebanon offered an example of the high intellectual price the modern Arab world had to pay for sectarianism.

The assassination of Malcolm Kerr, the president of the American University of Beirut, was particularly ominous. Kerr, a Beirut-born American citizen, was a compassionate writer and a true sympathizer of the Arab world. One year before his assassination in 1984, as Israel overran Lebanon, the Syrian regime silently quelled the Islamic opposition in Hama, and the entire region stood on the verge of falling apart, he wrote, "For the time being, we must remain isolated from the conflicts of the country and the region. We can survive if we persuade everyone that A.U.B. is purely and simply a professional institution of good educational quality. Naturally, we sympathize with all the people of Lebanon and the Middle East on a human level, but we are not involved in any of their factional conflicts."[62] Kerr's attempt to insulate his institution was not successful. The war engulfed every corner of Lebanon, and Kerr's talk of inoculating higher education proved premature. He seems to have ignored his own insight, as expressed on the first page of his milestone book, *The Arab Cold War*, in 1965: "Arab politics have ceased to be fun."[63]

The grinding war in Lebanon not only eliminated Kerr, but also unleashed a process that by its end undid Beirut's role as the beating intellectual heart of the Arab world. The unmaking of the intellectual class in Beirut is perhaps the most important event in the history of Arab thought in recent decades; the 1970s was the last period in which more books were published in Beirut than in the entire Arab world put together. Describing the scene, one Arab commentator writes,

> It was a generation ago, in the mid-1980s, that a whole world slipped through the fingers of the Arab elite, formed on the secular ideals of nationalism and modernity. A city that had been their collective cultural home—Beirut—was lost to them. A political culture of nationalism that had nurtured them had led to a blind alley, and had been turned into a cover for despotism, a plaything of dictators. A theocratic temptation blew into the political world like a ferocious wind, and the secular Arabs were left thrashing about. Nothing today, no ship of sorrow can take these men and women of the secular tradition back to the verities of their world. A political inheritance has been lost.[64]

The war precipitated the dispersal of Lebanon's intellectuals far beyond Cyprus.[65] Distraught by the escalation of mutual sectarian manslaughter, especially the violence that breached the taboo on killing intellectuals, many of these scholars were looking for ways out of the beleaguered city.

No account of Arab thought can afford overlooking the fall and decline of Beirut, the traditional seat of Arab intellectual thought. The city's destruction sapped the vitality of the cultural institutions that for years had driven up intellectual productivity and wages. As Beirut shattered into pieces, the appeal of other stable regions (especially Tunisia and Morocco) increased, and an entire class of intellectuals dispersed with it. On the margins of the Arab world, scholars like Jabiri in Morocco emerged as the new challengers of the traditions fashioned by Beirut. Indeed, Beirut's eclipse demonstrates less how the project of Arab modernity veered off course than how the project of turath began to take shape. The very foundations that supported Beirut and its intellectual community were erased, and a more vigorous tradition rose to replace it. Without a historical appreciation of the decline of Beirut and the passing of its intellectual community, it would be hard to understand how turath emerged to govern the intellectual conversation in the wake of the 1970s.

Among those who risked their lives and fled war-torn Beirut was the Syrian writer and translator Jurj Tarabishi. For many years, Tarabishi waited patiently, holding on to hope that the end of this irrational bloodbath was around the corner. But in 1983, with his hopes of seeing the end of the war diminishing, he decided to leave Beirut and go to Paris like Adonis, Nizar Qabani, Amin Maalof, and hundreds of other intellectuals, to avoid the fate of Malcolm Kerr. Ironically, as he tendered his resignation letter to Bashir al-Daouk, the publisher and owner of Dar al-Taliah, where Tarabishi had been an editor, he was surprised to learn that his publisher had already left Beirut for Paris as well. This irony fully captures the tragic fate of Arab intellectuals in Beirut. The once-bustling publishing house turned off its lights as many of its translators and writers flee the country, seeking a safe refuge and a better future. It was in the wake of these tumultuous events that the question of turath began to emerge.

Ever since the beginning of the twentieth century, turath had come to be recognized as the source of a lost Arab authenticity. During this time period, turath transitioned from an almost unthinkable entity to a thinkable object in Arab intellectual debates. As this chapter demonstrates, the evolution of turath into a central framework in contemporary Arab thought captures the shifts in modes of Arab intellectual production in the postcolonial era. Starting with the massive archival works that Badawi represented in Egypt, the advent of the Center for Arab Unity Studies that increasingly sought Arab authenticity, and, finally, the eclipse of Beirut, the city that safeguarded and checked the slide backward toward turath, this chapter set out to empirically reconstruct the ways in which turath gained more ground in the republic of Arab letters. In the wake of the destruction of Beirut, the time was opportune for the coming of age of intellectuals from the margins, like Jabiri. The intellectual void that Beirut left pulled in a new guard who took issue with the question of turath. The combination of these factors reshaped intellectual sensibilities in the Arab world, sensibilities that drew much of their references from turath.

Turath should not only be understood as a limited conversation within the intellectual sphere, but also as a discourse that transformed daily practices. What cultural references were facilitated in the wake of turath? What sort of Arab *self* did this discourse fashion? To what kind of intellectual persona did this field of turath studies give rise? The following chapters attempt to answer these questions by examining the manner in which the discourse on turath redesigned intellectuals' lifestyle and ordinary conversations in the Arabic-speaking region. The overriding aim of this chapter was to show how the question of turath was consecrated as the Arab intellectual landscape grew more inclusive. As in politics, the democratization of the intellectual field led to intellectual polarization and, as we shall see in the following chapter, a cultural war between a rising guard of intellectuals who sought to voice their concerns with past traditions and those who felt that their cultural capital was shrinking.

2

THE GREAT CULTURAL WAR

The Social and Connected Critics

The advent of the problem of turath gave rise to a new breed of Arab intellectuals in the 1970s whose scholarly assumptions were at odds with many of the widespread intellectual orthodoxies of the 1950s and 1960s. The new intellectuals whom I call here "connected critics" embraced turath as a framework of reference—as a tradition that "engages a conception of truth, reason, and ethics different from those proposed by the traditions of the West."[1] More than the connected critic is concerned with European theories, he (usually a male) is keen to explore the intellectual potency of his own cultural heritage. While he is critical of the Islamic right or what is commonly known as political Islam, he is also discontented with the progressive Arab left, with whom he broke ranks. The ambition of the connected critic—especially in the wake of the defeat of the postcolonial project—was, and remains, to reclaim the study of heritage from Islamists, who considered themselves the only guardian of the Islamic canon. This newfound cultural orientation not only increased the friction with the Islamists, but also, and probably more important, with social critics, deepening the level of distrust among old friends.

This chapter aims to historically account for the connected critic as a product of the social formations that emerged in tandem with new regimes of power and new forms of governmentality in the postcolonial state. It will show that his emergence was a necessary result of the cultural disenchantment with the politics and sensibilities of the postcolonial project and the social critics of the 1950s and 1960s. The controversy over turath best captures how the ideas and perspectives promoted by the connected critic diverge with the rest of the intellectuals and political activists subsumed here under the designation "social critics." While the social critic firmly believed in the inevitability of emancipation from arbitrary cultural traditions and feared the authority of the past, the connected critic emphasized values of connectivity and continuity with the past. Put differently, if the social critic wished to disassemble cultural norms, traditions, and practices to set the ground for the rise of the new Arab subject, then the connected critic wished to connect to the heritage in order to create historical continuity. Rather than stressing the primacy of overcoming the ancient reliance upon cultural traditions, the connected critic regarded relationality with those traditions as foundational for the making of an authentic postcolonial subject. The differences between the social and connected critics have increasingly been at the forefront of Arab thought and political imagination since the 1970s.

Before the question of turath had been established at the center of Arab thought, the connected critic was a marginalized figure. He stood little ground against the two main adversaries who dominated the intellectual field: the Islamic scholar and the social critic. Despite the major ideological differences that separated the Islamist and the social critic, they shared the same rejection of reality. In their writings they deployed a total critique of Arab society. In the 1970s, however, three developments made it historically possible for the connected critic to claim and assert himself as a significant player: the decline of class analysis, which dealt a harsh blow to the social critic who drew on Marxism; a collective disenchantment with the state, especially in the wake of the defeat of the postcolonial project; and, lastly, the decline and breakdown of the nationalist agenda. These were not the only factors that facilitated the emergence of connected critics, but merely historical contingencies that helped create amenable cultural circumstances that laid the groundwork for his ascent.

Who is a connected critic? What mode(s) of critique does he deploy and privilege? What intellectual genealogies and historical sources does he draw upon? How did he come to impose his questions and presence on the Arab intellectual landscape in the post-1970s? For years, the connected critic was misconceived as a bridge builder, a centralist figure who occupied the unmarked terrain between the Islamist writer on the right and the revolutionist-socialist thinker on the left; more than a bridge builder, the connected critic functioned as a bridge destroyer, denouncing the former as idyllist and idealistic, an ideologue who portrayed the past as a dreamland, and rebuked the latter as nihilist, a writer who insisted on severing ties with the Arab cultural repertoire.[2]

The ascending power of the connected critic has disrupted the intellectual conversation in the Arabic-speaking world in diverse ways, changing its registers of valuations. If Arab intellectuals of the 1950s and 1960s were wary and skeptical of values gleaned from turath, then their attitude was turned on its head. The connected critic would fashion past traditions of turath as one of the nurturing sources of the Arab subject. He would call into question the cultural dilemmas (e.g., individualism, self-autonomy, and secularism) that haunted the social critic in the 1950s and 1960s. His interest lay in investigating concepts like authenticity, cultural heritage, historical continuity—issues that rendered many of the old questions of the social critics irrelevant. If formerly Western theories emerged as the only theories to deliver the Arab world from social and political ills, with the rise of the connected critic turath traditions were seen in the same vein: a valuable source to draw on in order to provide alternative trajectory to social progress, emergence and growth.

THE CONNECTED CRITIC IN CURRENT HISTORIOGRAPHY

Despite the great shuffling within the Arab intellectual landscape in the 1970s, little scholarship has been dedicated to this new breed of Arab intellectuals, whose endeavors have escaped serious academic attention. With very few exceptions, neither the politics and sensibilities that the connected critic had ushered in nor the field of turath that he helped to institutionalize are adequately addressed within the current historiography.[3] The toll of this negligence has been high. The current focus on Arab leftists, nationalists, Marxists, and Islamists has limited the scope of historical investigation, making it impossible for historians to see beyond the limits of their own generic expectations. This is why it is important to ask what a history of contemporary Arab thought might look like if the modernist vocabulary through which this historiography gets written is parochialized and marginalized—that is, what kinds of subjects and agents will take center stage if we dispense with the dominant narrative that bifurcated postcolonial writers as secular/religious, modernist/traditionalist, liberal/conservative? As societies of the Global South entered the 1970s, many turned to study their suppressed past, rendering many of the questions and concerns that preoccupied the 1960s less compelling. Arab intellectual engagement with the topic of authenticity in the 1970s was in sync with the discourse of authenticity in other ex-colonized nations, reflecting the spirit of late modernity.[4] Authenticity, as Charles Taylor shows, has come to pervade and define the late modern period. In what follows, I suggest accounting for the rise of the "persona" of the connected critic, who wrestled authority from and undermined the intellectual supremacy of both the social critic and the Islamic critic. This historical explanation aims to place the connected critic front and center by marginalizing the persona of the social critic, whose dominance limits our ability to see good works of art, philosophy, and cultural criticism as more than polemics between secularists and Islamists.

Many scholars have expressed great dissatisfaction and concern with the terminology and narratives that characterize the field of contemporary Arab thought along modernist dualities. The growing angst over these persistent errors of misclassification can be seen in the writings of Omnia El Shakry, who underscores the "need to denaturalize the dominant categories and dystopic narratives of Middle Eastern social and cultural history." These narratives, she writes, have "occluded key elements of the history of decolonization from our view."[5] The intriguing rise of the connected critic, I argue, affords a new opportunity to subordinate, or even do away with, the misguiding taxonomies perpetuated by the modernist/development narrative. How to classify an intellectual who is critical of the Left and the Right, one who is neither modernist nor traditionalist? What to call an intellectual who asserts the need for democracy, human rights, and freedoms, yet rejects the liberal order and secularism? The connected critic is an unorthodox writer in that he embraces progressive politics but shies away from secularism, emphasizes democracy and human rights but denounces the liberal notion that one must sever ties with past traditions in order to embrace an autonomy of the self.

The cultural war between social and connected critics affords an alternative way to do justice to the intellectual debates that the current historiographical arrangements won't allow. As a way of introduction, one can characterize the social critic by his desire to create a *traditionless* society. In other words, he is a writer who aims to create a free society and an emancipated individual unconstrained by past traditions. Ever since World War II, the social critic enjoyed unrivaled epistemological authority, at least in the Mashreq, in articulating the national aspirations and expectations of the Arab people. As a secular-nationalist-socialist writer, the social critic—for example, Sadik Jalal al-Azm (Syria), Hadi al-Ulawi (Iraq), Mahmood Amin al-Alim (Egypt), Suhayl Idris (Lebanon), and, of course, Jurj Tarabishi—espoused ideas like social change, progress, autonomy, sovereignty, development, growth, and modernity to redeem a society that he considered in the grip of traditional frameworks. His feat lay in propounding a revolutionary sensibility that had percolated under the Arab national movement for years.

The social critic formulated a template of the decolonized Arab world and the new Arab subject, one who is emancipated, sovereign, and modern. He valorized a model of the detached and disinterested pursuit of learning, fought against imperialism and colonialism, and wrote profusely on Western philosophies. An array of cultural institutions, peer-reviewed journals, dailies, magazines, and books gave material expression to the politics that animated the social critic. Yet his decline began at the start of the 1970s, when he and his old questions, especially with regard to the shape and value of Arab cultural heritage, were shown to be meaningless—that is, when it began to dawn upon him that his intellectual frameworks and Western cultural references were not even capable of providing answers to his own perplexities: What to do with the sheer heritage of Arab history?

The connected critic—for instance, Hassan Hanafi, Abed al-Kabir al-Khatibi, Taha Abed al-Ruhman, and Jabiri—came along to answer this question. He had no wish to obliterate the past in order to create a new society from scratch. The connected critic took his cues for intellectual production primarily from Arab cultural heritage. Defined by his affiliative relations with past traditions and cultural references, he deemed Arab cultural legacy a rich and essential foundation of pertinent philosophies, theorizations, and tested wisdoms that lend him crucial epistemological tools with which to criticize modern forms of Western philosophies. While critical of the social critic, the Marxist, and the nationalist, the connected critic was also critical of Islamists who conceived of turath as an idealist place. His advent, however, heralded not only the decline of the social critic but, most significantly, also marked the beginning of the cultural war on the place of turath in the postcolonial world.

Rejecting the view of turath as an intellectual wasteland, a cultural burden on future generations, the connected critic instead forged a new associative relationality with heritage to launch an authentic project of modernity that by no means imitated European models and prescriptions. While finding his references for the present in the past, the connected critic was unlike the Islamist, who wanted to repeat the past and copy its ideas. While Islamists understood turath as either a set of unchanging habits or a set of fixed rules, the connected critic rejected this static view of the past. He called for a return to the past—not to stay there, but to critique the present. One of the issues that best illustrate his cultural positioning is the complicated question of secularism.

THE CONNECTED CRITIC AND THE QUESTION OF THE SECULAR

In the spring of 1989, the French-based Arabic journal *al-Yaūm al-Sābiʿ* (The seventh day) embarked on a series of debates between two celebrated intellectuals: the Moroccan scholar Mohammad Abed al-Jabiri (1935–2010) and the Egyptian philosopher Hassan Hanafi (1935–2021). Circulating for over ten weeks under the title "Ḥiwār al-Mashreq wal-Maghrib," the series covered ten hotly debated topics from the perspective of two connected critics.[6] While Jabiri represented the Maghreb in this dialogue, Hanafi—as an Egyptian—represented the Mashreq.[7] The debate drew much public interest, propelling once-indifferent TV networks to engage scholars in interviews and talk shows, which led to the making of "star" Arab intellectuals.[8] The reactions following each weekly debate brought into the open pent-up disagreements not only among individual intellectuals, but also among journals and publishing houses.

One of the topics that created much commotion was, predictably, secularism, the subject of the third debate.[9] The secular idea had grown more contentious during the 1980s,[10] as many Arab Marxists who had renounced Marxism adopted an explicitly secular identity.[11] Yet it was intriguing that both of the debaters, whose critical writings against Islamists qualified them as progressives, deemed the secular question in the contemporary Arab world a "spurious question" (*mas'lah muzayyafah*). They unanimously called for purging "the secular slogan [*sic*] from Arabic dictionaries," given the complexity and ambiguity that shrouds the term. The true cultural demand, they proclaimed, is not secularism, but democracy and human rights first, and individual and collective freedoms second.[12]

Jabiri's and Hanafi's retreat from secularism signaled a radical move within the progressive Arab Left, an act that jolted many of their colleagues out of their complacency. The Arab Left, a hodgepodge of Marxists, nationalists, communists, and socialists, had previously branded itself as the predominant revolutionary party in Arab politics and fashioned itself as inherently secular, forward-looking, anti-past, and anti-religion.[13] Despite the fact that Arab secularism was still a nebulous idea, it nonetheless unified the Left as an organic whole and pitted them against Islamists.[14] In the wake of these exchanges, Jabiri and Hanafi insisted on forging a new definition of the Arab Left, one that was less revolutionary and more attuned to Arab cultural heritage. Displeased with the secular thrust and excessively Westernized references adhered to by progressive intellectuals in Beirut and Cairo, Jabiri and Hanafi called for a new cultural framework grounded in turath.

This call did not go unanswered. Many writers wondered whether Jabiri and Hanafi had abruptly abandoned their previously progressive positions and ended up embracing atavist/Islamist stances after years of criticizing Islamists for their ahistorical narratives of medieval Islam. Western historians came to share this view: that Arab intellectuals took a sweeping turn to Islam. The assumption that Islam and turath are the same misled many of these otherwise shrewd observers. Within the Arab intellectual landscape, the apparent turn in Jabiri's and Hanafi's attitudes promptly instigated a torrent of reactions from old and close friends on the left, who felt betrayed. The emerging intellectual configuration led to the creation of new intellectual factions, each with its own publishing houses, journals, scholars, and even affiliated universities. In light of these newfound polarizations among postcolonial Arab intellectuals, one must ask to what degree the old dichotomies of secular/religious and modern/traditional are still viable analytical categories.[15] Do these modern but archaic categories clarify the heated debates within the Arab intellectual scene, or stifle them altogether? Jabiri and Hanafi demonstrate that one can be progressive and still embrace turath, that one need not do away with turath in order to be progressive and maintain a coherent leftist identity. Jabiri's and Hanafi's decampment from the revolutionary Left did not lead them to the Islamic Right, as many of the early critics wanted us to think. Rather, their migration from the left marked the first feature of the age of authenticity.

It is not easy, however, to pin down the causes that led two eminent intellectuals to ditch secularism while holding on to progressive politics. Remarkably, the ground upon which Jabiri and Hanafi had come to rebuke secularism appeared flimsy when compared to the rigorous Western scholarship on the secular. These two eminent connected critics fell short, for example, of demonstrating that secularism in the Arab world has instigated more interfaith tensions, infighting, and civil wars than it has resolved, as Saba Mahmood has amply shown in recent work.[16] Nor did their misgivings toward the secular idea stem from secularism's hidden Christian genealogy,[17] or its unmistakable Protestant implications.[18] In fact, Jabiri and Hanafi did not take such a path in their repudiation of the secular. Their resistance to the secular appeared (oddly enough!) to be Orientalist in nature, describing the secular as an "imported problematic" (*Ishkāliyyah Mustawradah*) imposed upon an Arab society insufficiently trained in and unacquainted with secular logic.[19]

Jabiri and Hanafi claimed that, since Islamic historical experience lacks an analogous concept of the separation between church and state, secularism remains foreign to the Arab world and extraneous to its intellectual traditions.[20] This absence explains why Arab societies should not endeavor to embrace or accommodate secularism.[21] Jabiri and Hanafi proposed a different kind of separation, based upon an Arab genealogy. Rather than a separation between church and state, they called for a separation between reason and religion, one that is more embedded in Arab turath—most remarkably with the work of Ibn Rushd.[22]

This rejection of the secular idea does not illuminate the connected critics' penchant toward Orientalism so much as it implies a more complicated contest at work. I argue that at the root of this rejection stands a coherent "intellectual" agenda that has to do with their cultural anxiety about the intellectual superiority of the Mashreq and its intellectual models of cultural imitation of the West. Put simply, Jabiri and Hanafi explicitly claim that the secular question that preoccupied the Arab intellectual class was introduced specifically by Mashreqi writers. Only if one manages to dispense with the Mashreq and, in particular, the hierarchy of knowledge to which Beirut and Cairo had given rise would the "spurious question" of secularism be dissolved.[23]

In the wake of Jabiri's and Hanafi's fierce rebuttal of the secular, how should historians narrate the history of nonsecular Arab progressives?

Jabiri was a progressive who did not want to cut his ties with the modern age he inhabited in order to reproduce a past heritage, like the Islamists. In fact, Jabiri remained a secularist in the Rushdian sense, rather than the Western sense, for he called to separate reason from tradition the way the medievalist Islamic philosopher Ibn Rushd did in the past.[24] To historically contextualize the place Jabiri and Hanafi carved out in the current Arab intellectual landscape, it is important to acknowledge that the two dominant narratives in the field of Arab intellectual history are growing anachronistic. They do much disservice to historians, since they limit the field of investigation. According to the first narrative, political Islam is seen as the ideology that compensated for the waning ideologies of nationalism and the depleted Arab Left. A second narrative—also omnipresent—fashions a rise-and-fall story line that depicts the rise of the Arab world along the nahda/naksa (awakening/setback) narrative—in other words, the Arab renaissance, touched off by the contact with Europe but reaching its end in the Arab-Israeli War in 1967.[25] These two overriding narratives have failed to bring to view the unmarked domain of experience that scholars like Jabiri and Hanafi were encountering; tied to a modern framework, which bifurcated the postcolonial writer into secular/religious, they rendered the connected critic into practically an invisible writer. To give voice to the connected critic, one should forgo the taxonomic impulse to organize Arab intellectuals into preconceived categories like religious and secular, liberal or conservative.

As the connected critic gains more ground and visibility in current Arab intellectual debates, the historical agents and the cultural institutions they generate take primacy—and precedency—over a focus on ideologies (e.g., Islam, nationalism, Marxism, Pan-Arabism). The shift from big ideas opens the field for a new set of questions, which the former focus on Islam and nationalism rendered unthinkable. Rather than ask what politics Islamic sensibilities entail, one should start with an agent-oriented inquiry: What kind of politics did the connected critic generate or foreclose? How did he proceed to triumph over the social critic, who was characterized by his aversion to political conformism? What social expectations and intellectual references has each type of critic drawn upon? The exploration of the dynamic debates around turath, which prescribed new terminology and posted new queries, through nonsecular agents, institutions, and conferences, help us see more than what the current historiography has so far allowed.[26] While the secular/Islamist contrast worked well for years, it had grown outdated, superseded by the new affiliations dictated by the field of turath studies. The notion of the critic, however, imposes itself as a more suitable title, since it carries a less charged connotation than the secular. It is to the formation of the critic as cultural institution, and later on as an intellectual persona, to which we now turn.

In seeking an answer to this historiographical issue, I adopt Michael Walzer's terms, the connected and social critics. The social and connected critics are "ideal types" that conceptually help us illuminate the sensibilities that animate different groups of Arab writers and intellectuals. My understanding of these "ideal types" takes its cue from Gadi Algazi's concept of the "intellectual persona" as "an exemplification of a philosophical stance, of one's commitment to basic values, or of the epistemic virtues cherished and cultivated within a specific scholarly community."[27] The two terms carry great explanatory power for the cultural war in which these critics were engaged and that called for this terminology.

THE TIME OF THE SOCIAL CRITIC

The new political conditions created by World War II thrust the social critic into the center of the intellectual scene, allowing him to steadily encroach on the authority and domain of the *Adeb* (old writer).[28] The social critic, a middle-class writer defined by secularist, nationalist, modernist, and anti-imperialist sensibilities, had conquered the intellectual field by the early 1950s. As a critic who superseded the Adeb, he forged a radical sensibility in politics and philosophy, with a proclivity toward a total revolution that compared with the timidity of the Adeb, who were willing to accommodate mild traditionalism. For the best part of the

1940s–1970s, the Arab intellectual landscape was shaped and defined by these social critics—of which the new generation of post–World War II scholars like Michael Aflaq, Yassin al-Hafiz, Mahdi Amil, Suhayl Idris, and Tarabishi and their acolytes are good examples. They valorized translated literature over local cultural references, took the Mashreq (especially Cairo and Beirut) as their natural habitat, and fostered intellectual and literary sensibilities developed in the West. As Egyptian writer Yahya Haqqi writes, the social critic has an "intuition" that "[was] available exclusively to writers intimate with Western culture."[29]

The advent of the social critic who prevailed over the Adeb marks the beginning of a new chapter in Arab history. This social critic promoted a revolutionary sensibility because he thought of the current political class of landowners as lazy inheritors, time servers, and adept players of office politics. As a writer, the social critic of the mid-century gave rise to novel intellectual assumptions and expectations that render the Adeb obsolescent, out of sync with the newfound revolutionary proclivities that pervaded Arab politics in the postcolonial condition. The social critic established new publishing houses like Dar al-Adab, radical socialist publications averse to turath like *Dar al-Taliah*, and radical journals like *Mawaqif*, *Majallat Shiʿr*, *Dirasat Arabiyya*, and *al-Adab*, all of which had sustained the social critic's work and galvanized his image in public.

In her writing on Arab existentialism, Verena Klemm makes use of the term "socialist critics" to refer to a group of writers who "eagerly attacked the literature of 'the ivory tower' where, so they believed, the traditional cultural elite embraced the myth of artistic autarchy."[30] The revolt of the socialist critics—whether existentialists, Marxists, positivists, or nationalists—against their predecessors is also discussed in the writings of Yoav Di-Capua. Ironically, in his own writings Hisham Sharabi proposes the title "cultural critics" to refer to this group of nationalist/secularist writers, who were marked by their revolutionary sentiments. These cultural critics who called the social order in question, Sharabi writes, stand in opposition to their adversary, the Islamists, with whom they find themselves caught in the crosshairs of secular logic (that no longer holds true): what Sharabi describes as "the opposition between two radically different positions . . . one seeking total salvation through return to religious truth and the Islamic ethic, and the other advocating radical social change through rational analysis and the establishment of the modern secular state."[31]

One of the primary reasons that Sharabi's version of the cultural critic has not taken hold in the field was due to its inherent contradiction in his terms. While Sharabi is right in referring to postcolonial secular scholars as critics, his description is misleading, since these critics were not inspired by their own culture to criticize their societies. Rather, they took their cues and references from social sciences originating in the West, as Sharabi avers later in the same article. "The Arab scholar or man of science," he affirms, "is the translator and articulator of a methodological and theoretical body of knowledge that has been formed in a different language and in other countries."[32] Given that this writer is "satisfied to remain in the shadow of Western knowledge," the term "cultural critic" seems inappropriate. A more precise term might be Klemm's notion of the "socialist critic," or, in a less ideologically charged sense, the social critic. This seems a more apt designation, especially when compared with the work of his antagonist, the connected critic, whose vision and theoretical references stemmed directly from his own cultural repertoire, as we will see.[33]

What is a "social critic"? To describe the Arab social critic as a writer who meekly agreed to live "in the shadow of Western knowledge" might underestimate his work and stature. Alas, Sharabi was not the only one to refer to the postcolonial scholar in such a high-handed manner; Yahya Haqqi, an Egyptian novelist and editorialist, describes the social critic as someone who is bestowed with an "intuition" of foreign languages and knowledges. Indeed, the social critic is defined by Western epistemologies, not least of all Marxist, existentialist, socialist, and positivist theories.[34] Yet the Arab social critic was not simply an "imitator" of Western theories; he stood at the forefront of Arab intellectual experiments in nationalism, Marxism, and existentialism. He articulated the first postcolonial writings and aspired to liberate human reason from the impact of religious myths. His critique is heightened by a sharp sense of self-awareness and self-criticism. Taking advantage of mid-century political upheavals in Cairo and parallel mayhems in Beirut and Damascus, he was able to replace the Adeb, a figure of the nahda who was deemed, rather condescendingly, by the guard of the social critic as a timid, docile, institutionalized writer.

The social critic reached his peak and secured his intellectual hegemony in the early postcolonial era (1945–1970). He dominated the most prestigious university ranks, daily news, and publishing houses. One of the most vocal social critics was Sadik Jalal al-Azm, the author of confrontational titles like *Self-Critique After the Defeat* (1968) and *Critique of Religious Thought* (1969). While Azm's writings were by no means the most genuine and thought out, he nonetheless represented the rising symbolic capital of the social critic in the 1960s. He was part of "an intelligentsia who had launched a war of position in the 1940s and 1950s against intellectuals of the previous generation."[35] In other words, Azm was not only an individual, but part of a larger generation who came of age in a postindependence context.

The Arab social critic was informed by a domain of experiences that profoundly influenced his predilection to radicalism and revolution, first and foremost the experience of defeat. The Arab-Israeli War in 1967, the dissolution of the United Arab Republic (1958–1961) between Egypt and Syria, and the unraveling of the postcolonial project constituted a domain of experiences that left an enduring impact on the social critic. As he came to witness the upheaval caused by these events, which shook his existence and faith, he applied new terms and categories that helped his readers and followers to sort out social interaction along his taxonomies. No wonder that the social critic fashioned a literature awash with panic, chaos, and desperate hope. As a writer who lived in the weeks and months after the defeats in 1967, which came on the heels of postcolonial setbacks and long stretches of turmoil, he described only uncertainty and horror. The pain inflicted on the social critic through these experiences soon gave way to an anger that has in many ways determined the course of Arab history ever since. His call to take the state by revolution, for instance, stemmed directly from a life that had been shaped by tragedy. The calamity of the historical war in 1967 underwrote and articulated the politics the social critic undertook, forcing him to break with the utopian visions that marked the writings of his predecessor—the Adeb.[36]

As a pioneer of a vanquished society, the social critic invented all sort of scapegoats. His blame for the defeat in 1967 was immediately attributed to Arabs' entrenched traditionalism. It took only a short step from this initial realization to disseminate the conviction that contemporary Arab peoples are better off doing away with their cultural turath altogether. Traditions that had held Arab society together were made the main subject of critique, the primary impediment on the way of development and growth. The cultural imperative to disengage turath was placed suddenly on the cultural agenda of the Arab world. It was considered the most efficient way through which social critic could cathartically cleanse himself of any responsibility or guilt.

As a class of writers who came of age in the post–World War II era, a time informed by Third Worldism and culminating in the upheavals of the 1960s, Arab social critics embraced the same vivacity that empowered the student movements in Europe and the United States, movements that unflinchingly believed that "men have unrealized potential for self-cultivation, self-direction, self-understanding, and creativity."[37] Past traditions, according to the social critic of the 1960s, inhibited the realization of these pent-up capacities. The social critic Tarabishi, for example, based his views on a manifest hostility to turath because it encouraged a "submission to authority"—a sensibility that ran counter to his revolutionary feelings. For Tarabishi, the return to turath was no less than a grim reminder that prejudice knows no borders, a reversion to premodern status quo. As we will see in chapters 5 and 6, Tarabishi's intellectual career presents a quintessential example of the dreary fate of the social critic in the Arab world: rising hopes in the 1940s–1960s, and the dashing of dreams in the closing decades of the millennium.

Indeed, as young middle-class writers and translators, social critics like Tarabishi and Azm were keen to bury a past that they believed slowed the march toward modernity. In their writings, they placed added value on the new and novel, an emphasis that entailed the denunciation of the old and outdated. The consensus they helped to forge was that a society attached to its dark past could not aspire to a brighter future.[38] The dailies that emerged during the 1960s like *al-Fajr al-Jadid* and the journal *Shiʿr* reflected this spirit in different and diverse ways. But it was the thriving publishing houses like Dar al-Adab (1953) and, most remarkably, Dar al-Taliah (1959) that captured the social critic's historical moment.

As a rising generation of writers and activists, the social critics employed new categories and evaluation systems that afforded them the power to hail or condemn, fashion or undermine local values and norms. As they came to control most registers of valuation, they came to label that which appeared new and up-to-date as "good," and that which seemed stuck in the past as "bad." Under their watch, turath, the repertoire that for centuries provided the cultural compass for Arab societies, lost its former ability to define itself and the things around it. They hollowed out turath, emptied it of its content until it ceased to function as a reference. If, previously, social innovations and practices had been measured against turath, to social critics turath had lost the capacity to fulfill this mission. No other generation of Arab intellectuals went to such lengths to disparage and undermine the authority of past traditions of turath. The idea that history's calculus cannot be trusted is perhaps the most striking aspect of the social critics' entire corpus.

Interestingly, despite their attempts to set themselves apart (and above) the "Udaba" of the nahda, they were very much alike in their embrace of a crude modernist worldview. Central to this modernist vision is the assumption of "the theology of progress," which "constantly points to the future as the site of a better life."[39] This sense of crude modernity, which condemns past traditions, is shared by the middle class of Arab scholars that emerged in the late nineteenth century. This class came to claim modernity by incorporating "into their daily lives and politics a collection of manners, mores, and tastes, and a corpus of ideas about the individual, gender, rationality, and authority actively derived from what they believed to be the cultural, social, and ideological praxis of the contemporary metropolitan Western middle classes."[40] Therefore, despite his attempt to steer clear of the Adeb, the social critic remained in the end like his predecessor in his views.

Like their Euro-American counterparts in the 1960s, this generation of Arab social critics considered themselves not only modernists but also outsiders, displaced and exiled, even though they lived in their own societies. They conceived of themselves as alienated writers and their criticism as an external activity. Michael Walzer's description of the modes and lifestyles that characterized the Euro-American social critic applies to Arab writers as well. "The conventional view," writes Walzer, is that they had "to stand outside the common circumstances of collective life" to be able to critique their society and culture. In the world of the social critic, "criticism is an external activity; what makes it possible is radical detachment—and this in two senses. . . . First, critics must be emotionally detached, wrenched loose from the intimacy and warmth of membership: disinterested and dispassionate. Second, critics must be intellectually detached, wrenched loose from the parochial understanding of their own society: open-minded and objective."[41]

Feelings of strangeness and alienation in their own society, values that for long had been condemned and rejected by Arab society, now appealed to Arab social critics. Adonis, a prominent poet, publisher, and editor, saw marginality as an index and a condition of originality.[42] He described the human condition of the social critic in his poem "On the Life of Solitude and Marginalization," where he writes that "we [social critics] live in the folds of the city, / like snails behind their shell." Other social critics seem to agree with Adonis. Hayder Hayder, a Syrian novelist and a translator known as "the voice of a black future" (*al-mustaqbal al-Aswad*), writes that he "set himself in opposition to the social order, which he wished to destroy to enable the coming of the new."[43] Hayder introduces himself as "the writer of despair and cruelty; the daylight that is taken by darkness; [I'm the writer of] sadness and death that hangs over our despondent and alienated souls."[44] Arab social critics like Hayder and Adonis shifted the way in which they demonstrate approval and disapproval of the new condition of alienation. If, formerly, the conditions of cultural alienation and marginality were classified as inferior, with the advent of the social critic they take on a positive connotation. As Walzer comments "marginality has often been a condition that motivates criticism and determines the critic's characteristic tone and appearance."[45] With the establishment of the institution of the social critic in the Arab world, the aesthetic metric began shifting away from traditional norms. Whatever object Arab society revered began to draw social critics' attention.

The new class of social critics intended to transform society rather than reform it. Questioning the normal, in their eyes, was predicated on slandering the authority of the past. This is why social critics like Tarabishi, Hayder, Azm, Aflaq, and Adonis propounded a comprehensive critique, a new mode informed by a mixture of Marxist and existentialist beliefs. Previously, the Adeb employed literary criticism as a means of interpretation and revision; the idea was to reform, not to condemn, to accommodate rather than repudiate. Unlike the interpretive framework of the Adeb, who drew his strength from the fragments of two seemingly incommensurable traditions,[46] the social critic was a total revolutionist, a radical in his visceral rejection of reality as a way of transforming it.[47]

The social critic's main objective was not to criticize, either, but to overthrow the bourgeoisie. Michael Aflaq, the ideologue of the Baath Party, gives a concrete example, in 1959, of the differences between the Adeb's dwindling power and the advent of the clas of social critics when he writes, "we feel that what we need is not the reform of the state apparatus or the repair of any objective flaw, but rather a deep and comprehensive overcoming [*inqilāb*]." According to Max Weiss, "Here is a program for total human transformation, at once moral and material."[48]

During the three decades that followed World War II, social critics ascended to the role of mainstream intellectuals with enough symbolic capital to design the architecture of the Arab intellectual landscape, in virtue of their critique, new translations, and new language. Their opinions and reviews proved to be crucial for other writers as well. Armed with a revolutionary "truth," social critics could brand any individual or entire societies who dared to disagree with them as backward, fanatical, tribal, and parochial. Enjoying the benefit of powerful institutional protections (e.g., prominent publishing houses and daily newspapers), it seemed in vain to resist them. Neutral and even unaffiliated writers felt the pressure to think like social critics—to agree with them not only about class struggle, colonialism, imperialism, and Palestine, but also about the dysfunctionality and futility of turath. Any social critic could wield power through behemoths like the publishing houses Dar al-Taliah and Dar al-Adab and the journal *Shiʿr*, platforms that have delivered the tools of reputational annihilation.[49] Under their hegemony, many of the artistic modes introduced by traditional writers had largely been written out of the literary mainstream, despite a sizeable readership. The canon was theirs to design, enforce, and protect. As pacesetters, they saw themselves as "modernist prophets and agents of change."[50] Despite the differences among them, social critics wanted to be modern and to control the production of modern literature. By being modern, the social critics "declared their intention to take a preeminent role in the production of knowledge and culture, not just for themselves, but for society at large."[51]

THE ECLIPSE OF THE SOCIAL CRITIC

The end of the reign of the social critic came as a surprise and provided a glimpse of things to come. Interestingly, the intellectual infrastructure established by the class of social critics (i.e., publishing houses, the literary canon, freestyle poetry, and translation movements) proved no guarantee against the cultural assault unleashed by the connected critic during the 1970s. The cultural institutions that the social critic had painstakingly established over the course of thirty years (1940–1970), which withstood the pressure of the state and the vagaries of time, proved remarkably vulnerable in the face of the connected critic's scathing critique. This new challenger did not attack the social critic for his lack of piety, the way Islamists had done, but for calling to abandon turath and perpetuating a lifestyle of inauthenticity and inferiority. Indeed, the conversation on turath that began in the 1970s reached its crescendo with the overthrow of the social critic. The triumph of the the connected critic stands out as the most remarkable event during the 1970s. It is worthwhile to elaborate on the rise of the connected critic, whose main goal was to dethrone and defeat the social critic, and to place it in the appropriate historical context.

The political and economic transformations of the 1970s surveyed in chapter 1—the defeat of the postcolonial project, Nasser's death, the rise of new cultural centers and the Lebanese Civil War that dispersed important intellectual clusters in Beirut—had the effect of changing the public perception of the social critic. He was no longer viewed as a Pan-Arab hero, who fought in the name of the masses. Quite the contrary, the social critic who made himself an outsider was increasingly seen as hostile.[52] In the wake of the crumpling of the postcolonial project, his numbers grew smaller, and his social reputation was destroyed.[53] As many Arab intellectuals' positioning had vacillated from an emphasis on external ideologies to a new attention to internal politics, social critics who continued to maintain a distance from society, championing their marginality and alienation, came under fire as outsiders, spectators, or, as Walzer writes, "total strangers, men from Mars."[54] The social critic who "derives a kind of critical authority from the distance he establishes" found himself on the losing end in the new age of authenticity. Walzer compares him to the "imperial judge in a backward colony":

> He stands outside, in some privileged place, where he has access to "advanced" or universal principles; and he applies these principles with an impersonal (intellectual) rigor. He has no other interest in the colony except to bring it to the bar of justice. . . . He has gone to school at the imperial center, at Paris or Oxford, say, and broken radically with his own parochialism. He would have preferred to stay at Paris or Oxford, but he has dutifully returned to his homeland so that he can criticize the local arrangements. A useful person, possibly, but not the only or the best model.[55]

The intellectual ambition of the social critic of the 1960s appeared in the late 1970s as morally corrupt, practicing an unattractive form of social activism, because the intellectual bet he made on radical change proved vacuous.[56] The 1960s, which aimed for a total replacement of society, appeared in the the 1970s as a bitter dream. A change in the intellectual guard was brewing.

THE ARRIVAL OF THE CONNECTED CRITIC

The totalizing agenda the social critic valorized as a way to replace the social order with a new order (through *inqilāb* or *thawra*) left many Arab intellectuals rattled and outraged. The thick volumes through which he spoke highly of the merits of social revolution and emphasized the value of effecting a radical rupture with past traditions proved no more than futile talk; on the ground, the postcolonial reality looked gloomier. The vast majority of peasants who had been promised social mobility to the middle class remained poor. The social critic acknowledged that reality and that failure. Even though there was a palpable change in education and relative progress made in transitioning away from a Bedouin to an urban lifestyle, writes Hayder Hayder, the overall outcome was disappointing. The ambition of the social critic to "completely and radically destroy [*al-taḥṭīm al-kāmel wal-Jathrī*] the economic, societal, and cultural relations with the old world [*al-ʿalam al-Qadīm*] was not accomplished."[57] While initially the call to break ties with the past in order to pave the way for unmaking the social order appealed to many Arab writers and activists, the project came up short.[58]

Indeed, the social critic's insistence on nothing less than a total transformation of society began losing its credibility by the beginning of the 1970s, as many Arab regimes settled in and gave rise to new power structures that the social critic had not anticipated. The new Arab rulers had to enforce new policies to secure their authority, which, in turn, placed serious strains on the social critic's key demands, chipping away at his status and intellectual capital. In the summer of 1970, two "progressive" Arab regimes ended their scramble for power. In Egypt, Sadat, the so-called "liberator of Islamists," secured the most coveted position, while Assad assumed power by ripping through political codes and forcing his way to the presidential office. One year prior, Qadafi maneuvered his way into becoming the unrivaled leader of what then looked like an oasis brimming with oil. While the Arab world seemed to be resolving its political melees, there remained a pressing feeling that the 1970s marked the loss of cultural anchors. This sense was reflected in the rise of Saudi

Arabia, which would also subsidize new agents determined to question the cultural canon that the social critic tenaciously guarded. Empowered by the petrodollar that endowed it with an unprecedented surge of confidence, Arabia emerged eager to undo and replace the cultural institutions the social critic spent years making. Put simply, the political scene that had ushered in the social critic in the wake of World War II had reached its end at the start of the 1970s, altered partly by new players and new presidents. In light of all these changes, the political and cultural milieu had never been more primed to the rise of a new breed of Arab intellectual: the connected critic.

The connected critic was defined chiefly by his rejection of the social critic and the revolutionary politics of the 1960s, which fell victim to its own excesses. The connected critic, by contrast, aspired to emancipate the Arab self from the national and ideological pretentions that his predecessor (social critic) imposed on Arab people. Untroubled by the differences between secular and religious domains, the connected critic was hell bent on developing an intellectual agenda shaped by its distance from the social critic's radical paradigm; he fashioned a modest, humble intellectual agenda instead. If the social critic sought social change through discontinuity, then the connected critic thought that continuity could provide the necessary means for change. For the connected critic, past traditions of turath contained possibilities and trajectories yet unrealized. If the social critic was obsessed with the new and the novel, the connected critic refused to privilege the present over the past, fully convinced that certain elements of the past can be used to disrupt and dismantle the conformity of the social order.

Mohammad Abed al-Jabiri embodies the intellectual sensibilities of the connected critic more than any contemporary Arab intellectual, with the possible exception of Hassan Hanafi and Taha Abdulrahman. Despite the copious commentaries on Jabiri's works in the current historiography, his writings were rarely seen in the context of his opposition to the social critic. For the best part of his career Jabiri railed against the intellectual premises that guided the social critic in the Mashreq, especially with regard to their unduly reliance on Western frameworks of reference and the break with turath. Yet he was often seen as part of the category of intellectuals that he mostly condemned. Subsuming Jabiri in that category has limited historians' analysis of this scholar. Part 2 attempts to redeem Jabiri from this position.

Over the last three decades of his life, Jabiri developed a fully fledged framework that laid the scaffolding of the intellectual presuppositions of the connected critic. Central to this "new positionality," as he called it (and as we will see in chapters 3 and 4), is the understanding of the shaping power of past traditions of turath in contemporary life. Instead of breaking with the past, Jabiri calls to connect to it in order to change the present. No change or reform of the social order can ever take hold except if this change is inspired, and rooted in, cultural frameworks, he argues; change is always internal to culture, rather than external to it.

Unlike the confrontationalist social critic, Jabiri is an illuminator of the unrealized possibilities of the past traditions of turath. He shows how certain norms and habits can afford new forms of life and new ways of being. He retells the story of Arabs in history in an attempt to create a new Arab identity. His narrative informs Arabic speakers of who they are. He deals with the historical material of Arab culture rather than canceling it out for modernity, as the social critic would do. Jabiri believed that the social critic's prescription for social change and advancement were based on wrong assumptions; rather than a total revolution, he insisted on the inauguration of a new age of codification, not unsimilar to the age of codification in medieval Islam. "It would be impossible to achieve reform in thought," he writes, "except through the culture to which one belongs."[59]

Jabiri primarily chafed at social critics' aim to unmoor Arab society from its traditions, the most trusted sphere of spiritual and cognitive experience. According to Jabiri, this effort left Arab society adrift, suffering from a lack of direction and the loss of its most authentic cultural compass. He argued that the social critic's insistence on forgoing the cultural repertoire that gives a society its symbolic structure and meaning had also left Arabic readers vulnerable to the attacks of conservative and fanatic Islamists. Rather than weakening their adversaries, the politics ushered in by the social critic had in fact empowered them. Specifically, Jabiri claims that there is little hope to cutting people's ties to their traditions. "We are not calling to break with turath. . . . What we are calling for is to relinquish the traditional understanding of tradition. Namely, to let go of the traditional sediments in the process of [a new] understanding of tradition."[60] With this insight, the connected critic positions past traditions as the ultimate guard not only against Islamic obscurantists, but also against the unguaranteed wagers that the social critic had made—gambles that seemed to have pulled Arab societies one step closer to the brink of the abyss.

The connected critic is by no means a traditionalist or a writer who suffers from political nostalgia.[61] Instead he offers a new mode of affiliation with turath, one that is more complex and nuanced. His relation to turath is not functional, as though it were a sort of intellectual ware to be customized and adjusted to the exigencies of the present, as the nationalist writer of the 1950s–1960s thought. Nor does the connected critic share the social critic's view of turath as a relic or collection of inert traditions. Rather, he wants to create a society attuned to its turath, to seize upon its forgotten opportunities in order to give rise to a new Arab subject who is an active agent rather than an imitator and a follower. Yet, for their detractors, the connected critic was seen as neotraditionalist by virtue of his reliance on traditional sources of the self. However, the fact that the connected critic takes his cues from Arab cultural heritage, which equips him with epistemological tools that resonate with Arabic speakers everywhere, doesn't make him neotraditionalist. His agenda is premised on connectivity with turath rather than dispensing with it altogether.

Elaborating on the work of two major connected critics, Hassan Hanafi and Jabiri, Yasmeen Daifallah writes that these two had "concluded that any attempt at sociopolitical change [by] calling for a 'rupture' with Islamic tradition, whether in theological or cultural terms, was bound to fail." Daifallah rightly points out that these two scholars, who at an earlier point in their lives had been radicals, found a detour through tradition to be effective. For Arab intellectuals to effect change, Daifallah writes, they must "rise to the double challenge of both historicizing and preserving turath." Intellectual discourse, she adds, "had to be *critical* of tradition while also paying *allegiance* to it, to re-examine the historical rationale of traditional Islamic knowledge, to relativize its value for the present, but also to commit to its preservation."[62] What Daifallah establishes is that these scholars are neither traditionalist nor nostalgic. The connected critic is, rather, an author who articulates a different vision of turath, based on the premise that it could offer an alternative trajectory for an Arab modernity.

For the connected critic, there is no singular modernity but multiple modernities that exist simultaneously (see chapter 3). Central to this conception is the understanding of the relations between present and past. If the social critic, as we saw earlier, furnished a total critique of society because of his belief that nothing in the current order is salvageable, the connected critic starts from a resolute belief in the intellectual and cultural prospects locked within the status quo but not yet realized. More interesting, the idea of multiple modernities, which gained cultural currency among Arab intellectuals in the wake of the 1970s, amounts to a devastating rebuke to the intellectual presumptions of the social critic of the 1960s—most important, the idea of catching up with Western modernity by imitation.

As a connected critic, Jabiri was among the first writers to challenge the dominance and supremacy of the social critic, whom he hastily (and quite haphazardly) associated with the Mashreqi scholar. To end the long period of intellectual purgatory and cultural stagnation, Jabiri proposed marginalizing dominant perspectives inspired by Western models that limited the critic's scope of investigation. The connected critic that Jabiri exemplified thought of his predecessor—the social critic in the Mashreq—as a defeated writer who caved to colonialist, Europeanized models of scholarship. As such, Jabiri wrote, the social critic followed the winner, or the West, by every move. Taking his ideas from Ibn Khaldun, the fourteenth-century Arab philosopher who developed a theory on the relations between vanquished and victorious nations, Jabiri argued that social critics in the Mashreq are like the "losers who imitate winners almost by reflex." From the perspective of the connected critic, this cultural imitation created an unhealthy dichotomy between belittled "borrowing" nations like the Middle East and other ex-colonized nations, on the one hand, and superior "credited" ones like the West, on the other.[63]

The connected critic was not only troubled by the idea of "imitation," but also irritated by the social critic's resolute determination to create a tradition-free society. Though a connected critic like Jabiri might condemn conventional readings of turath, he nonetheless appreciated the hidden potential inscribed within them. Traditions might have disappeared during the three decades following Arab states' independence, but traditional concepts did not, he argued. Therefore, turath should not be overthrown or overlooked. Jabiri's emphasis on authenticity and turath led him to the conclusion that Arab hadatha (the Arab version of modernity) should emerge from within (*min al-dakhil*) turath, rather than from outside of it. "Nations do not rise by tugging themselves under other nations' traditions," he writes, "but by aligning in their traditions."[64] If read and examined from a nonideological position, Jabiri contended, turath could provide a new trajectory for Arab modernity, from within Arab cultural soil. He viewed any version of modernity external to the domain of turath as doomed to fail because it is borrowed, imitated, and imposed from above. This was one of the primary critical takes Jabiri directed against Mashreqi social critics.[65] In the second volume of *Naqd*, he made this conclusion crystal clear: "There is no path to renewal and Hadātha except from within al-Turath, its mechanisms and possibilities."[66] This was a direct rebuttal to the social critic, who viewed European modernity as the only pathway out of Arab postcolonial plights.

The growing critical exchanges between the social and connected critics, bordering on hostility, began to polarize the postcolonial intellectual community in the Arab world. Scholars, writers, publishers, translators, and readers sympathetic to Jabiri would convene intellectual meetings and conferences without extending invitations to social critics like Tarabishi. The connected critic slowly began to distance himself from the vocabulary of his adversary. Gradually, he centralized his analysis on notions like authenticity, alternative modernity, and autochthonous identities, ignoring the social critic's idiom: vanguard, revolution, catching up, development, emergence, and class analysis. If in the 1950s secularists and Islamists spoke two languages, now social and connected critics offered two starkly different social and cultural imaginations that set them on a collision course.

The following chapters elaborate on this cultural war. I start with Jabiri's project of cultural emancipation through what he calls "historical independence of the Arab subject."[67] His central idea of *intithām* (alignment), discussed in chapter 4, betrays a swift rejection of the agenda of the social critic. Jabiri assailed the condition that the social critic lauded and appreciated—of the necessity of being an alienated and marginalized writer in order to objectively observe the social structure of Arab society. Critics who are defined by a condition of exile and emotionally detached from their traditions would not bring about change, he rebutted. Alienation from one's own culture, he asserted, gives rise to revolutionary commitment rather than to an organic cultivation of cultural wisdom. Unlike the "imperial judge" positioned above his society, Jabiri represented the new Arab critic who is connected to his society and culture. As Walzer writes, the connected critic is the local judge "who earns his authority . . . by arguing with his fellows. . . . This critic is one of us. Perhaps he has traveled and studied abroad, but his appeal is to local or localized principles; if he has picked up new ideas on his travels, he tries to connect them to the local culture, building on his own intimate knowledge; he is not intellectually detached. Nor is he emotionally detached; he does not wish the natives well, he seeks the success of their common enterprise."[68] For the connected critic, critique must arise from a common cultural reservoir of knowledge—that is, from references familiar to native people. His critique should be viewed as "an internal argument." For Jabiri, the social critic must draw upon familiar "frameworks of reference" like turath and collective memory that resonate with Arab speakers if he wishes to be heard again. As Walzer clearly articulates, the social critic must "manage to get himself inside, enter imaginatively into local practices and arrangements," since there is little "advantage in radical detachment."[69]

In sum, with the advent of the connected critic, turath has shifted from its position as a cultural burden that keeps society behind to a corpus of unexplored authentic traditions that provide diverse untrodden paths to modernity. This relocation of turath from the margins to the center of Arab thought set in motion the first campaign in the great cultural war. Simply put, if turath had lost the authority to define itself and its surrounding intellectual milieu during the social critic's heyday in the 1950s and 1960s, the arrival of the connected critic restored its legitimacy.

The debate between the social and connected critics affords a new lens through which to scrutinize contemporary Arab debates. This debate on the place and value of turath has scholarly merits that, if taken seriously, could offer a new framework for revising much of the geographical, idiomatic, and historiographical axioms that have shaped—and continue to shape—the field of Arab intellectual history. Narrating current Arab debates through the paradigm of the connected and social critics creates new modes of investigation and could degrade the emphasis on Islam. Above all, the rise of the connected critic diverts the focus from the Mashreq and invites historians to take note of writers in North Africa, where new and exciting intellectual hubs are taking shape. Moreover, exploring these turath-informed debates attests to the establishment of new hierarchies of knowledge in the Arab world, at the center of which one can recognize a dramatic shift from a once-passionate opposition to turath as an obstacle to development and growth and a force to be defeated to a position that embraces and celebrates turath's intellectual affordances.

This chapter has recounted the erosion in the social critic's social standing and intellectual stature. The diminishing power of the social critic—or the "unmaking of the Arab intellectual," as Zena Halabi puts it—marks a foundational event in Arab intellectual history. This event facilitates two critical developments: the slow death of the social critic accelerated the emergence and rise of the connected critic, but also enlivens the decade of the 1970s, in its way no less eventful than the 1960s. The connected critic came to question the social and intellectual assumptions of the social critic, who, in turn, triumphed over the Adeb.

As a new challenger, the connected critic assailed his predecessor for his apparent failure to bring about social change, for ignoring cultural references and frameworks that resonated with local populations, and most importantly for failing to making good on his promises to help the Arab subject lead an authentic life. The new modes of engagement with turath raised questions: Why did Arab scholars overlook their cultural heritage for so long? Why did they launch a cultural war on turath only at the beginning of the 1970s? To answer them, I investigate the intellectual career of the connected critic Jabiri and the social critic Tarabishi in order to better understand how the field of turath became a highly controversial issue that informs and forms the Arab intellectual landscape in the postcolonial condition.

II

CURATORS

Mohammad Abed al-Jabiri, arguably the most important postcolonial philosopher in the Arabic-speaking world since the 1970s, passed away in 2010. Jabiri has seen his work commented on, written about, and engaged with more than any other intellectual in the Arab world, with the exception of Mohammad Arkoun and Edward Said, who never published in Arabic or wrote for Arabic-speaking audiences. Some of Jabiri's writings have been translated, into sixteen languages–an unrivaled feat in contemporary Arab scholarship—and his works have provoked much debate and prompted many symposia and conferences. As one of his contemporaries has observed, Jabiri's writings "left no one indifferent; intellectuals throughout the Arab world were either passionately for or against him."[1]

Thanks to an engaging writing style and a compelling mode of analysis, Jabiri has been read on a massive scale. Even if he aimed his writings at a limited class of intellectuals, Jabiri endowed his work with a simplicity that rendered many of his books approachable to a wider educated population—a far cry from the clunky writing of other Arab philosophers such as Abdalruhman Taha, Abdallah Laruoi, and Abed al-Kabir al-Khatibi. In his life Jabiri was also the winner of the most prestigious literary prizes in the Arab world, including the Ibn Rush Prize and the Prize of the Philosophical Association in North Africa, and he enjoyed so much symbolic capital in Morocco and elsewhere that he turned down many others, like Saddam Hussein's book prize ($100,000) and Muammar Qadafi's book prize ($25,000).

Jabiri's reach and impact is not limited to his own generation. The shaping power of his intellectual analysis and diagnosis is particularly palpable among the younger Arab generation that took to the streets in 2011. As anthropologist Sonja Hegasy noted while doing field research into Morocco's sociocultural opposition in the early 1990s, "Participants would refer to al-Jabiri in order to claim the right to speak out against Islamist proponents, patriarchal authorities or state propaganda representatives."[2] Young political activists read and referred to him so they could "substantiate their claim to apply their own reasoning and voice their own convictions." Hegasy writes, "I gained insight into how his works indeed influenced young politicized adults: they rejected an understanding of society in which religiously conditioned norms could not be applied in a metaphorical sense. . . . They wanted to base their visions on doubt, personal reasoning with all its insufficiencies, and on the heterogeneity and contingency of the past."[3] The influence of Jabiri's ideas could be seen among diverse segments of the public, including civil rights groups, creative writing workshops, and informal circles in Morocco and beyond, as well as with political activists and environmentalists. Who was Jabiri, and how did he chart his way from modest beginnings to the pinnacle of the Arab intellectual sphere?

Until the early 1970s, Jabiri was a little-known writer from Morocco, without the purchasing power or intellectual stature of thinkers such as Zaki Najib Mahmud and Amin al-Alim in Cairo or Suhayl Idris and Yassin al-Hafiz in Beirut. Nevertheless, Jabiri's early writings stirred much debate among the larger intellectual community, which his articles and questions began to steer in new directions, forcing haughty intellectuals in Beirut and Cairo to pay attention. The next two chapters grapple with the institution of the connected critic that Jabiri endowed with both meaning and substance; taken together, they offer an elaborate profile of the man and his ideas, intellectual career, and trajectory, in order to demonstrate the ways in which he curated the field of turath anew.

3

JABIRI AS A THINKER OF (INTERNAL) DECOLONIZATION

In the late 1970s, Mohammad Abed al-Jabiri wrote in *Nahnu wal-Turath* (Turath and us) that "no other thought tradition in the entire history of human thought has suffered, and is still suffering, from historians' injustices as the philosophical tradition in Islam."[1] What most upset Jabiri was his conviction that historical analysis of these traditions made little sense of these important tradtions. This may sound peculiar, even ludicrous, given the massive efforts that Orientalists, Arab countries, and individual intellectuals have made to excavate and explore valuable and hitherto unknown philosophical traditions over the last century. Despite recent headways in the field of turath studies in general, Jabiri deemed this work less than satisfactory. Past turath traditions "remain meaningless, fragmented and disembodied ideas," he argued. "Our work in the field of turath studies has been focused exclusively on collecting and anthologizing [*al-jamʿ wal tajmiʿ*] . . . but we are still short of earnest and original studies of these raw and valuable materials."[2] A decade later, Jabiri reminded his readers that the cultural mission of Arab intellectuals to bestow meaning on turath traditions remained incomplete. "The philosophical history in Islam," he stated, "has not been written yet."[3]

For anyone familiar with modern Arab thought from the late nineteenth century, when the study of Arab and Islamic traditions began in earnest, Jabiri's grievances about "historians' injustices," "unwritten Arab history," and the abject shortage of "earnest and original studies" of "raw and valuable" medieval traditions sound not only puzzling, but intriguing. Though Jabiri is by no means the only intellectual to voice alarm over the state of turath studies in the Arab world, he certainly was among the first to offer the most resonant articulation of these concerns.[4] His observations raise urgent questions: Have not Arab intellectuals been studying their turath since the late nineteenth century, when the term *turath* was coined? What does Jabiri mean when he rails against the state of history-writing in the Arab world? Why does he insist on the primacy of studying turath in the postcolonial era? The main purpose of this and the following chapter is to address these questions by outlining Jabiri's intellectual project, by dwelling on what he called the "new vision" that he rolled out in the 1980s. This new vision gave rise to new interpretations and intellectual undertakings that posed a challenge to different modernist concepts and assumptions that many intellectuals and activists took for granted. Jabiri's new vision meant not only to divert attention from the cultural anxiety Arab intellectuals harbored with respect to Western traditions (i.e., catching up, imitation, and the diffusion model), but also to establish the responsibility of this Western-bound knowledge for the positioning of turath within the broader structure of knowledge in the postcolonial Arab world.

Jabiri offered a fully fledged diagnosis of the Arab intellectual condition in the colonial and postcolonial eras. His project amounts to one of the most original interventions in the collective effort to decolonize the Arab self, for two reasons. First, he underscored the need to connect the postcolonial subject to its past histories when the vast majority of Arab intellectuals proudly asserted their independence of them. Second, he insisted that this connection (*itsal*) provides antidotes to the cultural woes that colonization inflicted on the Arab people. Connection to turath, per Jabiri, will usher in a new era of self-decolonization that restores a sense of continuity and wholeness. Well before the advent of the European colonizer, the Arab self was complete, unfragmented, and reconciled with its past and cultural heritage. But the advent of modernity, through colonialism, deformed and split the Arab self, especially in the wake of the historical break that took place in the nineteenth century.

While not the first, Jabiri's analysis of Arab colonial and postcolonial conditions is among the most profound, consequential, and elaborate, for the simple but always interesting reason that his works enjoy canonical status. While he adhered to the modern order and its political mechanisms (i.e., democracy and human rights), he nonetheless was critical of many aspects of European modernity. For Jabiri, Arab modernity must not follow the same path. The European "modern mind," Carl E. Schorske reminds us, "has been growing indifferent to history because history, conceived as a continuous nourishing tradition, has become useless to it."[5] Jabiri's call to *re*connecting to turath rejects this idea.

WHY JABIRI?

Jabiri launched his career by posing simple yet far-reaching questions: Where do we find our ideals? How do we decolonize the Arab self from Western or Islamic authoritative referents (*sultat marji'yah*)? And, most important, are ex-colonized nations well served by continuing to rely on universal principles and teachings that alienate them from their own cultural traditions? For many Arab intellectuals during the 1970s, these were not abstract questions, but inquiries into their freedom, self-determination, and self-realization. To Jabiri, many of the common European prescriptions imposed on decolonized nations have wreaked havoc on Arab peoples. He argued powerfully against casting away the past in order to usher in modernity. "Naturally," he writes, "it is impossible for the Arab nation with a steep history and traditions, to break free with past traditions by throwing them to the sea. This is absolutely impossible."[6] Rather than blindly embrace the European model, Jabiri firmly believed in the benefits of fashioning an Arab version of modernity with a distinguished Arab pedigree emanating directly from its vast historical experience. This is the ground upon which he emphasized the "need to rationally work out [*Isti'ab*] turath" to spawn a modernity that is Arab in character, features, and nature.

Marginalizing European frameworks and circumscribing the sway of its cultural models over the ex-colonized subject (i.e., conceptions, perspectives, worldviews, styles of analysis) has been the hallmark of Jabiri's project since the mid-1970s. For Jabiri, neocolonization as a condition of life was, and remains, a real condition. This reality could be reversed only by reaching back to local traditions and indigenous culture, rather than reaching out to modern and European traditions. With this new conceptualization, which calls for shifting the cultural gaze from the exterior to interior, Jabiri's analysis undermined many Arab scholars' assumptions that many of the postcolonial challenges could be solved coherently through progressive governmental and social policies. When governments fail to do their part, many Arab intellectuals and activists believed, then they must resort to more modernity. And when everything fails, these Arab activists and writers didn't hesitate to resort to revolutionary mean to force change. The results, in Jabiri's eyes, were devastating. At an earlier stage of his life, when he was still mired in national politics, Jabiri thought this mode of nationalism was working—until one day it didn't work. With the collapse of the postcolonial project, Jabiri came to conclude that any enduring change should originate in the past. Postcolonial failure convinced him that the ex-colonized Arab people can never be wiped clean, born again, or remade overnight by this or that revolution; any real and lasting change requires a long and persistent reckoning with the past if it is to succeed.

Ever since the nahda of the late nineteenth century, Arab thought had not been jolted and disrupted beyond recognition as it was with Jabiri's intervention in the 1970s. His proposals were capable of undercutting the normative reliance on European models and of delivering a trenchant critique of Arab intellectuals' disregard and negligence of their turath. But it was Jabiri's feat to demonstrate how Arab intellectuals continued to think of their turath through Western eyes long after colonism had ended (see chapter 4). In this regard his question "How do we read?" is, to my mind, among the most important of the questions he explored. In raising it, he prompted a cultural shift in the attitudes of many readers, from a wholesale rejection of their past traditions to a willingness to revise their attitudes about turath. It also forces his readers to consider questions not only about the form of colonial and postcolonial thought, but also of its location, geography, and meaning.

Despite his scathing critique of certain European concepts of modernity, Jabiri is classified as a modernist in the current historiography.[7] Curiously, no elaborative intellectual biography of Jabiri has been published to date, despite the overwhelming acknowledgment of his central contributions to the (un)making of Arab intellectual debates over the last four decades. In historicizing Jabiri's intellectual formation, one can instantly register a historiographical note. The passage from the colonial to postcolonial condition, which accompanied an intellectual earthquake in the Mashreq, hardly affected Jabiri and other Maghrebis' styles of analysis and intellectual habitus. In other words, the transition left his writing style, modes of thinking, and cultural perspective untouched. Few of the ideological controversies that centered on the role of the writer, committed literature, and free poetry, which stirred so much debate among literary circles in the Mashreq, seem to have had any effect on his life, or on the lives of many Maghrebi philosophers. Although Jabiri wrote in Arabic and shared considerable intellectual and philosophical ground with colleagues in the Mashreq, his domain of experience and its particularities kept him independent.

The following intellectual biography shows that the primary turning point in Jabiri's life, which coincided with a shift in perspective for Arab intellectuals, came as late as the 1970s, spurred by the growing cultural anxiety with economic downturn, political repression, neocolonialism, and capitalism. It was at this time that he came to the realization that past traditions are not dead traditions, but influential cultural referents and frameworks with the power to shape tastes and realities. This agenda lies at the center of the new philosophical conversation for which Jabiri, among others, became the first to provide the necessary intellectual scaffolding. As we shall see, Jabiri's primary suspicion of radical change and his newfound appreciation of the inherited wisdom of the past were based on a new conceptualization of the notion of time. For Jabiri, the modern concept of time is fractured; therefore, he rejected what he called the continuous perceptions of time. The separation between past and present, Jabiri argued, is essentially artificial, arbitrary, a modern invention that he did not accept. During the 1970s, the conceptual approach to time and temporality had transformed in fundamental ways that helped Jabiri in his reckoning with past traditions and their "afterlives." As historian David Carr puts it, "Our conception of time is at the root of all our other concepts."[8] The moment the concept of time is disrupted and altered, many other conceptions are affected as well.

APPROACH AND METHOD OF INVESTIGATION

The urge to revisit Jabiri's work emerges first and foremost from the need to better understand the postcolonial condition in the Arab world. One way of grappling with that world is by understanding the conversation among native intellectuals: the questions they ask, the cultural concerns they cope with, and the fears and hopes they share with each other. In this sense, there is little doubt that Jabiri's philosophical intervention in the larger context of Arab thought is original and profound; even his many critics acknowledged his canonical status in contemporary Arab thought. However, despite the plethora of commentaries and essays that have explored myriad aspects of his work, it is not easy to escape the impression that Jabiri's writings remain elusive. In what follows, I refuse to "read" Jabiri as the author of thirty-one books, but rather the author who has written twenty-seven books *plus four.* This methodological separation of his works into two different groups is critical to my approach and analysis of his intellectual development.

The four books that make up his magnum opus, *Naqd al-ʿAql al-ʿArabi* (Critique of Arab reason) are commonly seen as the central part of his intellectual output. For reasons as yet unclear, the "plus four" garnered more academic attention than the rest of his works put together. Like Allan Bloom's *The Closing of the American Mind* (1987), a book that offers a profound and compelling diagnosis of the common illness infecting American society and institutions in what Bloom refers to as the "crisis of reason," Jabiri's *Naqd al-ʿAql al-ʿArabi*, which appeared in 1984, 1986, 1990, and 2001, offers a comprehensive analysis of the crisis of reason in postcolonial thinking by tracing back various strands of modern Arab thought to premodern patterns. Emphasizing structural continuity over historical breaks and ruptures, Jabiri concluded that, for the Arab people, the past is not only cohabitating but also coexisting with the present. The way out of this crisis of the postcolonial condition is, therefore, not by dispensing with the past, or by destroying the old order, but through recognizing, ordering, and forging new relationships with it. This embrace of turath, Jabiri warned, must be judicious. Jabiri proposed to Arab readers the development of a new relationship with the past, as lovers develop a new relationship after a crisis.

Yet the problem of the plus four is that they gave rise to a rather static portrait of Jabiri as, on the one hand, a modernist, secularist, and liberal, and, on the other, a chauvinist, Islamist, and conservative. In fact, what has been written on Jabiri's project has by far exceeded what he wrote himself. The current historiographical focus on the plus four is not the only way of approaching Jabiri's positionality; the disproportionate emphasis on those books has given shape to an arbitrary hierarchy of Jabiri's works in which the twenty-seven merely serve as an illustration and elaboration on the plus four. As such, they tend to be received as books that complement his magnum opus: sustaining his arguments, filling in the gaps, and substantiating his arguments. This view of subsidiary and primary books has distorted much of the writing on Jabiri's project, limited the scope of his philosophical intervention, and paralyzed the historicization of his intellectual project. Moreover, Jabiri's plus four is not a readily transparent source for historians in evaluating his work on modernity, the liberal order, secularism, and Arab reason, given that these books are often punctuated by fevered speculations on matters contradicted by Jabiri elsewhere. This chapter and the one that follows engage Jabiri's other works in order to decenter and disrupt this common reading. In short, my method of defamiliarizing Jabiri rests on the reading of the twenty-seven works, which suggest an estimation of Jabiri as less of an Islamist or a liberal-modernist, but simply a connected thinker in the postcolonial age.

MODEST BEGINNINGS

Mohammad Abed al-Jabiri was born in December 1935 in the southeastern town of Figuig to a family of Berber descendants. His father was a well-off merchant and an avid nationalist, his mother a divorced housewife whose husband mistreated her. Jabiri spent the preponderance of his early years in the household of his paternal grandparents, occasionally visiting his mother, who stayed with her family. He attended al-nahda al-Muhamadiyya, the national school in his town and, for two long years, studied at a French elementary school. As a young man, Jabiri knew little about the world beyond the limits of this placid place, with its routine, monotonous lifestyle, surrounded by an all-encompassing universe of untouched spaces filled with sand.

In his autobiography, *Hafriyat Fi al-Dhakira Min Ba'id* (A distanced archeology of memory) (1995–1996), Jabiri ruminated on the life conditions of Figuig's strained community, where he lived the first part of his life. Rather than elaborate on the economic misfortunes of townspeople, Jabiri opted to dwell on the many cultural codes and traditions that created resilient people and inoculated them from the vagaries of time and obtrusive French authorities. Though many of these traditions were outdated and obsolete, they bestowed his people with order, hierarchy, structure, faith, and a sense of place and belonging. The only disruptive force in this town was the intolerable presence of the French *colon*.

Remarkably, Jabiri spent little time talking about the big topics—of socialism, Marxism, or existentialism—that preoccupied the ideologists of his generation, primarily in the Mashreq. Instead he addressed the seemingly trivial, describing a place made up of slums and huts and populated by humble people. He wrote about his family's house in Figuig's center, a stone's throw from the only mosque in town. Jabiri seemed to like this early twentieth-century mud house. Porous and permeable as it may have been, Jabiri was proud to mention the snake that slithered in and out, undaunted by human dwellers of this house. He describe the social landscape at great length: he mentioned the people who suffered illness, as well as barren women, and others who prayed for rain. In his telling, most of the townspeople who suffered a dearth of resources beseeched God in each endeavor. It is truly remarkable how Jabiri and the other residents of the town cohabited with animals in their living spaces. The modern sensibility to dominate and control nature was nowhere in sight in this town. What held this community together was the invisible power of tradition, which gave life meaning, purpose, a reassuring sense of normalcy, and greater equilibrium.

Economic hardships aside, Jabiri painted the picture of a rather solid community with a sense of dignity. Many of the life stories he recounted would be seen as personal failures in modern-day metrics: a scarcity of food and basic needs; promising students whose studies were derailed by household commitments; poor sanitary conditions; excruciating domestic chores, such as the collecting of twigs by women to start a fire. In fact, the lifestyle Jabiri portrays seems almost medieval. Yet, in his depiction, Jabiri refrains from abstractions. Rather, he humanizes the people he lived among, gives them names, acknowledges their work: the man who makes a living in his meadow, diligently tilling the ground; another who builds his own shelter with his own hands; another who tours the town's myriad Sufi shrines; yet another, who is a brilliant storyteller. People who could easily turn to opioids or to religious agnosticism labored to keep their families afloat. Local and indigenous traditions, Jabiri showed, warded off extremities for the townspeople, provided them with strong coping mechanisms to overcome health crises and get through their days. "In Figuig," he writes, "people lived their lives with fidelity [to their families and traditions]. . . . Everything and everyone was inexorably linked to another with a strong link: kids, mothers, fathers, brothers and relatives; animals, birds, reptiles, jinns, and angels; moons and stars, all these creatures dwelled in the same space bounded by familiarity and cohabitation."[9]

In this peaceful, unassuming town on the Algerian border, where only Amazigh was spoken, Jabiri spent his early formative years. Yet, like many others his age, Jabiri picked up and left town after graduating from elementary school. His relocation demonstrates that the modernist myth that the poor are bound to the places where they are born rings hollow. After completing elementary school—a real milestone—he left for Oujda, an adjacent city, where his nationalist, womanizing father ran a tailor shop and sewing business with his brother. In Oujda, Jabiri was exposed to a larger society with a diverse array of peoples who spoke Arabic and African languages. For a short time, Jabiri worked as an apprentice in his father's shop, mostly supervised by his uncle. In this medium-sized city, he came to realize that cities featured not only people abiding by traditional social codes, as in Figuig, but also teemed with moral lapses, such as sexual and juvenile delinquencies. At this stage of his life, Jabiri was not particularly proud of his father's three marriages.

From 1949 to 1951, in Oujda, Jabiri attended the Tahthib Middle School. He was one of thirty students—all male except for six female students who spoke Darija (Moroccan Arabic). Despite his exposure to a strikingly different environment and his studies in Arabic, Jabiri's life in Oujda "was not particularly eventful." Jabiri's most salient memory from his stint in this gloomy, uninspiring city was the fate of his father's business, which was dealt a blow by French authorities. As a tailor, his father was accused of "trading in unauthorized garments" bound for the French army and charged with affiliation with the National Party, and for this "loyalty to the Independence party" he had suffered. With his father's business shattered, Jabiri's proclivity to nationalism grew stronger. He emerged more convinced of the disruptive power of the French *colon* and the need for independence. The French presence seemed to have generated a measure of existential anxiety for young Jabiri, a feeling that began to effect his nervous system, changing the way he understood and perceived the French threat. Jabiri soon learned that his nascent nationalism meant a desire for dignity, independence, and freedom—for, despite his murky relationship with his father, young Jabiri had always been proud of his father's untrammeled nationalism.

CASABLANCA: RALLYING BEHIND THE FLAG

Jabiri had mastered reading and achieved an intermediate level of Arabic writing before continuing his journey to Casablanca, where he spent the next five years. Finding a high school in mid-century Morocco proved a challenge. Morocco, Jabiri writes in his memoir, "had featured no more than four or five high schools, except in Rabat, where Mohammad V had built few other more." But Jabiri's resolve to continue his studies only increased with his growing awareness of the centrality of nationalism. During high school, he began reading a list of different nahdawi scholars (who go unnamed). His exhilaration at the liberating effect of these writings attests to their riveting power on his young self.

Jabiri sat his sights on enrolling in an Arabic school, one that would be administered not by the French but by Moroccan nationalists. In Casablanca, he attended Lycée Abdel Karim Lahlou, established by the Istaqlal (Independent) Party as part of its vision to create a generation of future nationalists who would lead Morocco in the postcolonial era. Though French was the language of instruction, it nonetheless made way for Arabic as a second language, as part of the new national curricula. In this institute, Jabiri was transformed from an unaffected town kid into a genuine Moroccan nationalist. In his memoir he elaborates on the different ways teachers had begun teaching Arabic literature, adab, and philosophy in civil studies classes, instilling in him a new sense of national pride and dignity. The school afforded an amenable atmosphere for young students to embrace Moroccan nationalism; as one of Jabiri's commentators writes, "This climate profoundly influenced al-Jabiri who saw Arabic as the tool for Morocco's political autonomy *ultimate*."[10] Indeed, if there exists a discernable milestone that clearly marked young Jabiri's movement toward nationalism, it would indisputably be this moment in the early 1950s. The young boy of Figuig is gone, and a national activist has taken his place.

Casablanca was a world apart from Figuig: a bustling city featuring diverse ethnic populations who proved capable of living in a multicultural world with little attachment to traditions. Unlike the town of his birth, the French authorities had turned Casablanca into a liberal project that assumed individuals to be freer than ever from accidents of birth, race, gender, and location: "From Figuig . . . to Casablanca . . . one thousand kilometers apart . . . from an oasis on the big Sahara to the business and industrial heart of the capital of modern Morocco."[11] In this city, far from his ailing mother and insolvent father, Jabiri rubbed shoulders with leading nationalists, many of them disguised as schoolteachers, party members, and union leaders. These people came from different walks of life, some emigrants, some locals, some religious, others less religious. Casablanca in the 1950s was poised to embrace young and ambitious nationalists like Jabiri, who blended in easily.

College had long been a hub for national radicalization in the colonial world. Jabiri's high school (also called "college" in colonial Morocco) changed his thinking in fundamental ways. His was the first cohort of young Moroccans to graduate from a two-year college. Jabiri's graduation was an exceptional event in the history of education in Morocco: it was attended by Mehdi Benbarka, the foremost leader of Morocco's Istiqlal Party, who delivered a zealous commencement speech. This event marked the beginning of Jabiri's enduring friendship with Benbarka, who offered him an invitation to Istiqlal headquarters when delivering his certificate. Jabiri's closeness to Benbarka set him on a new course. The mythical nationalist leader gave the young chap from Figuig a purpose, meaning, and unmitigated sense of belonging. The national party, desperate for young nationalist graduates, would offer Jabiri new opportunities. By recruiting him to translate and write, it secured him a decent job first at the national newspaper *Aqlām* and then at *al-'Ilam*. Jabiri started as a translator, but he advanced in the ranking and soon became a correspondent.

Unfortunately, the split that took place within the Istiqlal Party led to Jabiri's firing from his jobs at both newspapers. He followed Benbarka as the latter parted ways with the party and created his own, the National Party. The rupture within the Istiqlal Party did not mark the end of Jabiri's national experiment, however. He soon was assigned as secretary general of the *Tahrir* newspaper, established by Benbarka as the mouthpiece of his oppositional National Party. This is how Jabiri found himself imbroiled in the politicis of the Arab Left: as the new party formed, it struggled to cultivate a cadre of Arabic-speaking young nationalists to carry the agenda. To address this issue, Benbaraka decided to send a few Moroccan students to Syria to study Arabic. Jabiri was among those who were given a grant from the party to go to the Mashreq.

THE MASHREQ: THE SPIRIT OF ARAB NATIONALISM

Upon arriving in Syria in 1956, after a fourteen-day journey aboard a ship that made stops in France, Alexandria, and ultimately Beirut, Jabiri registered that "no Arab could feel alianated in Damascus." For years, Damascus had been the favorite destination of aspiring Moroccan students; Damascus University, as well as Syrian middle schools, featured a French curriculum that appealed to them more than the Egyptian system did. The Mashreq in general was viewed as a place of education and learning, nationalism and authenticity, and, above all, anticolonialism. As historian David Stenner puts it, "The countries of the "Arab East" remained points of reference for many Moroccans, because they symbolized the possibility of an authentic Islamic anticolonial modernity that could counteract European hegemony."[12]

At Damascus University, Jabiri enrolled in a general studies program and took courses in Arabic literature, philosophy, and history while working as a reporter for the newspaper *al-ʿIlm*, the official daily of the oppositional National Party in Morocco. During the academic year 1956–1957, he experienced many of the boisterous events that roiled Damascus, attended a rally in support of Nasser, mingled with young Arab nationalists he had read about back in Morocco, joined reading groups, and attentively listened to speeches by rising young Baʿthists. One of the young radicals that he befriended was Jurj Tarabishi, a little-known student who also enrolled in the department of humanities at Damascus University. At the time, Tarabishi was under the spell of existentialism, a keen reader of French philosophers and, later on, a prominent translator. As a good Syrian host, Tarabishi would extend an invitation to Jabiri, who seemed to Tarabishi a particularly diligent and hardworking young man but "not as good with girls."[13]

For Jabiri, Damascus was not only a place where he came to meet a new guard of Arab activists and intellectuals, but also a city where Pan-Arab politics took flight. He expressed fascination with young nationalists and social critics who threw their weight behind the political project of Pan-Arabism and debated passionately about the role of literature in politics, free verse, and total revolution. As a correspondent for *al-ʿIlm*, he reported how these young social critics went about their daily lives: obsessively reading literary journals and Michael Aflaq's statements, attending French-style cafés. Keen to join these circles, Jabiri thought that the Arab nationalist movement in Damascus could provide a blueprint and a practical program that the newly independent Morocco could imitate. These young activists believed that politics could provide the way to decolonization; they were idealists who subscribed to a Pan-Arab ideology that presumed the current nation-states were a transient state of being, having read the work of Sati al-Husari, who considered the Arab states to be artificial units and propounded the idea that the Pan-Arab nation was the only real entity. These social critics, whom young Jabiri admired, were also influenced by Michel Aflaq. The founder of the Baath Party, Aflaq disseminated an ideology of total revolution, one that is not limited to politics but includes a transformation in cultural norms, historical perspectives, and social standards. The social critics read about and admired Nasser's revolution and marveled at his revolutionary policies and nationalization project. Jabiri observed all this, taking note of how ardently these young, worldly nationalists in the Arab Mashreq read and translated Western philosophies; he also bore witness to the way notions like class analysis, existentialism, positivism, political awareness, and sovereignty animated the intellectual conversation among them. But no other notion struck him as more than that of revolution, the proponent of which despised not only the status quo but also past traditions that, in their eyes, seemed to sustain the old political order—a sensibility that seemed to have captured the students and social critics whom Jabiri held in high esteem.

The politics of revolution, social change, and struggle against one own's history greatly inspired Jabiri at this stage of his life. In fact, these encounters and exchanges with Arab nationalists defined and shaped his national politics. By the end of his academic year at the Damascus University, Jabiri returned to Morocco, unsure whether he would return to Syria. During the year he spent there, Morocco gained independence. In free Morocco, Jabiri was thrilled to disseminate the program of political decolonization through total revolution he saw unfolding in Syria, which was comprised of three components: personal freedom, national sovereignty, and Arab dignity.

Within the new independent state of Morocco, Jabiri doubled down on nationalism, manifested in a relentless pursuit of school building, creating an educational class that would salvage the country from the effects of French colonialism. During 1958, Jabiri could not make up his mind with regard to his future: Should he go back to Damascus to carry on with his education or stay in Casablanca and work for *al-Taḥarir*? Ultimately, Jabiri's aspiration to establish a high school for girls tipped his mind toward staying in Morocco. Though he seemed restless about the state of education in his new country, he realized that a newly independent Morocco could offer new beginnings, where a better school system could emerge. After all, the highly prized education system in Damascus was not as rigorous as it seemed in Morocco. The deep traditions of learning flaunted by Mashreqi intellectuals left little impression on Jabiri as he settled in Casablanca.[14] Some distressing questions began gnawing at him: Why does the Mashreq view the Maghreb as a periphery? Why is the Maghreb commonly categorized as culturally and intellectually inferior to the Mashreq? Jabiri's journey to remake the educational landscape in Morocco—an endeavor that dominated the next two decades of his life—was heroic. Like a true nahdawi, Jabiri located in education the promise to deliver the Arab world from the clutch of colonialism, the only way to correct the imbalance relationships between the two wings of the Arab world.

EDUCATION IN MOROCCO

Jabiri's career path remained unchanged by the transition to the postcolonial state. He continued to read Western literature like the rest of his peers. "Between 1958–1965 I read the majority of the socialist thought canon that includes works by Marx, Engels, Lenin," he writes, "and I was not the only one- not in the Arab Maghreb nor in the Arab Mashreq- who immersed himself in reading such works."[15] His enthusiasm for nationalism, which translated to his work in the educational field, continued unabated. With the establishment of the new socialist party of National Unity for the Popular Forces (UNFP), which split off from the Istiqlal Party, Jabiri was elected a permanent member in 1962, while writing a weekly column in the newfound leftist journals *Aqlām* and, starting in 1964, at *al-Taḥarir.* Meanwhile, he took a position as a high school teacher but was soon promoted to principal of a girls' school and for a couple of years worked as an educational inspector. In the late 1960s, he enrolled in the department of philosophy at Rabat University (later Muhammad V University). After graduating in 1967 with a master's degree in philosophy, he took a position as assistant professor in the same department. In 1970, he defended his dissertation in front of a committee of French and Arab professors.[16]

Intellectual historians are hard pressed to make sense of Jabiri's career during the early years after independence. Little evidence exists to demonstrate serious breaks or shifts in his overall intellectual journey. No meaningful change in his choices of topics, approach, or styles of analysis and writings seemed to have occurred. Quite the opposite: Jabiri's intellectual trajectory up until the 1970s provides further evidence of a structural continuity with the preceding era, or the preindependence era. Even though the velocity of his writings and publications increased, the basic approach remained the same. It is important to emphasize, though, that, unlike his counterparts in the Mashreq, where the new postcolonial condition brought about vast changes to trends in poetry, translation, and philosophical approaches, ultimately ushering in a new guard of intellectuals, few changes of that scale and type could be seen at work in Morocco.

Jabiri's political interests and tastes also remained constant. In 1966, for instance, he coauthored his first book, *Dirus fi al-Falsafa* (Lessons in philosophy), with his colleagues Mustafa al-Umairi and Ahmad Sultani. A textbook for Moroccan students in the humanities, which became a mandatory reading for generations, *Dirus fi al-Falsafa* includes many entries on Western philosophy and gives little attention to Arab philosophers or classic Islamic works. In 1974, Jabiri published his second book on the educational system in Morocco, *Min Ajil Ru'ya Taqadumiya libaʿd Mushkilatina al-Tarbawiya wal-fikriya* (A progressive vision of some of our educational and intellectual problems). Comprised of a collection of articles and other weekly columns he had previously published, nothing in these books attests to a radical change in Jabiri's modes of thinking. The content and issues they grappled with carry an indelible universalist tone; little in them foreshadow the Jabiri who emerged post-1975.

A WORLD SPLIT APART

The first and most concrete shift in Jabiri's thinking came in in the mid-1970s, in the form of an article on medieval Arab philosopher Abu Nasr al-Farabi (870–950). Published in 1975, the article made a splash; it offered a corrective reading to the common categorization of Farabi as the first rationalist philosopher in Islamic history, whereas prior scholarship assumed that Farabi's translation of Aristotle had launched a new Islamic engagement with philosophy. Jabiri argued that Farabi in fact had been less of a radical. Despite the fact that he was among the first to propound Greek philosophy in Islam, Jabiri argued that Farabi was not unlike other medieval Islamic philosophers, since he combined "philosophy in Islam, and Islam in philosophy." Rather than break new intellectual terrain, Jabiri contended, Farabi ended up showing that religion is not inimical to philosophy. "At its depth," Jabiri writes, "[Farabi demonstrated that] religion does not contradict reason and does not oppose it but superficially. The world of religion is rife with exemplars of the world of reason."[17] Depicting Farabi as a philosopher embedded in Islamic traditions rather than a radical, Jabiri redeems a forgotten genealogy worthy as a model for contemporary Arabs. But the call to reconsider Islamic philosophy as an alternative to modern Western philosophy touched a nerve among Arab intellectuals. Jabiri's detractors thought that he dragged the Arab world back to medieval times.

This was the beginning of a shift in Jabiri's approach, writings, and thinkings. Here Jabiri stood face to face against the Arab intellectual community: he had to either endorse the position that past traditions post a threat, or stick with his new findings about Islamic philosophy. Jabiri's new approach stunned many. What is at stake in this early text, Jabiri said, is the question of how to think about turath. Here Jabiri implies that the common assumption among Arab intellectuals that turath is less worthwhile should be reconsidered. The next chapter dwells at length on the new reading philosophy Jabiri proposed in the wake of what he considered, after Roland Barthes, the death of the author; however, it is important to register here the remarkable departure in his thinking, conceptualization, and epistemology. The reactions to his article would prompt Jabiri to rethink the order of knowledge in the Arab world and raise questions with regard to the collective assumptions that structure and shape the intellectual canon in the postcolonial world. His abiding interest in epistemology would lead him eventually to publish the two-volume book *Madkhal ila Falsafat al-ʿUlūm* (Introduction to scientific philosophy) in 1977, for which he became popular outside of Morocco for the first time. In this work Jabiri centralized the questions at the core of the postcolonial intellectual agenda those of knowledge, references, ideals and epistemology, or *how* we know what we know. He realized that the arranging and ordering of knowledge determines the type of persons this knowledge generates. The questions Jabiri posed regarding the sources of knowledge, myths, ideals, and collective memory that had come to the fore in the postcolonial condition as Arab intellectuals engaged the question of how to be creative in the postcolonial world, rendered him a rising star. Jabiri insisted that rethinking the massive philosophical traditions in medieval Islam provides the answers to these dilemmas. This was both a fascinating yet haphazard proposal. Jabiri proved that he was willing to take the risk.

It is important to register in this regard that Jabiri's earlier faith in following European philosophical traditions began to shake. "Revitalization of knowledge," he argued, "must start from within the culture to which it belongs. . . . This process of knowledge revitalization cannot take place except through a thorough archeology of knowledge in the culture of this [Arab] nation."[18] This was the most audacious call coming from a progressive nationalist to attend to past traditions in an effort to marginalize European epistemology.

This statement makes for a radical conclusion and perhaps marks a turning point in Jabiri's perspective, not only on what kind of education Arab students should receive, but also on what framework Arab culture should draw upon. His declaration assumes two suppositions: first, it undermines the modern belief that learning unfolds through exposure to foreign and exterior knowledge unavailable to ex-colonized nations. Formerly, many believed that exposure to and contact with external (European) knowledge via translation and adaptations of modern frameworks were necessary to the modernization of the Arab world. This view had prevailed since the time of the nahda, until the 1980s, when Jabiri called for turning the gaze inward. According to Jabiri, this predominant model of learning by following external sources and references must be secondary to the exploration of the internal knowledge of Arab culture. Second, Jabiri's statement not only reverses the modernist arrangement according to which Europe is always conceived as the primary source of knowledge (epistemology) and the rest as exemplars (imitation model), but it also disrupts the idea of a single modernity, calling for multiple modernities that draw on local cultures and indigenous traditions.

After forty years of little change, in the span of one year, Jabiri changed greatly. It is curious that Jabiri, writing on the margins of the Arab world in the mid-1970s, was endorsing the marginalization of European epistemologies by placing Arab turath front and center. Rather than breaking with Arab history and collective memory, he insisted on breaking with European forms of modernity and called to ditch "history writing that is informed by eurocentrism."[19] More curious still is that his initial excitement about nationalism, political independence, and social critics began to sudside, giving rise to new cultural questions and concerns with regard to turath that would soon redefine Jabiri and, with him, the entire Arab intellectual landscape. As his commitments to the ideals that animated the nationalist social critic gave way to new sensibilities, Jabiri began to appreciate the power of connectivity and continuity with past traditions, a power that would later give rise to the connected critic. Jabiri's rethinking of his pledges to modern principles and assumptions—which formed the backbone of many Arab intellectuals—began to reconfigure his thinking. Like many disenchanted Arab intellectuals, Jabiri looked around and saw little promise. The problem of the deformed Arab subject was his alienation from his culture. The rupture with the past seemed to have amplified, rather than alleviated, this condition of alienation. During the 1970s, as many Arab intellectuals came to realize that the postcolonial state had fallen short on its promises, the turn to turath offered a new hope—the only hope. With the pervasive anticipation of the postcolonial project diminishing, Jabiri realized that turath could provide the only hope for the retreating ex-colonized world.

THE ROAD TO A NEW NORMAL: A SEARCH FOR A NEW VISION

In 1977, Jabiri published an article entitled "Fi al-Baḥth ʿan Rūʾya Jadīdah: al-Turath wal-Fikr al-Alʿālami al-Muʿāsir" (A search for a new vision: turath and contemporary global thought), which reflected many of Jabiri's working assumptions and captured early on the new intellectual sensibilities that began informing the cultural persona that he came to embody: the connected critic. In this article, he reprimanded Arab intellectuals, especially his previous colleagues on the progressive Left, for their disregard of turath, and, most notably, for failing to appreciate its tremendous impact on the constitution of the Arab self. No grand schema for cultural change, nor any analysis of the Arab reality, can afford eschewing turath, Jabiri argued. He called for foregrounding the question of turath and addressing it first before thinking of changing the corrupted social order by deploying Marxist analysis: "Changing the present no longer means to start from scratch," he contended. Turath, he explained, provides the traditions that sustain and feed Arab's sense of wholeness. To think with Jabiri that the main problem in the ex-colonized world is a distorted sense of wholeness is to acknowledge that the postcolonial Arab is the product of a historical rupture. If Europe emerged out of itself, the modern Arab world emerges out of a historical break with its past. With this new understanding, Jabiri wondered how Marxists could ignore turath's sway over the Arab subject. Turath is made up of "Arab collective memory and [provides] the social imagination" of the postcolonial subject. Grappling with it, therefore, is the first step in decolonizing the self. "Turath," Jabiri expounded, "is everything that co-exists in and with us from the past, whether ours or others' pasts."[20]

The main thrust of Jabiri's new vision was that the place of turath should be changed in the current order of knowledge in the Arab world. This is no slight bid. Rather than framing turath as secondary to translation and importation of Western teachings and theorizations, Jabiri powerfully advocated for turath as the central domain of contemporary Arab thought. By bringing turath from the darker corners in which it had been hidden, Jabiri's new vision held the promise of effecting a comprehensive restructuring of contemporary Arab thought, or at least a reconfiguring of the intellectual conversation along a new set of questions and concerns. This call was destined to gain more ground in the Arab world, not only because Jabiri adroitly tied turath into the central debates, but also because he billed it as a new beginning of intellectual investigation.

In historical retrospect, it is easy to see how Jabiri reorganized the intellectual field to facilitate a new engagement with turath. His rigorous framing of the main cultural questions was not the only quality that riveted his readers; his unique talent for deconstructing many of the issues that consumed Arab intellectual debates appealed to them as well. Embarking on a series of books published in 1980, 1982, 1989, and 1991, Jabiri addressed Arab Marxists as well as Arab liberals and questioned the logical assumptions upon which they based their arguments. It is a curious, yet rarely acknowledged, fact that Jabiri's intervention was among the first to precipitate the decline of class analysis in the Arab world. The downturn of Marxism during the late 1970s was a remarkable event in the postcolonial world, and Jabiri's work accelerated it. Yet

Jabiri was rarely acknowledged, much less given the credit, for decentralizing Marxist assumptions in the Arab world.

To establish his new vision, Jabiri started by demonstrating the outdatedness of the ongoing conversation among Arab intellectuals, a discourse he described as "repetitive and cyclical."[21] Jabiri singled out two problematics that framed the Arab intellectual conversation in the second half of the twentieth century: Islam vs. Arabism, and authenticity vs. contemporaneity. Coming to grips with the way Jabiri displaced and disrupted these issues helps us appreciate the novelty of his work and his interventions.

Islam vs. Arabism, Jabiri acknowledged, was one of the dualities that had for a long time polarized Arab thinkers and intellectuals. The main question that stirred this conversation was the question of priority: "What is the first and basic feature that determines the identity of the populace of this region: Arabism or Islamism? Does Arabism come first? Or the opposite, Islamism is first . . . and perhaps first and last?"[22] Deconstructing the question by demonstrating the ways in which the debate was meaningless, useless, and even anachronistic, Jabiri called for an end to this ludicrious conversation. Historically speaking, Jabiri argued, the question emerged in a particular context and in a specific region of the Arab world (Mashreq). Time had rendered this debate unworthy of any further intervention, since "each one of these sides of the argument is right . . . but what is needed is not to express yet another perspective [on that matter] but a [cultural] revision of these perspectives."[23] Any step forward must first dispense with this "false question" of what comes first: Arabism or Islamism.

Emptying this question of its content, Jabiri convincingly showed that Arab thought had been bogged down by this artificial question, and others like it. For the sake of propelling Arab intellectual debate in the right direction, Jabiri pleaded with Arab intellectuals to let go of cultural problems that bear little contemporary significance. He suggested instead that they grapple with the "primary absence" in Arab thought—namely, turath. Here Jabiri turned to address the assumptions liberal Arabs took for granted, in particular their disregard of turath and their presumption that any engagement with it amounted to a futile debate on the moribund past. In response to this modern assumption, he claimed that "it is impossible to thoroughly adopt turath, for it belongs to the past . . . but it is also impossible to swiftly reject it . . . since it makes for a fundamental component of the present."[24] The way Jabiri questioned the modernist separation between past and present, time and temporality, as implied in this statment, will be addressed in the next section.

The question of authenticity vs. contemporaneity was also a pervasive problematic that had preoccupied the Arab world since they launched the project of the nahda. For Jabiri, however, whole debate surrounding this question are mired by ambiguity; in fact, he found little justification for pitting authenticity against contemporaneity. "What is indeed intriguing," he wrote, "is to find the Arab intellectual asking, and repeating the question, continuously: what must be taken from turath and what must be taken from the West? He never asks, not even once: who am I now and what does it mean to be me. We [Arab intellectuals] keep asking what we should take from turath as if we haven't taken anything whatsoever; we ask what to take from the West as if we haven't been linked or integrated into its culture."[25] The dilemma, therefore, lacks originality and solid framing and represents a sort of cultural compromise between Islamists and nationalists, and "nothing could make these questions more complex and unresolvable than framing them in a wrong way."[26] The debates within "contemporary Arab thought do not reflect objective reality," Jabiri argued; rather, they are often "hollow, empty debates that reflect the fears and hopes [of the Arab intellectual] no more; what render them to reflect psychological conditions rather than objective facts."[27]

The conclusion Jabiri drew is that the first and basic mission on the postcolonial agenda should be to achieve a "complete historical independence" (*Istiqlal al-thāt al-ʿArabiya*) of the Arab self. "Only *by* and *through* such a historical independence" may the Arab subject be poised to "break free of patterns of thought that stand behind these frameworks" that compel and impose spurious patterns of thinking.[28] Jabiri wrote, "The path for historical independence of the Arab self is to wrench loose of the two frameworks altogether; meaning breaking free from the predecessor's authority."[29] For Jabiri, what was urgently needed was to disengage Arab thought from liberal conceptions.

CRITIQUE OF LIBERAL MODERNITY

Jabiri's new vision was radical not only because it linked the theme of change to the past rather than the future, but also for the way it undercut the very assumptions of the liberal project upon which many Arab intellectuals proceeded. In its crude version, the modern-liberal project assumed that human beings are by nature nonrelational creatures, separate and autonomous individuals. Arab liberals embraced the notion that humans must dispense with old culture, past traditions, and superceded values in order to be free and modern—premises that run in opposition to the compelling sense of connectivity with past traditions for which Jabiri's new vision advocated. Yet, despite his trenchant critique of several aspects of modernity, Jabiri was accused of embracing modern taxonomies.[30]

The liberal project rests on the idea of liberating people from their embedded relationships, replacing custom with abstract and depersonalized law. Liberalism looks at past traditions askance, as a constraint on expression and pursuit of individual freedoms. Liberal Arab intellectuals based their understanding of European liberalism on three main aspects: progress, time, and individualism. The omnipresent idea of progressivism took hold of the Arab public and intellectual imagination early in the twentieth century. Originating in the West, but embraced by many ex-colonial subjects in the Arab world, progressivism "is grounded in a deep hostility toward the past, particularly tradition and custom."[31] Though many Arab intellectuals used this idea as guidance in their writings and analysis of Arab society, it also misled them into disparaging their past traditions in the name of progressivism. No Arab writer has promoted this idea more strongly than the leading Egyptian philosopher Zaki Najib Mahmud. In his memoir, *Ḥaṣād Al-Sinīn* (Years of harvest), Mahmud writes that "of all the ideas that he lived through, he came up with one, which he made central to his intellectual activity . . . and this central idea is 'progress.'"[32] What did Mahmud mean by "progress"? Essentially, he writes, it means "looking at the later stage of human life as doubtlessly higher than the preceding stage in history. Later stages are more knowledgeable, better, abler and closer to fullness . . . than preceding stages. The general arch of development is directed forward [toward the future], as is [the case with] a growing baby."[33] In this sense, then, progress requires a traditional society to free itself of traditions to facilitate for growth and evolution, or what Samir Amin calls "emergence." This progress implies a commitment to destroy the past for the new to emerge, which is what Mahmud meant when he asserted the "necessity to obliterate [hadm] to make way for the building of the new."[34] For Jabiri, however, this conceptualization of progress cancels out the past as an entity, rendering it as inimical to the future and the present. Worse, it displaces the meaning of the past from a force that may bear an inspirational significance to a heavy burden that modern people should shed: "The progressive awareness meant that the past, with all its pages, whether enlightening or not, are deemed transcended."[35] What benefit would the postcolonial world receive from forgetting its past? For Jabiri this misguided view is based on a modernist concept of time, an idea that he elaborated in detail.

The modern liberal project rests on the notion of fractured time and discontinuous contexts and entails a separation of the past from the present in order to proceed. In this understanding, the past is regarded as "other," or, as historians say, a foreign country. This division of time is neither natural nor neutral, Jabiri contends, but a modern European arrangement that gives priority to presentism at the expense of the past and future. Presentism, in Jabiri's eyes, is very dangerous, due to the fact that it encourages individuals to think only within the context of one's own lifespan and to focus on the satisfaction of immediate pleasures. In practice, this means less attention to past generations' concerns and fosters a carelessness toward subsequent generations. But what do Arab liberals mean by fractured time besides the focus on presentism? The best way to understand Jabiri's analysis here is to think of premodern temporalities and compare them with the liberal conception of fractured time. Turath, Jabiri writes, promotes a concept of continuous time that morally binds the individual to his ancestors, compels him to care for shared traditions and ideas, places him in a continuous conversation with preceding generations, and ultimately pulls him from the obscurity of presentism. The liberal conception of time deplores this traditional/turathi conception of continuous time, which was predominant in Islamic societies, because within the frames of continuous time the individual is saddled with past traditions that constrain his choices. Thus, there emerges the need to set him free by a different concept of time—the fractured time that separates past from present concerns. However, this narrowing of temporality, in the liberal sense, encourages the self-actualization of the individual while also instilling indifference toward community, family, religion, and society. For Jabiri, prioritizing the present means in practice weakening or even severing the personal obligations toward those with whom one shares a past. The effects of this fractured time are especially pernicious in non-Western societies, since they tear apart the social cohesion; therefore, Jabiri's proposition is that Arab intellectuals do away with this conception of temporality, urging that planning for the future cannot be done effectively without taking the past into full consideration.

A third component prioritized by the liberal order is the individual, the liberated and self-governed subject who wrenches himself free from the constraints and limits of the community. With the advent of modern conceptions of the subject to the colonized lands, long-standing local codes that shaped behavior through education and the cultivation of norms, manners, and morals came to be regarded as oppressive limitations on individual liberty.[36] Resolving these newly reviled social bonds seems to lift the burden from the individual; any sort of affiliation—family, community, past traditions, religion, ethnicity—that stands in the individual's way is met with suspicion. For Jabiri, such a concept of individualism is highly problematic, in that it tears the individual from the undiminished merits of connection and filiation.

This understanding of the liberal project, to which many Arab intellectuals subscribed, disguised a commitment to a misguided conception of European modernity that detested the past, cultural heritage, and local customs and cultures. This critique of some of the constitutive principles of the liberal-modern project raises a challenge to researchers who have categorized Jabiri as a modernist or liberal. Though Jabiri did call for democracy and human rights and insisted on the liberation of the human from established structures of authority, his project does not easily fit into these premade taxonomies. As a connected critic, Jabiri accepted the configurations of modern life, but unlike the modernist project, he rejected the assumption of emancipation from arbitrary culture and tradition. Jabiri insisted on connecting the postcolonial subject to his tradition and culture, thereby radically questioning the commitment to the liberal project.

Jabiri's new vision and critique of Arab liberals demonstrates that, since the beginning of the nahda, the subject of turath had been addressed and treated rather perfunctorily, seen as extraneous rather than integral to the making of the Arab self. In his book *Khitāb al-Arabi al-Muʿasir* (Contemporary Arab discourse), Jabiri demonstrates that the common way to deal with turath was to dispense with it, outlining in detail how liberal nahdawis were studiously silent on the role turath had occupied in the technologies of the Arab self. No other nahdawi was more hostile to turath than the celebrated Salama Musa, who said, "I cannot imagine a modern nahda (awakening) to any eastern nation unless it is based on European principles."[37] Jabiri's new vision questions that common assumption. It asserts that a true liberation, a true decolonization of the self, would remain incomplete without first addressing, processing, and taking stock of turath.

One of the distinctive markers of Jabiri's writings is his framing of the ontological problem of the Arab self as a matter of its relationships with past traditions. Though he enrolled in the Pan-Arab project and climbed up the ranks of the national party in Morocco, by the mid-to-late 1970s Jabiri's private feelings diverged from those of the rest of his generation in the Mashreq. His reaction to the defeated postcolonial project differed from the way society told him he was supposed to react. This dissonance between how he felt he was supposed to react and his actual feelings led him to develop his new vision, which questioned many of the intellectual axioms he grew up taking for granted. He thought that the dismissal of past traditions was wrong, that progress must not conform to European prescriptions, and that cultural translation should be internal rather than external. Social change, Jabiri believed, should not follow a revolution, but proceed directly from an indigenous cultural repertoire rather than European modernity. Jabiri would articulate a new philosophy that can be described as no less than a rebellion against the incomplete experiment of the decolonization era.

This chapter shows that Jabiri's intellectual trajectory had not seen the fundamental shift that apparently impacted Arab intellectuals in the Mashreq during the turbulent period from the colonial to the postcolonial eras. What, then, accounts for the shift in Jabiri's own life? The preceding pages give credence to two main arguments: first, that historians should pay more attention to the untouched continuities between the colonial and postcolonial eras in regions beyond the Mashreq. As Jabiri's biography and an analysis of his new vision demonstrate, very few Arab writers could illustrate the relentless continuity between the pre- and postcolonial eras as vividly as he, a scholar who lived at the far end of the Arab world. While the transition from the one era to the next affected cultural production in Beirut, especially in literary and poetry circles, Jabiri's life project remained constant as he traveled from colonialism to independence.[38] Historicizing his intellectual career, which spanned across sixty years of intense activity, attests to the deep rupture in his mode of thinking that took place in the wake of the 1970s, giving historians new questions to grapple with.

Second, Jabiri's intellectual biography indicates that historians should not take for granted the common interpretation that the dismantling of the Pan-Arab project led to political Islam. Rather, they must treat the disenchanting effect of the postcolonial state as a condition that drove many intellectuals to seek new cultural references that gave rise to the connected critic. Reconstructing Jabiri's intellectual trajectory has many merits for historians of the region, aside from correcting historiographical distortions. It pulls them away from focusing on Islam/secularism;

it invites them to think beyond common categories, which often distort as much as illuminate Arab history. The fact that in the post-1970s, for instance, the cultural emphasis on revolution and nationalism has given way to the idea of authenticity could mean not only the rise of Islam but also the rise of scholars like Jabiri. It could mean the writing of a history of the connected critic, rather than the Islamist.

It is my argument that the kind of person who emerges from the new order of knowledge in the 1970s is markedly different from the kind of person generated by the previous order. As we will see in the next chapter, the cultural turmoil of the 1970s has remade the Arab intellectual landscape, giving rise to new forms of discursivity and cultural personae. In many ways, Jabiri's analysis helps us appreciate the way Arab intellectuals deployed (modernist and turathic) categories, drew boundaries between different realms of knowledge (left and right), marked geographies of knowledge (Mashreq and Maghreb). He helps us see the power of context and the contingency of ideas on historical development. Above all, he shows us how ideas define people and remake their identities.

4

RESTATING TURATH IN THE POSTCOLONIAL AGE

So long as we do not establish our past on rational foundations," Jabiri warned in early 1981, "we will not be able to establish for a present and future rationality."[1] With this statement, Jabiri came as close as one could get to articulating the meaning of authenticity and the working assumptions of the connected critic. Here he assured his readers that while the Arab past was made to be irrational, it can be rearranged to be rational. For Jabiri's project, remaking the Arab past is essential, because not only does it provide cultural references in the postcolonial era; it also provides a moral ground for critiquing European rationality. Implicit in this is Jabiri's idea that the development of the ex-colonized Arab people hinges less on imitating Western rationalism than on the formation of indigenous rationality.

Jabiri's profound distrust of exogenous (European) rationality and his persistent emphasis on endogenous (turath) rationality constitutes the main thrust of his intellectual output. To be sure, Jabiri did not rule out cultural borrowing so much as he opposed common models of cultural diffusion that implied cultural imitiation. In making sense of his thought system, marking the differences between these two cultural mechanisms is important. As Ivan Krastev and Stephen Holms write in *The Light That Failed*, borrowing is not the same as imitation, since the former "does not affect identity, at least not in the short term," while the latter "cuts deeper and can initiate a much more radically transformative process, veering close to a 'conversion experience.'" Because imitation is a more sweeping process, when compared to the limited nature of cultural borrowing, it usually "generates resentment" and "cultural backlash," as Krastev and Holms show.[2] While accepting early Islamic philosophers who borrowed diverse ideas from the Roman Empire as well as India, Jabiri inveighed against the wholesale imitation of Western models that was, in his eyes, typical in Cairo and Beirut. Instead, he called for embracing a more measured, cautious model of borrowing that had prevailed among medieval Islamic philosophers but was superceded by Arab nahdawis in the late nineteenth century.

The critical venues that Jabiri opened up in the 1980s have rarely been explored in full. His critique of intellectuals in Cairo and Beirut goes beyond their failed attempts to catch up with the West by imitation. In his campaign to decanonize the political agenda of the social critics in the Mashreq, Jabiri demonstrated the tendency of these intellectuals and activists to think about their past through Western eyes. They "read" their reality not by native cultural references but "by and through" European references. The nature of this critique set him apart from the rest of the group that emerged in the 1970s commonly called *turathiyun* (partisans of turath, or heritage thinkers). The members of last group "have a great interest in reviving the Islamic legacy of rational thought, such as the tradition developed by the School of the Mu'tazila . . . and the ideas of Ibn Rush." To be sure, Jabiri shared with these "heritage thinkers" many of their working presuppositions, as they too celebrated Islam "as a civilization with important and wide-ranging intellectual, cultural, and artistic achievements that should inspire Muslims to reassert themselves."[3] Yet, while many heritage thinkers marked political Islamists as their ideological nemeses because the latter group claimed the exclusive right to represent Islam, Jabiri's main concern was the formation of a new cultural canon—one that had more to do with warding off political nationalists and social critics whom, he deemed, guarded the current one. In other words, Jabiri's critical writings against political Islamists is dwarfed by his expansive critique of Arab liberals and Marxists of the Mashreq, with whom he'd shared political views before changing course. Jabiri protested against their propositions because they assumed that rationality is universal, and therefore pliable for cultural appropriation in the ex-colonized world.

Jabiri's critical project was certainly not the first to invite scholars to attend to turath. But his project was among the first to mark Arab cultural heritage as an epistemological ground for endogenous Arab rationality. His call emphasizes not simply the exploration of the unutilized trajectories in the past, but also the exploration of the unrealized possibilities of past traditions in the modern age. It represents a profound change in Jabiri's personal career as well as a broader rejection of an earlier cultural agenda that rests on the unconditional following of Western rationalism.

Scores of Arab intellectuals embraced the diffusion model, including heritage thinkers. Like their metropolitan interlocutors, Arab intellectuals too credulously believed that, with the diffusion of European-originated ideas and teachings, the Arab world would be delivered from tyranny to freedom, from its state of darkness to the light of modernity. Even heritage thinkers, who leaned heavily on indigenous traditions, considered European teachings indispensable to the Arab people. Egyptian Nasr Hamid Abu Zayd, a quintessential heritage thinker, thought of himself as a mediator between two cultures; as Carool Kersten notes, his critical writings expressed "a desire to act as a translator between cultures."[4] Jabiri, however, contested this logic. For him, the futile attempt to graft European frameworks to turath and vice versa was not a victimless crime. If the drive behind heritage thinkers' cultural excavation of bygone tradition meant to "form a counter-narrative to the puritanical religious revivalism and uncompromising politics of the Islamists," Jabiri's motive was an abiding concern to decolonize the Arab self not only from the narratives of puritanical Islamists but also from European cultural references.[5] The way to do this, Jabiri believed, was to loosen the grip of Beirut and Cairo on Arab intellectual production. Attenuating the cultural dominance of the intellectuals in these two cities would provide the path to genuine decolonization.

Ironically, Jabiri was not always critical of Western modernity or the intellectuals who clustered in Cairo and Beirut. Before the 1970s, he conceived of Europe as the source of all theories (epistemology) and the Arab world as a place where these theories were tested (exemplar). Like many progressive Arab leftists, he also subscribed to the notion that one must relinquish his past in order to embrace the modern. As Jabiri puts it, "The ideology of modernity calls to effect a break with the past."[6] As a nationalist, too, he thought that modernity negates and stands in contradistinction to cultural heritage. Yet, by the late 1970s, Jabiri placed these modernist assumptions and principles under scrutiny, paving the way for the rise of a new conception of Arab modernity that appreciates the epistemological power of turath traditions. In one of his most evocative statements, Jabiri writes, "Modernity, in my view, means not to reject turath nor to cut ties with the past so much as to rise to a new level of dealing with turath."[7]

In addressing the cultural concern around how to deal with European ideas, Jabiri posed the question of how to deal with turath. He was not alone in recognizing its shaping power, but he was undoubtedly the most eloquent protagonist of the cultural shift that took hold of the Arab imagination in the wake of the defeat of the postcolonial project. His rejection of his former self—that is, of the intellectual presumptions he had held and that for so long sustained his thinking—opens a window through which to examine transformations in postcolonial thought. This particular transformation in the order of knowledge is best reflected in the cultural appreciation of turath. For the better part of the twentieth century, Arab intellectuals and activists had classified past traditions negatively when measured against the value of Western and modern knowledge. Starting in the 1970s, however, these same intellectuals saw the perception of past traditions and turath shifting from negative to positive. The upending of this order of knowledge is not only Jabiri's life story, but the story of an entire generation of postcolonial intellectuals who came to reexamine their modernist presumptions and biases against their own cultural heritage. It is important to ask what kinds of conversations, queries, criticisms, and questions were raised in the wake of this transformation: How did Jabiri and his peers manage to shed their previous attitude, which conceived of turath negatively, in favor of a more positive position?

Jabiri's new positionality, which reflected his newfound commitment and adherence to turath, prompted some critics to ask whether or not he had broken ranks with the progressive-liberal-leftists. Can one choose to honor his past and remain a progressive? To what degree can the Arab subject live authentically without feeling that he is being locked down by his past traditions? Had Jabiri given up on the present and retreated to the past? In response, Jabiri asserted that the Arab intellectual consensus about disremembering turath had proved ineffective, unhealthy, and even dangerous. Reiterating Freud, Jabiri argued that Arab writers initiated an active forgetting of turath, with little success, since they did so in such a fashion that the harmful effects of turath lingered in the unconscious. More convincingly, Jabiri argued that it is impossible to talk about the present as if it is cut off from the past; any analysis of the present must start by identifying the past traditions that continue to shape and inform it. In other words, in order to probe deeply into the structural of the present, one must reckon with the past that dwells inside of it. "What concerns me in the critique of the present," Jabiri writes, is the "invisible past that continue to configure it." The past "is the hegemonic power that resides in the present."[8]

In pursuing his project, which aimed at dismantling the authority of European references and the agendas of social critics in the Mashreq, Jabiri embraced an immanent critique, or critical realism, which he drew from medieval philosopher Ibn Rushd. Unlike the total critique that deployed by social critics in the 1950s and 1960s, Jabiri's critical realism sought to take the best of turath and move it toward fulfilling its potential. The total critique of the social critics had ruthlessly critiqued everything existing in order to destroy the status quo and hasten the coming of a new order to replace the corrupt one. Jabiri was against this approach. His restlessness about critical realism is rooted in his wariness of ostentatious, aggressive projects that aimed at altogether transforming the current order. Instead, he urged intellectuals to take stock of the traditions that can be salvaged—that is, from turath. Seen from this perspective,

Jabiri founded a whole new way of being that didn't amalgamate different aspects of Islam and modernity in a compromised fashion, but instead offered a new cultural positionality marked by rebutting Islamists's claims on the representation of turath, on the one hand, and progressive leftists and their radical critique of society, on the other.

To illuminate Jabiri's new positionality and elaborate on his critical realism, this chapter examines five themes that illustrate the main intellectual agenda of the connected critic. As mentioned in the previous chapter, the idea here is to marginalize the "plus four" books that for too long provided an overly rigid profile of Jabiri's expansive and complex philosophical project. Though Jabiri's plus four are the most debated, my focus here decenters them and prioritizes the rest of his works, which more directly engage contemporary Arab intellectuals. For intellectual historians of the modern era, however, these works are no less significant than the plus four; in fact, they afford the opportunity to examine the practical consequences of the theories put forward in his plus four. The choice I make here to foreground Jabiri's less-read works is not arbitrary; it is an attempt to contextualize his major contributions to Arab thought in the last decades of the century, to provide a more comprehensive explanation of his critical realism, and to extend the discourse beyond the usual commentaries that have focused on his plus four. Analysis of his writings suggests that what often remains out of view is Jabiri's critical engagement of his progressive leftist colleagues in an effort to decanonize their writings. This chapter aims to excavate the often-forgotten critique of his national colleagues: social critics who often presented themselves as free intellectuals, liberals who called to break with the past, and, finally, Arab Marxists who deemed tradition as the source of all of Arab society's ills. In what follows, I examine five subjects that figured prominently in his complete works: the dominance of European thought, the Andalusian school, the deorientalization of Arab-Islamic philosophy, the revision of the nahda, and the call for the creation of a new Arab intelligentsia. The exploration of these themes affords a better understanding of the connected critic that Jabiri exemplified.

THE DOMINANCE OF EUROPEAN FRAMEWORKS

One of the most salient arguments that Jabiri brought to the intellectual conversation during the 1980s was that the disremembering of the past and turath does not achieve liberation but, rather, powerlessness and bondage. The suppression of Arab cultural inheritance during the three decades after independence (1945–1975) was supposed to set the Arab subject free; instead, Jabiri argued, it emerged fragmented, less emancipated, and less liberated. Put simply, the Arab subject emerged less authentic. This was the context in which Jabiri impugned the embedded assumption among Arab intellectuals that everything must give way to the development of the new Arab subject. This critique of the Arab intelligentsia led to a new realization that past traditions are no longer to be feared, mocked, or viewed as a threat to the creation of the new Arab subject in the postcolonial era. The assumption that authorizes and endorses these understandings should be questioned and thoroughly examined.

The cultural mood of the late 1970s was primed for this interrogation and revision, especially with the weakening and gradual eclipse of the social critic and his institutions that had emerged two decades earlier. One needs only to think of the waning power of journals like *Shiʿr*, which shut its doors at the beginning of the 1970s, or other Marxist-nationalist publications. It is no surprise that Jabiri, a remarkably gifted reader of his historical moment, noticed this point of transition, when the order of knowledge was in flux, which propelled him to raise serious questions about the way Arab intellectuals had alienated the reading public from turath and past traditions. Rather than scaring away the Arab reader from his turath, Jabiri presented it as a more complex phenomenon, remote yet accessible, ancient yet a propos, intimidating yet fascinating, mystic yet rational. These contradictory attributes rendered typical framings of Arab turath less compelling, clearing the way for it to move from the margins to the center of Arab discourse. Vindicating turath from the contempt attached to it amounts to Jabiri's most enduring legacy.

The political moment of the 1970s also helped Jabiri to popularize his ideas. With the unraveling of the postcolonial project, the disillusionment with colonial modernity, and the growing sense of political desperation, a cultural context emerged that proved highly amenable to new ideas and new beginnings. Unlike revolutionary intellectuals and social critics, Jabiri grew convinced that to achieve some degree of freedom and human dignity one should start with the indigenous past, rather than with Europe. After completing his work on Ibn Khaldun, Jabiri began to grasp the meaning of history and past traditions and their scale in defining and shaping the social order in the contemporary Arab world, which led him to conclude that social and intellectual change starts by reckoning with and reconfiguring the place of past traditions in contemporary life. This reflects Jabiri's growing realization that history and turath are central, rather than marginal, to any lasting change in the Arab world.

Yet Arab history and turath are not givens. For Jabiri, the most difficult task was demonstrating that Arab history is narrated along European lines. This narration was endorsed and normalized by a particular class of Arab writers—specifically, social critics in Beirut and Cairo—who did not see turath's merit or value. Jabiri even grew convinced that Arab history and turath had never been written by native Arabs or from an Arab perspective in modern times. Seeking to dispense with prevailing European classifications, he stipulated that the first principle in reading turath is to marginalize Europe. Therefore, he inverted the formula of the social critics by calling to break with the traditional understanding of tradition rather than breaking with tradition as such: "Let us break free of a Europocentric history, a history that takes European civilization as its [primary] frame of reference."[9] The question remains: How does one let go of European conceptualizations through which generations of Arab intellectuals read and conceptualized their turath?

Ultimately, Jabiri addressed this question by examining the way Arab intellectuals (mis)perceived Europe and assimilated European categories. He called on his peers and colleagues to revise "our one-dimensional understanding of European modernity."[10] Jabiri dared Arab intellectuals to historicize what he called the "Arab reading" of European thought, which "turns Europe to a subject."[11] Europe always dominated as the subject, Jabiri complained, while other colonized nations were presented as the object. For Jabiri, this formula should be revised and reversed, since "the project of European modernity played a destructive role in the history of modern Arab nahda." This critical reading of European modernity would "emphasize the historicity, contingency, and limits," of European thought, rather than affirm its universality.[12]

Central to Jabiri's worldview are the notions that Western modernity is not universal, that turath can provide a trajectory for an alternative modernity, and that connectivity with the past allows the cultural decolonization of the Arab self. By urging his peers to reclaim and reconnect with turath as an intellectual tradition, Jabiri embedded his positionality in the cultural repertoire of Arab history and created a genealogy for the intellectual persona of the connected critic, whose raison d'être was found in a double critique of Europe and its Arab protégés, the progressive social critics in the Mashreq. In doing so, Jabiri not only took a position adopted by no other contemporary Arab intellectual before or since, but also paved the way to take on the social critics in Beirut and Cairo. Conforting this established class of intellectuals head-on was like putting his career and prestige on the altar. On the one hand, this move flanks Islamists who claim to speak on behalf of the past and, on the other hand, undermines progressive leftists who disdained and condemned turath as a domain that perpetuates religious wars, ethnic hostility, and communal prejudices.

A deeper analysis of European thought "would lay bare its tendency to hegemony and its penchant to reduce the old and modern worlds in European experience only."[13] For Jabiri, the way forward for the Arab people was to forge an "Arab philosophical project or Arab rationalism that is based on a critical reading of turath."[14] The notion of "critical reading of turath" is essential in Jabiri's thought because he realized that Arab history is rife with political and cultural events, many of which are not applicable to the modern age—or, as he put it summarily, "not all these [traditions] are redeemable." Unlike Islamists who glorified the past and called to restore it in its fullness, Jabiri insisted that only certain events or historical thoughts enjoy "future horizons." There are "exceptional" events that "we have to hold on to" like "the school of Maqasid in Sharia, and the rational-critical spirit of Rushdism."[15] The one particular school of thought that must lay the foundation for Arab rationalism, he believed, was none other than the Andalusian school.

THE ANDALUSIAN SCHOOL

Reclaiming the writing of history, Jabiri posited, means owning it. Owning history means decolonizing the self. Jabiri initially wanted to reclaim turath from Islamists, but he did not stop there. His intellectual endeavor deemed turath as a framework of reference that provides the teachings, principles, guidelines, and cultural references for contemporary Arab people to decolonize themselves from European neocolonialism. This was the context in which Jabiri made a major decision to rewrite the history of what he considered to be a forgotten school of rational thinking in medieval Islam: the Andalusian school. That decision soon amounted to a referendum on the way Arab history is written. For social critics and anticolonial nationalists in the Mashreq, Jabiri's project was a concealed attempt to break the grip of the Mashreqi intellectuals in the field of Arab thought. To Jabiri, however, the contempt with which turath had been regarded since the late nineteenth century remained scandalous. "The last century," he wrote in 1975, "has seen the awakening of Arab thought . . . and its gradual liberation from certain distortions, obscurity, and deviation that is attached to it. Yet, this [awakening] did not assist us to gain a clarity of vision and depth of foresight adequate enough to link [*rabt*] our present to our past."[16] The way Arab history was told was disjointed, illogical, and detached from the present, he argued. Jabiri also drew attention to the structural continuities within the discontinuities between past and present that influenced the way contemporary Arab nations told their story and ordered their lives. He believed that much of the Arab present was inexorably bounded up with the past—just not the rational past that he wished to promote.

The past for which Jabiri advocated was the past of North Africa and Andalusia, which fashioned a rare and unique school of thought that was "rationalist, critical and realist": specifically, the Andalusian school, which consisted of the finest philosophers the Islamic world has ever known, including Ibn Rushd, Ibn Khaldun, Ibn Bajaah, Ibn Tufil, Ibn Hazam, and al-Shatibi. What unified these philosophers was their untarnished rationalist tradition. All of them hailed from North Africa and worked and "breathed within this context . . . away from the Mashreq." Their philosophy was marked by a swift rejection of the philosophical traditions in the Mashreq, which Jabiri dismissed as a tradition drenched in *ʿIlm al-Kalām* (jurisprudence philosophy). For Jabiri the science of Kalam was not fully rational, since its goal was to address the apparent disparity and incompatibility between the revealed text (sacred) on the one hand and human reason on the other. This goal had attenuated and compromised the Kalam philosophy, which preoccupied eminent Mashreqi philosophers like Ibn Sina, al-Farabi, al-Ghazali, and Ikhwan al-Safa, among many others. This group of Mashreqi philosophers had indulged in esoteric and gnostic themes that muddled their philosophy, while the Andalusian school fashioned a rigorous rationalism.[17] As such, Jabiri asserted that it was a good candidate for the canon.

In Andalusia, Jabiri noted, Islamic rationalism reached its peak, specifically with the writings of Ibn Rushd, who debunked not only al-Ghazali, but also conveyed his repugnance toward the philosophy propounded by Ibn Sina in the Mashreq. "Ibn Rushd's critical realism," Jabiri wrote, "was the culmination of a critical stream that was going in one direction: to turn Eastern [philosophical] merchandise (ware) back to the East."[18] Jabiri was firm and consistent in his attempt to parse Islamic philosophy into distinct schools, commending the Andalusian school only to condemn the Eastern intellectual traditions. But, by redeeming Ibn Rushd, Jabiri meant to apply his critical realism—or what he metaphorically referred to as the "rationalist mechanism"—to contemporary Arab thought. The redeployment of Rushdian tradition, which contemporary Arab intellectuals had swept away, entailed calling into question the order of knowledge in the Arab world, which was dominated by Mashreqi intellectuals.

DEORIENTALIZING ARAB-ISLAMIC PHILOSOPHY

Among Jabiri's most radical moves was mustering the courage to assail an entrenched class of Mashreqi intellectuals whose command of Arabic thought, reviews, and publications was beyond all doubt. So was his well-established indictment of Mashreqi intellectual traditions as mired in ideology, which inflected contemporary Arab thought with many misleading concerns and questions, and his insistence on promulgating Maghrebi philosophical tradition as the only rational critical tradition in Arab medieval history while classifying Eastern philosophy as inferior. Another daring intellectual gesture that gained him considerable appreciation is his argument that Arab history has been derivative rather than distinctive. As long as Arab turath is not read on its own terms, independent of European conceptualization, the prospects of cultural change and social transformation hold little promise. This belief, from which much of his critique, views, and frame of analysis emerged, constitutes a significant part of Jabiri's intellectual standpoint. It explains why he felt that Arab people lead inauthentic lives.

Jabiri was firm in his conviction that, in the modern era, Arab cultural history had not been written from an Arab vantage point, except in rare cases. For Jabiri, even if Arab scholars endeavored to write Arab cultural history, these undertakings were bedeviled by modernist paradigms and Western categories. In fact, until the very last day of his life, Jabiri reiterated the same argument, insisting on the need to reconstruct and historicize Arab turath from "its own data."[19] Without the restoration of turath, Jabiri believed, Arab nations are bound to imitate the histories of Europe. The state of turath, he argued, is compromised, lacking in structure, independence, and ingenuity, subsidiary to European culture, subservient to European history. The way turath is being narrated serves only one goal: to bestow on European history its continuity and integrality. Indeed, the scaffolding of turath, which is designed by Orientalists, is adopted unconsciously by local intellectuals without questioning their main blueprints and interpretations. This is not a history of free, emancipated people; it is a history that perpetuates Arabs' condition of inauthenticity.

To decolonize Arab history means to de-Orientalize it by "achieving a historical independence"—specifically, from a prevailing European "reading." Jabiri called on his colleagues to dispense with what he termed the "objectivity" of Orientalists, which "is objective only for them not for us," he wrote, "not because they lack in impartiality and knowledge, a charge that we are not allowed to level against them all, but because the framework of reference that shapes, or is shaping, their readings [of Arab turath] is not the same framework of reference that we desire to shape our reading."[20] To set the process of decolonizing turath in motion, Jabiri suggested addressing the question of reading: "How do we read?"[21] Indeed, Jabiri would reiterate his concern with the question of reading on many occasions, in conferences, in interviews, as well as in his very last writings.

DECOLONIZING READING

No other tradition has been so unjustly subjected to a European reading as the vast philosophical traditions in Islam, Jabiri claimed: The ideas of [medieval] Muslim scholars "were read and examined through the ideas of Greek and Indian philosophers, rather than by, and through, Arab-Islamic cultural data, concerns and aspirations."[22] This lopsided reading led contemporary Arab scholars, in turn, to read their own turath in two divergent ways: some labored to demonstrate the "authenticity of forgotten Islamic philosophical traditions" vis-à-vis European philosophy while others endeavored to debunk and respond to "European distortions of this Islamic philosophy." Whether Arab scholars chose the former or the latter track, the result was the same: Arabic writing on turath was hampered by the concern with reacting to European claims. Instead of reading Arab and Islamic philosophy independently and through its "data" and within its "cultural domain," it was subordinated to a European frame of reference.[23]

In the nineteenth century, European philosophers launched a philosophical construct that marginalized Arab philosophy. The aim was to introduce "unity and continuity in the history of European philosophy that turned it from mere fragments to a coherent and harmonious construct."[24] Supporting the line of continuity in European history meant "bolstering the weakest link in this linearity, the medieval link, at the expense of the historicity of the Arab-Islamic philosophy, its particularity and authenticity, and its supremacy over Latin philosophy in the West, which was unremarkable in comparison with Islamic philosophy."[25] Jabiri therefore proposed that recuperating turath—and its philosophical traditions in particular—from its current readings entailed a deconstruction of the dominant discourse, which means "dissolving its authority over the Arab reader." Unfortunately, Arab turath, per Jabiri, is still fragmented and lacking unity and continuity, not unlike European philosophy before the nineteenth century; it remains an accumulation of ideas and schools of thought. "Our vision of Arab intellectual history is not subjected to reason," Jabiri writes. "We have not rationalized this thought and introduced it as historical processes and conflicts." Rather, turath is still regarded as a collection of jumbled texts, and the preoccupation with it remains limited to "reproduction of these texts."[26] To address this state of chaos and to present turath as distinctive rather than derivative, Jabiri suggested different ways of reading it.

PRELUDE: A DIFFERENT "READING" OF ISLAMIC PHILOSOPHY

Essential to Jabiri's thought style is the notion that every reading, analysis or interpretation is shot through a cultural mediator. "Cultural mediation [*al-wasāta al-thaqāfiya*]," Jabiri wrote, "is not a negatively [*sic*] neutral but one with effects."[27] While this observation is hardly novel, Jabiri spun this truism to assert that no one can write, produce, or even think without "predecessors" or "premade patterns" (*salaf*) or frameworks of reference (*ʾaṭur marjiʿīya*) or simply patterns (*namūthaj*). The way one reads is often predetermined by the cultural references one carries. What framework of reference do we lean on as we read? Jabiri asked. And in what ways does our background knowledge shape our dealing with past traditions? For instance, many scholars read the Andalusian philosopher Ibn Bajjah (824–887) "by and through" the philosophy of al-Farabi (872–950). Given that these two medieval Islamic philosophers wrote in the same language, shared a collective memory, and dealt with similar concerns misled historians to treat them as if one continued the work of the other; historians therefore read the latter "by and through" the works of the former.

Jabiri cautioned against this type of reading and stipulated its perils. Instead, he proposed a reading that established an epistemological break between the two scholars, rejecting the common conception of Arab philosophers as a coherent group. Closely attending to the issues that each one of these philosophers addressed led Jabiri to firmly warn against "reading Ibn Bajjah through Farabi's vocabulary."[28] Rather than claim continuity between the two, Jabiri established two separate philosophical traditions to which these philosophers belonged. Insisting on a definitive distinction between different strains of thought that were originally clumped together afforded Jabiri the opportunity to deconstruct the prevailing reading of turath.

With the impossibility of "reading" Ibn Bajjah "by and through" the philosophy of al-Farabi, how should the former's philosophy be read? Jabiri suggested that the only framework that helps in deciphering the works of Ibn Bajjah is the works of Ibn Rushd (1126–1198). Given that the latter lived after Ibn Bajjah, it seems that Jabiri was committing a historical anachronism. How could one read the works of a certain philosopher through a philosopher who succeeded him? To answer this question, Jabiri suggested reading Ibn Bajjah through the framework that reached its most remarkable articulation and fruition with Ibn Rushd. Here Jabiri's ideas take a complex turn, as he wrote that "the natural framework of reference to Bajjah's philosophy is the 'summit' to which his discourse belongs. We mean by that Ibn Rushd. It comes then that the [best] reading of Ibn Bajjah is through his afterlives, rather than through his 'predecessors.' . . . Ibn Bajjah had afterlives but he had no 'predecessors.' The Bajjahian discourse [*sic*] constituted a beginning to a philosophical discourse, therefore his framework of reference cannot be whatever was before him but whatever comes after him."[29] With this statement Jabiri demonstrated that each reading is also an interpretation.

In sum, the three sections surveyed in this chapter attest that the decolonization of the Arab self consists of three stages. The first calls to reclaim turath as a framework of reference to form a new cultural canon. The second insists on deorientalizing turath from European frameworks. The third calls for the development of a new reading methodology to set Arab philosophy free of the common readings that constrain Arab thought. In this regard Jabiri suggested a new method to help Arab readers "read" Arab and Islamic philosophy not through Western conceptualization but with terms drawn directly from the Arabo-Islamic historical experience. To grasp the rationale behind his realistic critique, we now turn to examine the ways through which he proposed "reading" contemporary Arab thought. Jabiri's growing confidence was rarely masked in this later stage of his life. Few intellectuals dared to stand up to the literary community to which they belonged the way he did. His defiance was reflected in his audacious call to replace the current Arab intellectual elite. Here too Jabiri would critique the nahda and call into question the Marxist and materialist reading of Arab history to pave the way for the rise of the new Arab intelligentsia.

THE QUESTION OF THE NAHDA

The nahda was a flagship project of the Arab renaissance. For Jabiri it was supposed to launch new social, economic, and political arrangements that would give rise to a free, modern, and sovereign "new Arab subject." Equally important to Jabiri was the fact that the nahda was also supposed to deliver the colonized from the bonds of colonial authority. Yet the nahda fell short in these regards. One reason for this failure is the fact that nahdawis drew on sources outside the domain of turath.

To Jabiri, they failed to fully enact historical experiences from the vast cultural repertoire of Arab history. The nahda never ascended to a true "awakening," he charged, because it was not founded on a new, fresh conception of the past. Quite the contrary: "The project of the nahda drew most, if not all, of its conceptions, ambitions, and idioms from the literature and jargons of European modernity."[30]

For connected critics like Jabiri, the vast repertoire of the past provided the necessary tools, conceptions, and ambitions for any serious project of cultural renewal. Given that many nahdawis leaned on Western frameworks, they doomed the nahda to failure from the start. In his critique, Jabiri appeared firm in his prescription of the way nations rise up or achieve nahda: "Cultural renewal is not carried out by borrowing [eclectically] from here and there . . . but from within [the cultural past], by enacting the features" that seemed amenable to "be renewed."[31] Any cultural renewal that builds solely on foreign borrowing is destined to fail; cultural canons can't be based on it. In this regard the nahda was a missed opportunity: it could have canonized turath, but instead nahdawis were more eager to imitate the traditions of Europe.

> Nahda, any kind of nahda, must proceed from a reconstructed turath in order to transcend it. It would therefore be a grave mistake to assume that the Arab subject might be awakened by returning to the past and "picking" what is "beneficial" from it. Equally mistaken is the assumption that this subject can be awakened by a total rejection of the past, aligning with other turaths or catapulting herself into the present [of others]. No, man cannot be innovative except through his own culture and from within his turath. Creativity, in the sense of renewal and authenticity, remains incomplete except if it is done on top of the past debris that was contained, assimilated, and transcended.[32]

Apart from Muhammad ʿAbduh's reformism, most nahdawis shied away from considering the past as the origin of the entire renaissance project. For Jabiri, no cultural renaissance could have proceeded without turath. While different nahdawi schools of thought did in fact make some use of turath, Jabiri considered such use as opportunistic and instrumental rather than an acknowledgment of turath as a fundamental part of the nahda project. As far as Jabiri was concerned, nahda must be rooted in past traditions to lay the foundation for the future. Unfortunately, wrote Jabir, "most of the intellectual currents that connected in one way or another with turath, did not aim to re-establish a new awareness of the nahda as an act of renaissance, nor did they establish new cultural frameworks to the new issues and ambitions [from the past.]"[33] The return to turath as practiced by nahdawis, Jabiri complained, "meant only to support temporary and contingent matters." This, he felt, was a wasted opportunity: "The return to turath during the era of the nahda remained moving on the pragmatic, temporal and functional level no more. . . . [nahdawis] did not endeavor to unearth and explore the roots [of turath]."[34]

Jabiri's critique of nahdawi discourse and thought stemmed from its authors' futile attempts to seamlessly attach one culture (Arab) to the other (European). The nahda was haunted by the obsessive "ambition to reconcile two irreconcilable traditions."[35] For Jabiri, nahdawis should have been more attuned to their own history, past traditions, and turath. For him, "nations cannot achieve their awakening [nahda] by lining up in other's [European] historical tradition but only by a firm and conscious alignment with their own history."[36] The road to a true nahda travels through history rather than bypassing it.

The nahda had spawned a twin, and the two forms of thought clashed against each other. On the right, it gave birth to the Islamic Salafi movement, and on the left it gave rise to a nationalist-secular movement. Neither of them bore much fruit. Jabiri's main critique of nahdawis was that many believed in the power of new ideas rather than the shaping power of historical experience. He condemned the idea common among Arab and Western intellectuals that the more one exposes colonized peoples to the genuine ideas of the West, the better. Jabiri considered this approach misguided for two reasons: first, because understanding ideas is not simply cognitive; and, second, because (historical) experience determines the way ideas are conceived and processed. In other words, Jabiri did not believe that there any such thing as disembodied understanding. Peoples' understanding of new ideas are shaped by experiences.

INTELLECTUAL OUTPUT AND THE SEARCH FOR A NEW INTELLIGENSIA

As the Arab world approached the end of the twentieth century, the name and work of Jabiri was foundational to the new intellectual landscape. His corpus of writings left an extraordinary mark on Arab readers, shaping their views and understandings of the world. Though he based his intervention on changing peoples' perspectives to help them understand the meaning of life under the condition of neocoloniality, Jabiri's oeuvre had had a long-lasting effect on the formation of Arab intellectual community. His call to think about the human condition of the ex-colonized reaches its peak in his call to replace the old revolutionary intellectual community.

One of the ideas that resonated with readers was Jabiri's idea of *intithām*, or cultural alignment, a guiding mechanism for effecting cultural change through turath. It means, as Jabiri wrote, to "line up behind turath [*al-intithām bil-turath*] to reform it from within . . . in order to rebuild the past, change the present and construct the future."[37] This idea takes on its full meaning if considered within Arab intellectuals' debates about how to bring about social and cultural change. Jabiri argued that the utility of new ideas (from the West) in changing people's perspectives was limited; instead, he thought that new taxonomies and classifications of shared knowledge would be more effective. New knowledge, Jabiri showed, depended on how the knowledge is expected to intervene in practical life. European knowledge, whether translated or Arabized, would always suffer from its Western genealogy.

The conclusion Jabiri reached was that change should always be internal to culture. For any agenda of cultural change to be legitimate, to gain the public's trust, it must commit and relate itself to Arab turath. So long as Arab intellectuals continue to overlook turath and imitate Western models, they would fail to prepare the ground for lasting change. Instead of trying to instill foreign ideologies, the Arab nation can become creative again through enacting its past traditions. Michaelle Browers has illustrated Jabiri's complex ideas with regard to this crucial point: "Expecting the Arabs to assimilate European liberalism as such is tantamount to asking them to incorporate into their consciousness a legacy that is foreign to them, a legacy that does not belong to their history but also has often acted as a tool for oppressing and suppressing aspects of Arab Islamic civilization. A nation can only experience the universal attributes of the human legacy within its own tradition, and not outside it."[38]

Another of Jabiri's ideas that resonated with Arab readers was the call to create a new Arab intelligentsia. Jabiri divided his rejection of the current intelligentsia into two parts: the liberal and Marxist elite. The liberalized intelligentsia as well as the revolutionary guard in Cairo and Beirut had not made good use of people's cultural repertoire, distrusting them and their knowledge. By choosing to overlook turath, the corrupted intelligentsia eroded Arab cognitive, economic, social, and personal systems—all the sources of resilience necessary for postcolonial nations to overcome setbacks with the least amount of damage. These writers overlooked the way turath provides the most trusted source of knowledge, one that nurtures the self and arms it with time-tested traditions in its pursuit to change the present and to plan for the future.

All the same, Jabiri also attacked Arab Marxists and revolutionaries, adamant in his rejection of their ideas. He said, famously, "Revolutionary culture is a smuggled ware."[39] Jabiri thought that he should counter Mashreqi revolutionaries the way the rationalist Andalusian school stood up to Mashreqi philosophers in the past. One of the most instructive lessons Jabiri derived from his study of Ibn Rushd was the life-changing principle that entails a cultural disengagement with the Mashreq. The establishment of an independent Maghrebi body of thought, Jabiri argued, required an epistemological break with Mashreqi revolutionaries, not with the past: "The Rushdian critical realism was the crowning of a critical stream that continued to move in one direction: turning away from Mashreqi [philosophical] idiom."[40] For Jabiri, this Rushdian philosophy provided the ground for both rejecting and replacing the Mashreqi thought system in the postcolonial era. But how was one to reject Mashreqi scholarship, which gave shape and content to Arab thought for more than a century? To resolve this dilemma, Jabiri called for the creation of a new class of Arab intelligentsia.

When Jabiri spoke of "the need to create a new Arab intelligentsia,"[41] to replace the one that, in the 1980s, was dominated by scholars from Beirut and Cairo, he meant replacing the established intellectual class in the Mashreq: the scores of writers, translators, authors, and publishers who articulated the main cultural questions in the Arabic-speaking world.[42] As far as Jabiri was concerned, the Mashreqi intelligentsia had propounded many ideologies that inflicted immeasurable pain on the Arab world—for instance, by disseminating misleading ideas like the idea of Arab unity "that spread more pain than happiness."[43] Though Jabiri acknowledges that the Mashreq had been the teacher of the Maghreb, he also thought that one should not overlook the fact that many Mashreqis were educated in the West and at the hand of Europeans: "The Maghreb's disasters, as well as its nahda, were imported from the Mashreq. Irrationality, for instance, had no roots in the Maghreb, but it arrived through books published in the Mashreq within the framework of particular Mashreqi conflicts."[44] Calling on Maghrebi scholars to view Mashreqi writings with skepticism, Jabiri prescribed the creation of a new intelligentsia that is "aligned in Arab turath."[45]

As we reach the end of our journey with Jabiri the connected critic, we must appreciate his least recognized intellectual output: debunking Arab Marxists. Indeed, no feat was more remarkable than Jabiri's willingness to take on Arab Marxists. In confronting and subjecting their complex writing to serious analysis, Jabiri was arguably the first to counter Arab Marxists, who enjoyed much cultural capital. Previously, very few Arab intellectuals would take a stand against the social critics and revolutionary writers, who wrote most of the reviews, established important publishing houses, and gave rise to many dailies and peer-reviewed journals. This, to my mind, is one of the most durable contributions that Jabiri has left behind, yet one that went unseen and underappreciated. "I came to discover . . . that the Marxist theory and scientific socialism are in true crisis [especially] when one thinks through them to inaugurate a socialism in backward states," he concluded in his very last work. "This crisis is reflected in the fact that the social theory as articulated by Marx, whose point of departure was European society, is not viable to a reality of the backward countries. It is impossible to think through it to solve social issues in the Third World."[46]

In the late 1970s, the prevailing sentiment was that Marxist theory was no longer applicable to Third World realities. Jabiri wanted to lay bare the reasons for that incompatibility. The main reason was that Arab Marxists viewed ancestors and the past as socially necessary inventions, rather than as a reality from which one could draw. When everyone has an ancestor backing him, Arab Marxists believed, all ancestors are devalued. For Jabiri, this Marxist conception of the past was neither helpful nor applicable to the Arab world. In particular, he opposed the way Arab Marxists wrote, thematized, and narrated Arab history. He called into question their very typology: "What benefit does the Marxist classification of classic Arab thought have? How is this classification of "idealist" and "materialist" currents useful? These are classifications that no longer classify."[47]

In diametrical opposition to Marxism, the main thrust of Jabiri's thesis was his insistence on the durability of ideas in history. This contention undermines the materialist approach, which overly emphasized contextualism, often at the expense of the longevity of past eras. Against this narrow contextualism Jabiri took the long view, believing that historical ideas from the past exert pressure and influence on the human in late modernity. For a scholar who thought that the borderline between past and present are not transparent, contextualism is dysfunctional. "Is there indeed a break that separates our past from present and future?" he asked. "When the past ends? Isn't it existing in our present? And when our future begins?"[48] Past epochs, Jabiri believed, are not totally isolated from the current epoch. For Jabiri, the contemporary Arab world was not completely detached from its past, and, under the surface of historical breaks that separated medieval and modern histories, there was a much-structured continuity through which past traditions continued to shape the modern age. This position, which Jabiri promoted, is in sync with recent scholarship in the field of intellectual history, which has begun to reconsider the methodology of narrow contextualism. As historian Peter Gordon has recently showed, a context-bound history deprives the historian "from imagining the possibility of semantic continuities across broad stretches of time," and, more dramatically still, Gordon rejects historians' skepticism "of the possibility that ideas from the past might still be available for critical appropriation in the present."[49] He recommends transcending the boundaries of the traditional contextualism that strives to defeat ideas—the same conceptions that Jabiri spent his life propounding.

When he passed away in 2010, Jabiri's foundational insights were a mainstay in Arab thought. He was able to establish a new approach to effecting social and cultural change, one that no longer denied the value of turath and indigenous cultural norms but regarded them as a basis for the future. What Jabiri achieved in his devastating critique of the Arab intelligentsia was revealing to the Arab reader the complicity of this intelligentsia in suppressing turath and past traditions, that these intellectuals were not unlike those colonial overlords who preached to the colonized Arab people to dispose of their heritage. In this intelligentsia, turath continued to be classified as inferior in comparison with modern knowledge. And, as Jabiri demonstrated, this classification was part of the working assumptions of Mashreqi scholars' worldview. Few other intellectuals have shown such critical depth and insight in deconstructing the entire project of the revolutionary Arab guard as Jabiri.

The distinctive positionality of the connected critic fashioned by Jabiri provides an alternative avenue to narrate the history of contemporary Arab thought. Neither traditionalist in its view nor modernist, Jabiri bestowed the intellectual persona of the connected critic with new content, which turned it into a fixture of the Arab intellectual landscape. Unlike any formal intellectual persona in the Arab world, the connected critic emblematized by Jabiri drew on turath without bogging itself down in past traditions; he believed that rationality can't and shouldn't be borrowed, but should emerge naturally from the past. The vast Arab-Islamic history that harbors many traditions has spawned one school that Jabiri saw as relevant in the present day, made of "free philosophers like Ibn Hazm and Ibn Rushd who left their rational-critical mark on the Cordoba School, and who passed down a tradition of free thinking which we are in desperate need to attend to for inspiration."[50]

To Jabiri, the challenge is to entrench the idea that no social change can take place without a preceding shift in cultural symbols: naming, language, narration, taxonomy and categories. Once readers take stock of the Arab cultural repertoire, once they comprehend the merits of connecting to past traditions, they will realize that changing the present cannot proceed without returning to turath. Though Jabiri has been critical of the nahdawis, Arab intelligentsia, Marxists, and Islamists, his critique never amounted to a total rejection of these intellectuals and their experiments. His work was informed by Ibn Rushd's "critical realism," which deconstructs the discourse to lay bare its false dichotomies. Jabiri demonstrated the ways in which many of the dualities and dichotomies that make up the nahda and contemporary Arab discourses are false and misleading. Speaking of Jabiri as a different kind of scholar, and accounting for his difference, remain challenges with which students of Arab thought must come to grips as they try to reckon with his unparalleled oeuvre.

III
BACKLASH

It is hard to think of another intellectual whose work has been more crucial in canonizing Jabiri's output than Jurj Tarabishi, a literary critic and prominent editor at Dar al-Taliah. Tarabishi was the first to recommend Jabiri's early works for publication. When Tarabishi read Jabiri's first manuscript in 1984, he couldn't conceal his enthusiasm for its originality. In one of his reviews, Tarabishi wrote that "whoever reads Jabiri would not remain the same person anymore. This book does not only educate but change you in radical ways."[1] Today, in the wake of the acrimony that developed between the two, it is almost impossible to believe these resounding words. The hostility between Jabiri and Tarabishi reflects the cultural war that rages on among Arab intellectuals—an antagonism that not only tells a personal story about two intellectual giants, but also faithfully reflects the careers of the postcolonial generation.

Despite their shared experience and involvement in national movements, Tarabishi and Jabiri were pulled in increasingly divergent directions in the wake of the defeat of the postcolonial project. For Jabiri, this defeat signaled the project's bankruptcy, shepherded by haughty social thinkers in Beirut and Cairo; for Tarabishi, it revealed Arab elites' faltering commitment to the project and its revolutionary ideas. The turn away from it bore witness to the fact that Arab progressives had never been truly progressives. As a social critic, Tarabishi believed that the postcolonial project intended to emancipate the Arab subject from the clutches of colonialism and liberate him from the burden of past tradition in order to pave the way for the creation of the new Arab subject, who is emancipated and politically engaged. As far as Tarabishi was concerned, Arab intellectuals failed to stick with the revolutionary agenda of the postcolonial project, resist the allure of past traditions, and rise above the sectarian and prejudices of turath.

Primarily for this reason, Tarabishi became one of the most critical voices of what he called domineeringly "the slide back to turath." Embracing turath, for him, meant further burying the postcolonial project under the debris of once-living secular rule. He deemed the mere proposition of reengaging turath in late modernity as a giant step backward, an idea that "ripped through Arab culture," as the title of one of his books conveys.[2] In his view, the resort to the turath framework afforded malicious actors the chance to willfully exploit the dynamics of aborted politics in order to normalize ideas about the past and authenticity. This precarious development inspired fear and perturbation in Tarabishi, who thought that Jabiri was trying to wind back the clock to more ominous times. If there is a cause at the root of the growing hostility between Tarabishi and Jabiri—which, unfortunately, was translated into a growing rivalry between the Mashreq and the Meghreb—it lies in the responses of each to the crumbling of the postcolonial project in the Arab world.

Born in Aleppo in 1939 to a middle-class family, Jurj Tarabishi was an enthusiastic translator and an energetic writer whose intellectual output and career have reshaped the contours of Arab thought. As a prominent outspoken social critic, Tarabishi was "one of the most prolific and powerful thinkers of the second half of the twentieth century."[3] He spoke of the recourse to turath following the 1970s in the most condemning terms, as a life-threatening project that breathes life into a "renewed and imagined medieval time."[4] At the beginning of the 1990s, he embarked on a project to debunk Jabiri and his followers, who presented turath as an Arab alternative to European modernity.

Tarabishi was the opposite of Jabiri in every respect. He advocated for more engagement with the West and denounced Arab scholars' engagement with turath. His career is much more expansive, however, than a mere dedication to casting off turath, and his biography conspicuously illustrious, a unique, personal story of a man who rose to the highest echelons of the Arab intellectual system. By looking into Tarabishi's life and the intellectual trajectory he charted, the two chapters in part 3 of this book examine the cultural temperament of his generation and the noticeable changes that occurred in their perspectives. Rather than focusing on the Maghreb, these chapters look at the ways the intellectual conversation developed in the Mashreq.

5

THE MAKING OF A SOCIAL CRITIC

Jurj Tarabishi

The Arab loss in the Arab-Israeli War in 1967 was the main event in Jurj Tarabishi's life. It interrupted his own story as well as the narrative of his generation. As a responsible intellectual, he felt under growing pressure to provide insight into the defeat. Vanquished nations always turn to intellectuals for clarity, and from the wreck of the war arose many responses. One curious yet elusive response cohered around Dar al-Taliah, a socialist publishing house in Beirut, where a small clique of young leftists came together. They were idealists who firmly believed in the power of political ideologies to transform life in the ex-colonized world, and, when normal political debate did not lead to change, they did not hesitate to force change by means of revolution.

Their reaction to the defeat was curious, as it originated from a relatively small group, whose interpretations of the war gained predominance across the spectrum in the Arab society. These young leftists were quick to leverage the historical experience of a postwar national ethos to confer import on the 1967 war. Not only did they assign it meaning, but, in even more important ways, they transferred that meaning from the military field to the cultural domain, turning the idea of "colossal cultural failure" (*fashal ḥaḍḍārī shāmil)* into their symbol.[1] The response they formulated was also elusive, as the bulk of contemporary scholarship shifted its focus to the reaction of the Islamic parties to the crushing defeat, while relatively few articles and books looked into the circle that formed around Bashir al-Daouk, the founder and owner of Dar al-Taliah.[2] Already active since 1959, this group consisted of previous members (dissenters and splitters) of the revolutionary Baath Party in Syria. Its evolution was made more visible in 1965 with the formation of the short-lived Arab Revolutionary Workers Party. One of its members, a twenty-five-year-old translator, stood out for his profound insight and commentary.

A young Syrian writer, Jurj Tarabishi (1939–2016) stepped into Arab politics at mid-century, during his undergraduate studies at Damascus University. At the age of eighteen, he was recruited into the Baʿth Party, where he avidly read the writings of Zaki al-Arsuzi, Michael Aflaq, and Salah al-Bitar, its three founding fathers. In the late 1960s, Tarabishi emerged as a central voice and an increasingly important figure in the nascent Arab intellectual landscape in Syria. Although he launched his career as a Baathist political activist, Tarabishi had to quit politics early on to make ends meet. His advocacy for the Baath's core principles, however, endured long after he turned his back on the party in December 1965.

Tarabishi made his way up neither through political parties nor army ranks. Instead he forged a career through translation and writing, which brought him much success. He translated existentialist literature (Jean-Paul Sartre, Simone de Beauvoir, and Albert Camus) into Arabic during the 1960s, when he was still in his twenties. Yet fame came to him with his remarkable renditions of Emile Brehier's seven volumes on the history of philosophy as well as works by Karl Marx and Hegel; Roger Garaudy and Herbert Marcuse in the 1970s; and, not the least, his translation of more than thirty of Freud's forty-third works.[3] In translating them from French rather than German, these volumes equipped Tarabishi with the vocabulary (trauma), method (psychoanalysis), and approach (Marxist critique) to articulate one of the most exciting analyses of the cultural transformations that swept Arab society in the last decades of the century. For Tarabishi, the Arab defeat in 1967 unleashed pent-up politics that changed the region. He felt deeply frustrated with the Arab armies that failed to repulse Israeli forces, a failure that troubled Arab intellectuals the way the atrocities of World War II afflicted postwar French intellectuals.[4]

Tarabishi, however, was not only a translator. In 1964, at the age of twenty-four, he published his first work on Sartre's critique of Marxism in a volume entitled *Sārter wal-Mārkissiya* (Sartre and Marxism),[5] an early display of his initial protest against the contemporary Arab intelligentsia, which would rise to climax in his *al-Muthaqafūn al-Arab wal-Turath* (Arab intellectuals and turath), a book that scathingly condemned Arab intellectuals' withdrawal from Western thought.[6] Before long, in the 1970s, he turned to literary criticism, writing copiously on Arab feminism and applying psychoanalysis to Arabic novels for the first time in the history of Arabic literature.[7] Even his most unforgiving critics concede that Tarabishi's "psychoanalytic approach is one of the more sophisticated critiques within current [Arab] debates."[8] It was during this period of his intellectual evolution that he famously stated that "the attitude toward women determines the attitude toward the world."[9] Although he remained a staunch advocate of women's rights, starting in the 1980s Tarabishi's interest shifted to the examination of the Arab past, its heritage and cultural repertoire. In one word, he zeroed in on turath.

In what follows I examine the ideological chapter in Tarabishi's life before he made this turn. My interest lies in examining why Tarabishi was consistent in his belief in the postcolonial project despite its failure when others like Jabiri turned away from it. One can begin answering this question by dividing up Tarabishi's career into two parts: the first period stretched from his birth in Aleppo in 1939 until his forced departure to Paris in 1984, and the second spanned his years in France as an alienated, exiled critic of Arab writings on turath. This chapter delves into the social and cultural milieux that shaped Tarabishi's life as well as his generation of social critics. It asks: What were the main ideological frameworks that he undertook in those years? What political commitments did these ideologies enable and sustain, and how did they frame his attitude toward the human condition in the ex-colonial world, postcolonial subjectivity, and turath? This chapter of Tarabishi's life is crucial to examine, for it lends us a window through which to view the formation of the Tarabishi generation's ideas on the West, turath, and Syrian nobility and peasantry through new lenses such as existentialism and class analysis in the heyday of decolonization and Arab nationalism. Paying close attention to the challenges Tarabishi faced in his life—his tribulations at school, his bitter arguments with Syrian Marxist comrades in Syria's dingy penitentiaries, his move to Beirut and integration into the intellectual community there—affords us the opportunity to grasp the ways through which the first generation of the postcolonial Arab world came to consolidate, and consecrate, a certain set of cultural assumptions, commitments, and political sensibilities.

BEING MODERN IN MID-CENTURY SYRIA?

Very few Arab intellectuals were as recognizable as social critics than Tarabishi, whose authority and influence came to him early in his intellectual journey. No doubt his broad interests and remarkable erudition helped him greatly navigate his way up, but it was mainly by virtue of the Syrian educational landscape that Tarabishi made a name for himself. Ever since the establishment of a new middle class in Syria, which bred new social manners according to a Western orientation that was not free of biases against local traditions, an educated intelligentsia began to forge and sustain its identity through notions of nationalism and Pan-Arabism.[10]

Tarabishi grew up to assume highly coveted positions in the small world of modern Arab letters. As early as 1961 he connected with the publishing house Dar al-Adab in Beirut and its formidable owner, Suhayl Idris. Between 1972 and 1984 he worked for Dar al-Taliah, undoubtedly one of the most esteemed publishing houses in the Arab world during the 1960s–1970s. As chief editor, Tarabishi was in charge of its influential journal *Dirāsāt ʿArabiyya* (Arab studies), the platform that set the tone for radical social critics for years. Tarabishi was forced to give up this position due to the escalation of the Lebanese Civil War. When he migrated to France, he served as the chief editor of the French-based nationalist journal *al-Wiḥdah* (between 1984 and 1989. Working in these positions kept him abreast of the flourishing Arabic publication industry from the early 1960s.

Tarabishi belongs to a generation that straddled the colonial and postcolonial eras, which experienced both the sting of colonization and the ensuing temporary euphoria that accompanied the rise of the postcolonial state. This generation—"the generation of losing wagers," as he referred to it—was defined by three events that partly explain its penchant for critique and its (one dares to say) embedded pessimism.[11] In its teens, this generation witnessed the spectacular upsurge in nationalism after the emergence of the postcolonial Arab states in the mid-1940s. The main event that validated and reinforced this elation was the gallant resistance that Egyptian leader Abed al-Nasser put up against Britain, France, and Israel in 1956, an event celebrated internationally to mark the end of the British Empire and colonialism in non-Western world. While this event echoes internationally with other postcolonial movements, in the Arab world it left young scholars with an inflated sense of their historical role as social designers of a new dawn. This war, though devastating to the Egyptian army, scored a vital political victory that propped up Arabs' morale, leaving intellectuals with the sense that they owned their future, which colonial states had for so long denied them.[12] The ensuing years, however, were less cheerful. From the heights of 1955–1959 to the crashing military defeat against Israel in 1967, things took a tragic turn, amounting to what Tarabishi called "a cultural trauma."[13] Six years before the milestone of 1967, Arab intellectuals witnessed the miscarried union experiment between Egypt and Syria in 1961, when Nassir sent General Hafiz al-Asad to Jail. This event confounded an otherwise exuberant generation of young Arab radical nationalists, dampening the triumphant mood of the 1950s. The third event that left a lasting mark on this generation, framing their mind for years to come, was the Arab-Israeli War in 1967. Impatient to see historical mistakes corrected, this generation was left disenchanted as Arab nations found themselves on the losing side. It was against this growing cultural background that Tarabishi relentlessly pushed back.

Within vanquished Arab nations, many intellectuals undertook the mission of critically engaging the past to offer a new reading of the present. Tarabishi thought that past traditions of turath were unreliable as a source of the self, much less of the postcolonial condition. Instead he called to assimilate the European model. Post-1967, Tarabishi would propound Western social theories on a large scale. No other idea had been closer to his heart than secularism, but embracing it cost him dearly in an age of authenticity, and Tarabishi quickly became the new outcast. Some have laid the blame for his marginality to his propensity for self-critique and self-flagellation, claiming that his writings have the effect of embedding yet deeper the sense of defeatism (*Tāʾṣīl al-Hazīmah*) in Arab culture.[14] As would become clear, it was less Tarabishi the man who contributed to entrenched defeatism than it was Tarabishi the social critic. Like many social critics in the Arab world who kicked off their career with an upbeat start, Tarabishi's career took him down the path of critique. Tarabishi's story is a story of an aborted generation, one that increasingly saw its values eroded, its sensibilities growing incommensurable with the new norm.

Tarabishi's uniqueness came to him not only by virtue of his firm belief in the power of secularism; it was also generational. Ever since Tarabishi's generation, which was born in the 1930s, came of age, it was obsessed with replacing the social order, upending its prevailing axioms, undermining the status quo, assailing cultural practices, and critiquing obsolete ways of being. Animated by a newfound national zeal, these young activists discredited what the "ʿAyaan" extolled as the value and sacredness of tradition. In a society swept up by iconoclastic fervor, past traditions seemed to bog people down, shackle them to dull, rigid, and routinized modes of behavior. As a "source of the self," turath was deemed at variance with the national spirit of the time. This was the first generation to dispute the order of things, to contest their naturalness.[15]

Tarabishi had many intellectual fathers who initiated him in the field, including Yassin al-Hafiz in Damascus, Suhayl Idris in Lebanon, and Mohammad Arkoun in Paris. The final "murdering of the fathers," a concept Tarabishi knew well through his translations of Freud, was central to his intellectual persona. Meanwhile, his persistent adherence to "crude" secularism drove a wedge between him and other Arab intellectuals. Tarabishi welcomed this moment of separation, not only because it enabled him to reexamine his previous ideological positions, but also because it offered him a rare opportunity to shed all intellectual godparents and authorities above him. "My desire to rebel against my father," he said, "was always stronger than my desire to tuck under the banner of a protective father."[16] The examination of Tarabishi's career in the first half of his life is a study of the revolutionary age in the Arab world, where different Western ideas crowded the intellectual field in the postcolonial world.

TARABISHI THE MAN

The study of Tarabishi's life and thought cannot be divorced from the familial, social, and cultural context in which he lived and worked. Though Tarabishi claimed that he had transcended his "roots," frequently changing his perspectives and worldviews, his experiences in Syria and Lebanon informed his literary tastes and intellectual vision. Whatever happened around him played upon his intellect and his psychology; the boisterous political scene in which he lived, marked by revolutions, social upheavals, and changing intellectual trends, contributed to his development into a social critic.

From modest origins to stardom in the world of Arab letters, Tarabishi trekked a long yet smooth way up. His life reflects the common story of a great hope that gradually vanished after the optimism of the 1950s–1960s gave way to the harsh realities of the 1970s–1990s. His writings reflect the rise and fall of the aspirations of a great swath of Arab social critics: the dream of independence, the ending of a humiliating chapter of neocolonialism and economic dependency.

THE BEGINNING: ALEPPO

The northern Syrian city of Aleppo featured a degree of modern facilities such as electricity and running water when Jurj Tarabishi was born on April 5, 1939, six years in advance of Syria's independence in April 1946. For years Aleppo was "one of the most important cities" in the eastern Mediterranean, sitting "astride global trade routes and served in the early modern period as a center of long-distance commerce in luxury goods, attracting merchants from all around the Mediterranean, north Europe, and South and Central Asia."[17] A remarkably multicultural city, Aleppo featured diverse groups of Arab Christians, Jewish traders like the Sassoon family, Venetian merchants and adventurers, Armenian silk merchants, and other peoples from various ethnicities who marked the city "with a tremendous ethnic, religious, and linguistic diversity."[18] Being the first Arab city to welcome travelers from the Turkish logosphere to the Arabic-speaking world, Aleppo had been functioning as a trade center between the Hejaz and Istanbul for generations. Yet it was during the much-hated French mandate (1920–1946) that its infrastructure developed rapidly, triggering a drastic shift in the status and well-being of the durable class of landowners.

When French colonial forces took control of Syria in the wake of World War I, they laid claim to a city that was immensely affected by nineteenth century reforms (*tanzimat*), including the tearing down of the city walls. After quashing a nascent popular revolution that emerged in full force in 1925–1927, French authorities began building wide thoroughfares, ramping up the city's industrial factories, opening new schools for its sizable Christian community, and connecting it to European centers.[19] Aleppo's noticeable economic expansion witnessed between the two wars would become more tangible only a decade after the mandate ended. With Syria's independence, Aleppo would retain this progressive edge, along with Damascus, both cities set in directions that depart from the vastly agricultural industry that reigned in the rest of Syria. The home of the first and only air force school in Syria, Aleppo further increased in significance as the army began to play a consequential role in directing Syrian politics. British scholar and journalist Patrick Seale, who gained unfettered access to Syrian state archives and befriended Syrian leadership, gave an informative description of the Syrian socioeconomic landscape shortly after the French mandate was swept away in 1946:

> Syria was a predominantly agricultural country, its backbone being two million peasants out of a then population of about 3.5 million, inhabiting some 5,500 villages built of mud and mostly lacking piped water, sewerage, electricity, tarred roads or any other amenity of modern life. Because of overcrowding and poor sanitation the population was ravaged by disease . . . In 1951–3, 36 per cent of registered deaths occurred among children under five. . . . Outside the two main cities of Damascus and Aleppo electricity was rare, serving fewer than a three-quarters of a million people in the whole country.[20]

Raised in Aleppo in a middle-class Christian family, Tarabishi was poised to pick a career in trade or education, but not in the army. Middle-class families in Syria looked down on army service, deeming it a low-status job track reserved for rural people. The modern reforms that the French authorities imposed on Syria further divided country and urban people, clearly depicted as the split between the savage and the civilized. Modernizing Aleppo, through tearing down the city walls that once separated the rural from the urban and paving new roads in and out of the city, had the effect of substantially increasing, rather than allaying, social tensions. Middle-class Syrians emerged more adamant about the differentiation of themselves from rural populations that walls once guaranteed. Seale and others, for example, have considered city dwellers' attitude toward rurals through the institution of the army as a "historical mistake":[21] "Scorning the army as a profession, they [urbanites] allowed it to be captured by their class enemies who then went on to capture the state itself."[22] As a city dweller, Tarabishi naturally shied away from the military. When the government called for volunteers in the early years of its independence, it was not urbanites who responded, but masses of "country boys." Alawites, long despised and derided, were among the first to embrace this opportunity: "The army was an attractive alternative [for country boys] because . . . fees had abolished at the Military Academy at Homs which thus became the only institution to offer poor boys a start in life: the cadets were lodged, fed and even paid to be there."[23] Since its inception, the Syrian army was a welcoming institution for rural folks, while being shunned by middle-class urbanites.

Tarabishi grew up with a grudge against the army, which he referred to with contempt as a "ruralized military force" (*qūwāt al-ʿaskar al-mutarayyif*).[24] In other words, while in many European societies the nation-state played a crucial role that, among other things, led to social integration between rural and urban folks, melting the social hierarchy, in Syria the nation-state had changed these social dynamics in a different way. Rather than alleviating tensions, it escalated them by encouraging different groups to emphasize their social standing. The attitudes of middle-class urbanites toward a "ruralized army" remains a constant in Syria today.

Although Aleppo sported a bustling urban space, it nevertheless offered only an array of religious schools, with the exception of European schools. Tarabishi attended a Christian school that instilled in him a religious sense. He spent his youth in Aleppo, where switching between a religious school and a practicing Christian household molded his early moralities and ethical inclinations. "I was born to a Christian family," he said, "and in the first stage of my childhood I was excessively religious to the extent that invoked the ridicule of my younger brother."[25] The oldest child of eight siblings, he took the name of his grandfather George (Jurj), to observe a customary practice, which still endures in many Arabic-speaking societies; later in his life, Tarabishi would lament this decision. In "Because of My Name," an article he wrote a couple of years before he passed away, Tarabishi chafed at the name Jurj for its religious resonance and clear connotation to Christianity. "Because of my name I failed to become an Arab hero," he stated.[26] Among his siblings (all male), he was the only one to take a name with a pure "sectarian and Christian ring" to it.[27] This demurring reflects a deeper concern that preoccupied Tarabishi, as a man who belonged to a Christian minority, which many deemed as starkly different, Western-sponsored, and, by definition, sectarian, and thus isolated from the rest of the Syrian Sunni majority. At the same time, Tarabishi claimed to embody Arab nationalism and advocated for Arab unity and nationalism. The discrimination against Arab Christians may have nagged him, but Tarabishi never let it overwhelm him.

EARLY SCHOOLING

While Syria's political scene was infamously unpredictable, the educational system fared no better. In 1943–1944, for instance, "less than a quarter of all Syrian children between the ages of six and twelve attended school."[28] In the village of Qardaha in the northwest of Syria where Asad was born, "a man would have to go round the whole neighborhood to find someone able to read a letter. The few people who could read were respected."[29] Syria had no unified curriculum and suffered from a paucity of qualified, competent teachers. This gave an edge to a host of religious school teachers and *ulama*, who held a larger sway over education. This state of art was stubborn, given the dearth in institutions: "In the 1940s there was only one secondary school along the whole length of the coast, from the northern frontier of Lebanon to Alexandretta, serving Latakia, Tartus, Jableh, and the entire mountain hinterland."[30] Unlike Lebanon, Syria had only one university: Damascus University, which was established in 1923. Aleppo, the second largest city in Syria, had no institution of higher education until 1957, the year in which the University of Aleppo was inaugurated. A high school diploma (baccalaureate) was the highest degree awarded in Syrian colleges, and it did endow some respectability and social status on its holders.[31] Yet the lack of a systemized and universalized educational order facilitated a relative mobility for any potential student to climb the social ladder. Tarabishi opened his eyes to the world precisely when this turbulent political landscape and educational chaos raged on.

In the Christian school Tarabishi attended, a sort of religious identity was taking shape among the students, instillied by zealous teachers by emphasizing Christian morality and spiritual conceptions while watering down national feeling. In times of high nationalist sentiment, minorities felt compelled to foster new awareness of their "religion and ethnicity." For many teachers in this Christian school, Tarabishi would write, the very bond that held Arab Christians together for centuries seemed imperiled. It was in such a school that young Tarabishi, who descended from a Roman Catholic family, became aware of his Christian identity. One morning in a theology class, a stern teacher who was also a priest in the Catholic Church of Aleppo taught a class on the idea of "sin" (*thanb*) and the fate of those who meet their "death in sin." The teacher faced a classroom of fourteen-year-old students who all came from Christian families. He began describing the "eternal punishments" God inflicts on people who commit "unpardonable sin." To simplify the meaning of "eternal punishments," the teacher asked his students to imagine a bird that touches the earth with its wings once in a millennium. He followed with a rhetorical question: "How many millenniums would it take the bird to eliminate the earth?" The punch line was, If you die in sin, you will be punished "eternally."[32]

The teacher staged drama to shore up students' fading Christianity in an age of ascending nationalism that seemed to render religious identity almost obsolete. The teacher wanted his students to acquiesce to God's ordinations, but his fear-provoking stories seem to have backfired. Hearing these dreadful descriptions of hell and God's merciless punishment, Tarabishi reportedly "trembled with fear" (*aṣābatnī raʿdah*). "The fear of eternal punishment is a cruel thing to instill in a child," he wrote. He then "exited school's gates with head down." He vividly remembered this moment, which reminded him of a girl who lived in a tall building next to the school. Anxious, Tarabishi could not afford lifting his head up to see his "beloved Italian girl on her balcony" as he made his way back, "fearing that the mere desire to wave her bye could be a reason for unpardonable sin."[33] Feeling that religion made impossible demands, Tarabishi recorded this episode as one of the first distressing events that undermined his belief in God. "I reached home with semi-derelict reactions and became sick for two days," he recounted. "When I woke up my only reaction was no . . . it is impossible that the God the teacher talked about exists and is cruel to this extent. Ever since that day I turned away from Christianity [*kafaftu ān ākunu masīḥiyyan*]."[34]

In 1954, three years after the pain inflicted on him by the religious teacher, Tarabishi endured a "second incident" that left him disenchanted with religion. This event took place in the newly introduced Islamic studies during his high school years—"a new thing in the Syrian curriculum,"

Tarabishi wrote. Teaching Islam was required only in elementry schools in Syria, but not in high schools and colleges; "Islamic studies became mandatory only after the coup that took place in 1955 that toppled Shiskikli."[35] Adib al-Shishikli's authoritarian rule was so intensely reprehensible that it drove otherwise antagonistic parties, including communists, Baathists, and the Muslim Brotherhood, to collaborate to bring him down—a once-in-a-century coalition. Indeed, it was under this totalitarian regime that the Baath saw its ranks swelling with the merger of Akram Hourani and other factions within it. These parties joined forces and colluded to put an end to the Shishikli's draconian regime.[36] The morning after he was forced out, Tarabishi wrote, the "Muslim Brotherhood refused to fill any [political] position in the newly formed government," stipulating one caveat that changed the educational scene in Syria ever after: instead of partaking in the new government offices, Islamists demanded to have Islamic studies introduced to high school and academic curricula. "Until 1955," Tarabishi wrote, "only elementary and middle schools taught religious studies."[37] Starting in the post-Shishikli era, "religious studies became mandatory for all [Syrian] students." Before that coup, "we used to learn national and civic studies" that now "turned to religious studies."[38]

Integrating "religious studies" left Tarabishi alarmed and petrified. For him it marked the beginning of the unravelling of Syria's secular curriculum, which had always been taken for granted. Witnessing the erosion of the secular legacy, Tarabishi chose to participate in religious classes. "I deliberately decided to take a class in Islamic, rather than Christian, studies to learn about the majority that I live within," he wrote about the experience that led him to leave religion behind entirely. During one Islamic class a round-faced teacher with a shortly trimmed beard wrote slowly on the board, "Who he is not Muslim is an enemy of Islam." Appalled and frightened, Tarabishi stood up, identified himself as Jurj, and asked a question of his own: "Would you consider me your enemy?" Tarabishi never mentioned the name of the teacher, whom he would meet with years later and recall the incident. This disconcerting episode hacked away at Tarabishi's already faltering appreciation of religion. A new realization began taking shape: that an unbridgeable gulf separated him from religion. Though he did not turn to secularism instantly, Tarabishi understood that religion drove a wedge among the different sects and diverse minorities in Syria.

It is hard to verify the accuracy of these stories. Tarabishi argued that he disavowed religion at very young age, but he invoked—or, rather, re-created—this experience only in the very last months of his life. The context in which he reproduced this experience left their marks on his retelling. I heard this story myself firsthand while interviewing Tarabishi in his apartment in Paris (see the conclusion). Seeing Syria "taking the plunge" and descending into a prolonged civil war that endangered his family in Aleppo, Tarabishi had nothing to say except to remind me of the sturdy defences that his generation built and maintained to keep away Islamists and that had finally fallen. But these stories are not far-fetched, either, since other Syrian intellectuals registered similar experiences. During the 1950s, as the new state reshuffled the curriculum, Syrian publisher Riyad Najib Rayyis cited a similar episode. He wrote that the introduction of religious studies increased the fractions and social marking among Muslim and Christian students: "It was common that Christian students skip religious classes entirely while Muslim students had to attend these classes," a formula that boiled up tensions among them.[39] What Tarabishi and Rayyis convey is that the nation-state in the Middle East did not lead to the expunging of religious differences, as it ought to do, but to the revival and incorporation of Islam in its functioning. The state's endorsement of Islamic studies emphasized the social and cultural differences among students, setting the stage for political and social polarization in the ensuing years.

POLITICAL QUAGMIRE: IN DAMASCUS

Tarabishi's dreadful experiences may not have made such a lasting impression on him had he not experimented in the cultural and political temperament of Damascus, where he moved to to pursue his studies in the department of Arabic studies at Damascus University.[40] In 1954, the year in which he arrived, he witnessed firsthand the chaos in the city that reflected the fierce fighting currently engulfing the nation. Damascus seemed barely governable, as it had yet to come to terms with the new reality of independence. As one observer succinctly noted, "Syria is a country that never wanted to exist at all, at least within its present boundaries."[41] Twenty years of French rule in Syria had pitted urban against rural, landowner against landless, old and complacent against new and radical. French colonialism, according to another observer, "undermined the old ways but failed to implant convincing new ones."[42] This partly accounts for the prolonged struggle to fix a broken system.

At mid-century, Damascus was brimming with national ideas and seemed poised to effect far-reaching changes. If Aleppo instilled in Tarabishi the first features of anti-religion, then Damascus trained him in nationalist sentiments, galvanizing new sensibilities that went into the making of a social critic. In the decade that preceded his arrival in the city, Damascus was roiled by the influx of many new migrants who flocked to the town after the amputation of Alexandretta-Antioch from Syria in 1939. This wave of dislocated Syrians instigated a flare of nationalism that had not yet dissipated by the time Tarabishi arrived. One of those dislocated was Zaki al-Arsuzi, the editor of a little-known journal, *al-Baʿth*, whose writings would vastly influence young Tarabishi.

Ever since its independence in 1946 until 1970, when Hafiz al-Asad wrested power, the Syrian government failed to gain popular legitimacy and stabilize its political system. The country's educational system was in tatters as well. Three years into its independence, Syria had descended into a political quagmire that stymied its efforts to put together a viable political order. Three forces were locked together in a fierce rivalry over the seizure of power: the old landowners who struggled for survival, the rising army officers, and the newly formed educated bourgeoisie who defined themselves against the wanton communists and archaic forces of the much-hated landowners.[43] The army was a new establishment that more than once had allied with the educated bourgeoisie to dislodge the notorious landowners and wealthy families from power.

The first destabilizing year came in 1949, when Syria was rocked by three coups d'état. The first, led by Husni al-Zaʿim (1897–1949), who ousted Shukri al-Qawatli (1891–1967), wreaked havoc on a fragile and still susceptible state—the first forbidden usurpation of power in postcolonial Syria by a military officer that heralded a series of putsches in the Arab world. Al-Zaʿim and al-Qawatli represented two starkly different political orientations and worldviews. Al-Zaʿim belonged to the rising rank of the army officers that challenged the hold of Syria's old nobility on politics.[44] Al-Qawatli, the guardian of the deeply entrenched interests of the big families and landowners, spent his political career warding off the mounting tide of change and ambitions set in motion by army officers like al-Zaʿim. While it is easy to sympathize with al-Zaʿim, from a historical perspective he set the course for the first precedent of *Inqilāb* that would repeat and recreate itself in different forms in neighboring Arab states. Specifically, his actions inaugurated political radicalism while breaking with a deep-seated tradition of political reformism. Like other coups in the Middle East, it reflected the scramble for power between the haves and have-nots, the old generation versus the emerging and radicalized generation. In Syria, al-Zaʿim was initially propped up by the highly politicized class of young Baathists, who hitherto had only fuzzy ideas about the political ramifications of the ideology they promoted. Al-Zaʿim, however, would not last more than few months in power, as he lost his head at the hands of his angered military Baathist allies, in a swift coup carried out by Sami al-Hinnawi (1898–1950), a cunning politician who also came from the officer ranks. Al-Hinnawi's fate was no less tragic than his predecessor's; he too failed to meet the expectations of the diverse and conflicting groups of the old landowners, the military, and the educated-radicalized class that pulled the political establishment in different directions. Not before long he too was overthrown in yet another coup, this time engineered by Adib al-Shishikli, a Kurd from the city of Hama. In the course of the first two decades after its independence, Syria would see a record number of eighteen presidents.[45] It was only with the arrival of Hafiz al-Asad that the scramble for power in Syria saw a cruel end.

In Damascus, as in Aleppo, the same patterns were at work, but with higher velocity and intensity. In Damascus three ideological forces grappled with each other for power: Baathists, Pan-Arabists (Antun

Saʿadah's circle), and communists. All three groups were anxious about the future of Syria, and all of them pushed for Arab unity as a remedy to what they deemed the social fragmentation that colonialism inflicted on Arab societies. In the Syrian limbo of 1955, however, communists seemed to stand a higher chance of gaining political ground. A number of events helped ensure the rise of communist power in Syria that appealed to newcomers like Tarabishi. In neighboring Iraq, opportunist politician Abed al-Karim Qassim seized power in a bloody coup that put a definite end to the monarchy. Qassim professed allegiance to no ideology other than his fierce opposition to Iraqi nationalists, and, to solidify his shaky status, Qassim gave a free rein to the communists who swarmed the streets of Rasheed and al-Mutanabi to eliminate the aggressive nationalist opposition. The Syrian communists took note of the drama unfolding in neighboring Iraq, bolstering their confidence in their cause. Moreover, the Syrian government's anticipated weapon deal with the USSR, signed in 1957, boosted Syrian communists, who blasted their adversaries by boasting deeds over words. Needless to say, communism held some allure for deprived people and newcomers, as it made grand promises to demolish all the social barriers that had stymied Syrian political progress since the nineteenth century.[46] Tarabishi found it natural to follow this party of change before he settled with the ranks of the Baath, but his involvement with the communist party did not last long; Tarabishi was disappointed with his comrades, who took orders from Russia.

After spending a brief stint in communist circles, Tarabishi found himself displeased with their dogmatism and joined the Baath Party, who were looking at Gamal Abed al-Nasser in Egypt as he began restructuring Egypt along new revolutionary lines. For young Baathists, an alignment with Nasser seemed to ensure a secure path to block the rise of communism in Syria. Few things can capture the political disorientation in mid-century Syria as the events in the late 1950s. In 1958, Syrian politicians, unable to settle on state policy, handed over their country to Nasser. Unhappy, Nasser accepted the offer, grudgingly stipulating one condition: the abolishment of all Syrian parties. For three long years the Baath Party dissolved itself and closed its main journal.

With his arrival in Damascus, Tarabishi entered a new world. The inflow of people and ideas to the capital animated the city, and Tarabishi's time there attests to a place that teemed with innovation and creativity. It offered Tarabishi and his generation a fresh opportunity to participate in the building of a fledging world of revolutionary literature. Here, he read Zaki al-Arsuzi, who praised Arabic and Arabs in history (he would be later called the philosopher of Arabic), and Antun Saʿadah, the genuine Pan-Arabist, who propagated the idea of Greater Syria that included Cyprus, for which he was executed in 1949. Damascus was a genuine postcolonial city in the Global South that heralded the promise to free young people like Tarabishi from the shackles of religion, dependency, and inferiority. Though Damascus was full of life, it offered a poor job market, particularly to young graduates.[47] Like other cities in the non-Western world, Damascus was unwieldy and not easy to restructure. After he obtained a master's degree in education in 1963, Tarabishi went back to Aleppo. On August 1963, he married Henriette ʿAbud, a young novelist who a few years earlier gave him Simone de Beauvoir's *The Makings of an Intellectual Woman* to read. Tarabishi set out to be a teacher, but, during a streak of misfortune, he was sent to teach in ʿAfrin—a small village far from Aleppo and his new wife. He couldn't settle into this job, since he had already developed rebellious sentiments that stood in contradiction with the nature of a teaching career. Later he would claim that "I quit teaching because I was assigned to teach in a desolate and far-off village away from my wife in Aleppo."[48] After unsuccessfully pleading with the education minister to be relocated to Damascus, Tarabishi decided to quit his job.

UNDER HIZB AL-BAʿTH

World War I terminated four hundred years of Ottoman dominance over Syria (1516–1918). In the wake of the Great War, Arab provinces were left to the vagaries of the two Western superpowers of the time: Great Britain and France. In 1916, in an infamous agreement known as Sykes-Picot, which every Syrian schoolchild learned to detest and vilify, these superpowers secretly arranged to divvy up the Middle East between them. France agreed to take control of the northern part—today's Syria and Lebanon—while conceding to Great Britain the areas that included Palestine, Transjordan, and Iraq. This haphazard breaking up of the Arab lands, which would prove permanent, was more than the inhabitants of Greater Syria could swallow—a colonial plan that would sow the first seeds of illiberal parties like the nationalist Baath Party. Before World War I, Syrians were accustomed to roaming the region that extends from Antioch in the north to Palestine in the south, enjoying free trade. When the mandate regimes restricted this free movement, it anticipated the first wave of Syrian nationalism.

The Baath Party came into being in Syria at the twilight of World War II (1943–1947), officially formed in 1946, though its ideological roots reach back to before World War I. The Baath is made of four factions, three with the name al-Baʿth, first coined by Zaki al-Arsuzi's journal *al-Baʿth* in 1940. The merger of these factions took place in Damascus between their representatives—ʿAflaq and Bitar in Damascus, Akram al-Hourani in Homs, Jalal al-Sayyid in Der al-Zur, Wahib al-Ghanim in Latikiya, and Anton Makdisi from Aleppo—and each faction's leader was sustained by a group of local supporters.[49] The party was revolutionary in its character. It did not grant titles of nobility. It didn't accept the social order and called for its replacement. Its main vision was to create a more just society based on equality and give rise to the new Arab subject. It denounced landlords and barons while deploring the feudalists (*iqṭāʿiyyūn*). Officially, the Baath put no limits on any Syrian citizen to entering the halls of power. In its early years, the Baath insisted on making state institutions and professions, which previously were out of reach for most Syrians, open for all. Here minorities and and the underclass saw opportunity.

From a historical perspective, the core ideas that informed the Baath Party could not have been conceived in any other Arab state but Syria. The French mandate that carved Syria up into four administrative enclaves had anticipated its emergence. France, the acting sovereign over Syria, not only took a huge mass of Syrian land in 1920 and attached it to Mount Lebanon, where its Maronite protégés had held sway since 1860, but it also yielded large parts of the former province of Aleppo to Turkey. In 1939, just few months before the outbreak of World War II, France officially ceded Alexandretta-Antioch to Turkey in return for joining the war on the Allies' side. This surgical amputation of Syrian land (Damascus in the south, Aleppo in the north) dealt the two major cities a serious blow, as they both lost direct access to the Mediterranean Sea (one was blocked by Lebanon, the other by Alexandretta). Concomitantly, as the British split up Palestine to facilitate a new "homeland for the Jews," the dreams of Greater Syria grew ever slimmer. This subtraction of land, one Levantine intellectual observed with sorrow, stirred "national feeling and opened Arabs eyes to the ghost that threatened to tear up and rip apart their land."[50] Thus, it seems only natural that the true founder of the Baath, Zaki al-Arsuzi, came from the ceded enclave of Alexandretta-Antioch. Deeply embittered by the colonial enterprise in Syria and other Arab provinces, Arsuzi called on Arabs to unify against the mandate powers. In his writing he extolled the pioneering roles of Arabs in history, vilified Turks, smeared colonialism, and called for a cultural renewal of Arab history, or, simply, Baath.[51]

Arsuzi was so deeply agitated by the seizure of land that, upon his relocation to Damascus, he wasted no time in launching his journal *al-Ba'th*. This journal, for which Tarabishi worked, came into being with a certain vision of Syria that was articulated in the late nineteenth century by Arab intellectuals who "reframed Bilad al-Sham / Suriya" as a geographical unit. During that time, writes Cyrus Schayegh, Bilad al-Sham "was declared a national space alongside, and comparable to, other national spaces around the world."[52] For Arsuzi and his generation, the colonial act of 1939 closed the final chapter on the dream of Greater Syria/Bilad al-Sham, which had been framed a century prior. Yet, to the consternation of Syrian nationalists, this was not the end, but the beginning of a series of amputations: "When the French finally withdrew in 1946, the country had shrunk to 185,190 square kilometers from the 300,000 square kilometers. . . . Syrians did not easily recover from the shock of these surgical operations, and the feeling that their country was made smaller, than meant to be, became a continued source of frustration."[53]

Despite its idealistic values, the Baath led scores of educated people astray. Though it started off deploying noble principles and articulating genuine public feelings, it had destructive ends. The Baath called for regrouping the now-fragmented Arab peoples through bounding them together into one single Arab nation. From its inception, the Baath made fighting Western colonialism and feudal landlords its primary goals, yet it had no intellectual backbone. For more than two decades, this party "lacked ideological writings," as Aflaq and al-Bitar's "improvised talks" on nationalism and anticolonialism constituted its main sources and frames of reference.[54] Al-Bitar quickly became known as the head of a party that pandered to the educated bourgeoisie. His criticism focused on the "prevailing order" of the old aristocratic elite and landowners, and, under his leadership, the Baath became the new challenger of the established system.

It is highly intriguing that the ideology of one of the most influential parties in the Middle East was developed by teachers, and that the bulk of its followers came from high schools. The party and its leaders, argues Muta Safadi, a Syrian author and political activist, were moved by emotions rather than cold, rational analysis of reality. Tragically, it figured prominently in creating the conditions that led the Arab world to its humiliating defeat in 1967. Safadi's scathing critique is spot on: the minority mentality making up this party stands as the prime culprit. Dominated by Alawites, who have been looked down upon and were considered unpolished and undereducated, the party would take great risks to gain legitimacy among the Sunni majority. A favorite strategy was to whip up hostilities against Israel—an easy way to prove loyalty to Arab cause. For that very reason, some Israeli army commanders, notably Yitzhak Rabin, loathed Syria the most among all of his Arab adversaries. As one journalist noted, "The easiest way for the Alawis to ingratiate themselves with Syria's Sunni Muslims, who were the majority, was to work even harder to heat up their border with Israel."[55] With little regard for accountability, the Baath Party dragged unprepared Arab states to one of its most searing defeats at the hand of Israel. Akram Hourani, a prominent Baathist leader, constantly pestered Nasser with regard to the presence of UN forces on the straits of Tiran; according to some accounts, Hourani constantly pushed Nasser to evacuate them, which were stationed in the straits after the 1956 war to prevent another escalation between Egypt and Israel. Harouni importuned Nasser in newspaper articles, but that was a less likely instigator of the war and the defeat in 1967. Yet if his cajoling should not be taken as the most significant cause for the outbreak of the 1967 war, Hourani certainly was a convenient enabler of it: a huckster who peddled magical thinking by assuring Syrian policy makers that they could take on Israel and gain victory. After the war, many received scorn and reproach for the defeat, while the Baath enjoyed full impunity.

When the Baath took power in the now-infamous coup of March 1963, Tarabishi "was mandated by the education ministry to work as the director of the Syrian Radio," a position that he held for "several months."[56] In its first year in power, the Baath revealed its true militaristic nature,[57] with "almost half of the members in leading positions of the Syrian Baath Party [coming] from officer ranks."[58] The Baath inaugurated a new era in Syrian politics by cracking down on Pan-Arabists, executing political dissidents and even persecuting Nasserists. In 1964, many young, educated Syrians left the party in the wake of the atrocities perpetrated across Syria. Tarabishi received harsh criticism for dragging his feet leaving the party.[59] Only when he fell out of favor with the Baath by 1965 did he decide to leave it. Yet his critical stance of the party had him "sent to jail for four months."[60]

While in prison, Tarabishi met other ex-Baathists, most of them Christian dissidents from Huran, who had been in contact with Akram Hourani. His multiple conversations with his ex-Baathist cellmates left him despondent that so-called radicals were actually reactionaries. In the course of one dispute over the phenomenon of honor killing of women for having sexual relationships out of wedlock, Tarabishi was aghast to realize that he was the only one to emphatically denounce the antediluvian practice. He was asked whether or not he would have his "daughter killed if she had an intimate relationship with someone who is not her husband," a question that shocked Tarabishi: "The mere idea of having a woman killed was [an] unspeakable atrocity."[61] At that moment, Tarabishi realized that a radical change in mentality ought to precede all social and political changes in society at large:

> Ever since [this argument] I learned that the issue is not between Muslim and non-Muslim, Christian and non-Christian . . . the problem has grown complicated. The issue comes down to the structure of mentality [*bunyat al-ʿaql*] in the first place. Inside [the] human brain, there are two stratums: one is on the surface that might be political, progressive, and socialist . . . beneath it the other stratum, structural to the mind, which is fatally regressive, whether the man is Christian or Muslim. Ever since that day I have a strong conviction that the attitude toward women in society determines the attitude to the world as such. Ever since that day my conviction was hardened more than any time before that we need to struggle in words to bring a change in mentalities, to alter the interior structure of mind, not only the political and ideological surface of the mind.[62]

Few other words can describe the mission the social critic took upon himself. The social change he aimed to bring about was radical, total, entailing the alteration of "the structure of the mind."

UNDER THE SPELL OF YASIN AL-HAFIZ

After parting ways with the Baath Party in 1965, Tarabishi joined a group of disparate young radical Marxists animated by class consciousness. A prominent figure in this group was Yasin al-hafiz, a genuine thinker and a sharp-minded commentator on Arab politics, who is known to have been the first Marxist in Syria. Hafiz was also the first to jot down the principles of the Baath in the late 1940s before ditching the party altogether.[63] Born in 1930 in the northeastern Syrian city of Deir al-Zur to a lower-middle-class family, Hafiz would become one of the most eloquent nationalist speakers and a founding father of the short-lived Arab

Revolutionary Workers Party in 1965. Before his ignominious departure from the Baath, embittered and disenchanted, he served as the party's education attaché. Hafiz is better known for propounding ideas of *al-fawāt al-Tārīkhī* (historical anachronism), *al-Waʿi al-Muṭābik* (corresponding awareness), and the popularizing of "Arab Marxism" instead of international Marxism. The terminology he coined in his analysis of Arab societies gained currency among the 1960s generation. In his fascinating autobiography, he writes, "It is imperative that Arabs would not be granted any moment of delusion, submission and surrender. We should make the present regression and oppression [*al-tāʾkhur wal-iḍṭihād*] more conspicuous by instilling an awareness of regression and oppression. Shame should be rendered more ghastly and horrid by spreading it out among people. We should teach people to panic from their reality to give them the temerity to fight back."[64] Hafiz launched two short-lived publishing houses in Beirut, yet his ideas left a lasting mark on a great number of present-day intellectuals, despite their misgivings on his Marxism: Wadah Shararah, Michael Klito, Haim Saghiya, Muta Safadi, and Yasin al-Haj Saleh, who belonged to the younger generation. Sadiq al-Azm is said to have taught his autobiography during his tenure at the American University of Beirut.[65] In 1965, when Tarabishi was released from jail, Hafiz's ideas were already firmly established. Like many of his revolutionary Marxist comrades, Tarabishi agreed with Hafiz's ideas on the incompetence of the Arab bourgeoisie, which failed to launch a frontal assault on the traditional forces in Syria. Instead of mounting a cultural attack on the traditional classes, Hafiz complained, Arab nationalists accommodated these anachronistic forces into the new state, who ended up forcing their traditional culture onto the modern Arab state.

In his autobiography *Al-Hazīmah Wa-al-Īdyūlūjiyā al-Mahzūmah* (The defeat and the defeated ideology), Hafiz takes what he calls Arab Marxism and applies its "tools" to criticize "traditional Arab societies." This work, Hafiz states in the introduction, "is a profound critique of the defeat [in 1967] by going, probably for the first time, from criticizing [Arab] politics to critiquing its society."[66] This shift from criticizing politics—prevalent prior to 1967—to critiquing society marked the growth of a new awareness that was specific to the clique that Hafiz fostered.[67] This was also among the first points of entry into the making of the social critique that would confer much distinction on Tarabishi's works.

The decline of the traditional European empires during World War II pressed Hafiz to embrace the causes championed by Arab liberation movements. He meant to raise awareness of the "regression of Arab societies" as a way to break what he metaphorically called "Arab cultural and ideological involution."[68] The idea of "regression" was still in popular usage as an economic aphorism before it assumed cultural signification at Hafiz's hands. As an Arab Marxist, Hafiz was incensed by the link "semi-Marxists" made between "backward and conservative politics, culture and ideology" on the one side and a "backward economic structure of Arab countries" on the other.[69] He chafed at so-called Marxists because of the "economic and industrial approaches" that seem to "prevail in the climate of ideas."[70] In describing his progress toward political maturity, Hafiz unapologetically thanked colonialism for paving the way before traditional and backward Arab societies to engage in politics without fear of punishment. Nowhere in his texts does he denounce colonialism outright. Quite the opposite: he identifies positive aspects in the detestable French colonial project in Syria for politicizing Arab society:

> The reality is that although the burden of French colonialism sparked my interest in politics, the (liberal) colonial French suppression did not reach a degree [of cruelty] that forced us to go back to a traditional-psychological temperament, where political tradition is absent and a temperament of escapism and aversion prevails. With colonialism, for the first time in modern Arab experiment, it was possible for Arab subjects to oppose existing authority without getting killed, or seized upon until succumbing on the one hand, and gaining some sort of passive and quiet solidarity from [the rest of] society on the other hand. One is ought to say that the colonial experiment set loose, with no intention, a process of politicizing Arab society, which had not known political tradition before. The removal of colonialism, which was

> followed by renewed Eastern despotism, marked the beginning of the reverse procedure of liquidating the remains of "the colonial democracy" and removing politics from society or forcing people to steer clear of politics.[71]

In the national ethos of the late 1960s, this kind of honest testimony is unusual, even if new forms of critique emerged at that juncture. Hafiz's type of social critique of Arab society, which "reverts to eastern despotism" and "fledging democratic tradition fostered by the colonial experiment," would later be taken up and developed by Tarabishi. As will be discussed in the next chapter, Tarabishi was profoundly influenced by the ideas of "cultural relapse," or the "reversion to medieval political thinking and practice," articulated by Hafiz. More than any other intellectual, Hafiz's vocabulary would frame and inform Tarabishi until the end of his days. This finds strong embodiment in the idea of *nukus* (regress, recoil, backsliding, and regression) that Tarabishi developed during his years in Paris.

Hafiz was fading from memory as many Arab intellectuals began to display some signs of disillusionment with Marxism during the late 1970s. His attempts to slow down the process proved futile. The publishing house that he established to disseminate his revolutionary ideas, Dar al-Haqiqah, lasted only three years, marking the passing of an intellectual brand. With his early death in 1978, at the age of forty-eight, Arab Marxism was in steep decline. It was in this year that Tarabishi declared his famous divorce from the Marxist ideology.

TRANSLATION

In 1964, Tarabishi made a general observation concerning the Arab intellectual scene that, to a certain extent, captured the essence of the historical moment of the time. "Until now," he wrote, "we have understood Marxism through whatever was written about it, not through Marx's own [writings]."[72] This statement betrayed his clear statement of purpose of embarking on translating Marxist literature into Arabic while also implying a break with previous generations who read Marxist literature in European languages. In the 1950s and 1960s, Arab intellectuals ushered in a new phase of translation of major Western intellectual projects. One scholar of the time remarked that in Lebanon alone the number of translated books exceeded for the first time those authored by Arab scholars.[73] The fact that translated literature outnumbered Arabic-composed books had tremendous effects on the development of the literary tastes and styles of reasoning that a social critic like Tarabishi grew up embracing.

Until the mid-twentieth century, very few Western works were available to mass readers in Arabic translation, despite the steep engagement with Western scholarship during the nineteenth century and the first half of the twentieth century. Indeed, Arab intellectuals and readers alike were, in general, aware of the extensive Western intellectual scholarship and traditions, as many of them mastered more than one European language. Some journals kept the Arab reader abreast of the latest intellectual modes in Europe, while Western philosophers also visited the Arab world and took teaching positions in the region, especially during the two world wars. The emergence of Arabic journals in the nineteenth century (*al-Muqtataf* and *al-Hillal*, in particular) had already created a space for Arabic readers to dabble in Western philosophy, theories, and sciences. These journalistic overviews, however, could not achieve more than what good journalism could offer in the form of presenting outlines and summaries of mainstream Western ideas. Although these scanty translations were necessarily patchy and brief, they nevertheless created social and intellectual commotion.

By the mid-twentieth century, however, the intellectual dynamics had drastically changed, and two groundbreaking literary endeavors were set to begin. The first was the establishment of the journal *al-Ādāb* in Beirut in 1953 (which expanded into a publishing house in 1956). Second was the founding of Dar al-Taliah in 1959. Dar al-Adab and Dar al-Taliah embarked on an unprecedented undertaking that systematically set out to translate works of Western intellectuals and philosophers. Unlike the characteristic cherry-picking of earlier translation projects, these publishing houses went so far as to render a large portion of existentialist and other Western literary works into Arabic.[74] The founder of Dar al-Adab, Suhayl Idris, underscored the significance of the project in an article entitled *Adabuna wal Tarjamah* (Our Literature and Translation.)[75] In it, Idris took issue with the quality of previous translations and the content of the books selected for translation and emphasized the necessity of translation as a medium through which to catch up with the West. Idris assailed translations done especially in Egypt, branding major Egyptian translators Ahmad Hassan al-Zayyat and Lutfi al-Manfaluti's selections as "unfaithful" (*Tarjammāt al-Khiyyānah).* He also brushed aside literal word-for-word translations as worthless and assailed what he characterized as *tassaruf* (excessive liberty) with original texts. Instead, he identified two objectives behind the process of translation: "First, reliability in rendering foreign text, and second, adapting Arabic and [Arab] reason to new styles of expression and thought."[76]

The desire to transform Arabic "styles of expression" is reflected in Idris's celebrated novel *al-Ḥay al-Lātīnī,* which Tarabishi appraised as the sort of new novel worth engaging with, the kind that contributed to the making of the social critic in its exploration of the cultural differences between the East and the West by demonstrating the Eastern protagonist's fascination with the West. Idris expressed a noticeable disdain of translations that "do not shed new light . . . on the path to freedom." Included in his list of useless translations were those of "Hugo and Shakespeare." He nonetheless highlighted the necessity of translating works that engage relevant and ontological issues,

> foreign works that address issues reflecting Arab concerns in this historical moment- for instance fighting colonialism in all its forms, denouncing cruelty and aggression, advocating for freedom and justice, struggling to liberate society from the shackles that impede creative possibilities and manifestly expressing different shades of anxiety that storm the subject in his pursuit of a meaningful existence—these foreign works that deal with this kind of issues, which every single Arab encounters today, are the most fruitful and valuable works.[77]

Born in 1925, Idris attended a religious school but continued his education at the Sorbonne between 1948 and 1952.[78] During his four years in Paris, Idris reached out to many Arab writers to prepare the ground for the creation of his journal *al-Adab*, which he later turned into a vigorous publishing house in 1956. As indicated in the letters he exchanged with the Egyptian novelist Anwar al-Madawi upon his return to Beirut, Idris quickly established the journal *al-Adab* in 1953. He received aid from veteran publishers in Beirut—namely, Bahij ʿUthman and Munir Baʿalbaki, who owned Dar Al-ʿIlm Lilmalayyin, established in 1945. Both of these publishers would also contribute articles to his embryonic journal to give it some prestige.

Idris excelled in fostering a broad network of scholars, of which his connections and acquaintances spanned a great spectrum.[79] Not only did he correspond with established writers from Cairo, the epicenter of Arab letters, but he also accepted submissions from semiperipheral places like Morocco.[80] A host of promising writers, poets, and journalists had expressed to Idris their desire to publish in *al-Adab*. Between 1956 to 1992, the years in which he was chief editor, he extended the journal's reach to Bagdad, Arabia, and further east. In the 1960s, for instance, Bagdad was a significant "center for the book market" for many Lebanese publishing houses, and "close to 1000–1500 copies of every book published by Dar al-Taliah would be sent to Iraq," as Tarabishi noted.[81] Numerous Baghdadi poets published in Idris's journal: Al-Bayati (b. 1926) Nazik al-Malaika (b. 1923), and, in particular, Badr Shakir al-Sayyab (b. 1926). Al-Sayyab wrote to Idris that "Iraqi radical writers and readers were more interested in new progressive values in economics, politics, and culture than in the values of the past," capturing the spirit of the 1960s, which went on making the social critic.[82]

In 1955, Idris founded the Independent Pen Association with Raʾif Khouri and Husayn Muruwwah. The following year he married ʿAida Matarji and, in the same year, founded the Dar al-Adab publishing house in collaboration with the Syrian poet Nizar Qabbani. The latter, however, opted out in the early 1960s, as he preferred to pursue a diplomatic career with the Syrian Ministry of Foreign Affairs. In 1967, Qabbani would resume his literary career, which placed him at heights to be envied by many.

Until mid-century, Idris wrote, "we have [had] very few translators with the proper skills and competency: technical proficiency in foreign languages and an expertise in its linguistic and rhetorical depths."[83] The urge to translate in order to catch up with the West, as defined by Idris, met Tarabishi, who was ready to take on this mission. At the turn of the 1960s, Tarabishi graduated from Damascus University to find a field that helped him cultivate his skills. The timing could not have been more apt, as the number of Arab universities in the Middle East began to surge, totaling twenty-three by 1969. Tarabishi rode the translation tide that swept across the Middle East; existentialism was all the rage, and he was the right man in the right place.[84] Tarabishi entered the field of translation in the early 1960s at the promising time of "translation outburst": "I resigned from teaching and from media and decided to live off a translation [career]. I remember translating Simone de Beauvoir's *The Makings of an Intellectual Woman* in 1000 pages for 2000 Lebanese lira. Obviously, the value of Lira was not that of today's. It was like $800 or $900 in today's currency value. At that time, I could live in Syria on $100 a month. Thus, I decided to live off translation, no matter the income. I left all of my previous jobs and dedicated my time to translation. Of course, not all my translations were good."[85]

Translation was indispensable in the making of the social critic in general and in Tarabishi's intellectual evolution in particular. It served as a source of income for him as well as for the new graduates. Idris commented on the way translation met his financial considerations: "Many asked me about the reason behind the paucity of my writings or even its absence in recent years. I respond that among other reasons, I needed to provide for my family. . . . I resorted to other activities to make ends meet. Among these activities was translating jobs or academic work [writing the dictionary]."[86]

Some scholars estimate that Tarabishi translated more than one hundred European classic works.[87] Far from making him rich, translating classical Western books only provided him with a meager sum. After 1970, the number of Arab students—the main consumers of Tarabishi's translations—rose tenfold. In Saudi Arabia alone, which had zero student enrollment in 1957, boasted seven thousand registered students in 1970. In 2010, it hit one million.[88] All these students around the Arab world read these European works in Arabic through the Dar al-Adab and Dar al-Taliah publishing houses with which Tarabishi worked.

The first literature Tarabishi translated was existentialist. As a student, he recalled, he was bombarded with existential literature throughout his studies: "My first dream in the cultural field was to translate the original text that contained the idea of iltizam-commitment [to Arabic], so that this idea comes out of its cloudiness and puts down roots [in Arabic literature]. As a freshman or sophomore at Damascus University, I started translating the complete text of Sartre's 'What's Literature.'" This was the first book Tarabishi had ever translated, at the age of twenty-one. "Since the idea of *iltizam* prevailed in [the] Arab cultural climate," he wrote, "it was not hard for me to find a publisher. It was Zoher Baʿalbaki, the owner of al-[M]aktab al-[T]ijāri li-Nashir, who paid me a symbolic amount of money so that I gave up the rights of its publication."[89]

The translation of *Mā al-Adāb* was not free of pitfalls, however. After some brief excitement, Tarabishi realized that mistakes had found their way into his translation. Luckily, the first edition ran out sooner than he had expected. Tarabishi's success surpassed his wildest dreams; his translations of Sartre brought him great popularity and more opportunities in the nascent job market. An offer came his way from Beirut, the cultural hub of the Arab world at mid-century. For years, the pull of the city attracted and then transformed newcomers. Tarabishi could not resist the offer.

IN BEIRUT

"On September 23, 1972 we arrived in Beirut," wrote Henriette ʿAbud, a feminist novelist and translator who was also Tarabishi's partner, in her memoir. This was after "Bashir al-Dauok—the owner of Dar al-Taliah—had given Tarabishi an offer during the summer to be the next editor of *Dirāsāt ʿArabiyyah*, as the late Sadiq Jalal al-Azm had given up the position."[90] Tarabishi embraced this opportunity. The Beirut of those years offered a vibrant social life, with cinema, theater, and intellectual salons being the beating heart of the city. Cafés were associated with certain publishers, streets were named after writers, and entire boulevards were dedicated to book vendors. Following its independence, Lebanon turned into an economic center in the Arab world as well, as petrodollars from the Gulf States poured in. Pioneering the drive to modernization, Beirut was the second city in the Middle East to electrify residences: "In 1912, light came to Egypt. Two years later it kindled excitement and bedazzled people by modernity in Beirut 1914."[91] The electricity projects reduced the burden of labor on women by making household work less time consuming, thereby freeing them for paid work outside the home. Women in Beirut and Cairo were the first in the Arab world to establish journals and to hold intellectual salons, when women in the rest of the Middle East were preoccupied with housework.[92]

What set Beirut apart was its expressive and educated middle class. Thanks to its diverse population, which ensured a relative freedom, it drew writers from all over the Arabic-speaking world; banished intellectuals from Iraq, Arabia, Tunisia, and Sudan all found refuge there. Since the nineteenth century, its coastline made it into a vast trading center, which sustained its middle class and intellectual spirit. Trade with other centers of commerce in the Mediterranean formed its backbone. However, Beirut's status as a hub of Arab thought was boosted in the wake of the Arab-Israeli War in 1948. According to Fawaz Trablisi, Beirut was arguably the only Arab city that benefited from the creation of Israel in 1948, before which the rivalry with the port of Haifa threatened to undermine Beirut's prosperous business, as Haifa's port was substantially expanding. Beirut's political and financial elites expressed concerns about the rapidly developing Jewish port in Haifa that might steal business; however, the 1948 war and the armistices that followed put an end to that threat. Arabs of the east blocked trading with and from Haifa's port while increasing their dependency on Beirut. After World War

II, the Lebanese markets showed an economic spike that in part sustained the effervescence of the intellectual community.[93]

Many Syrian writers, poets, and journalists with diverse intellectual records flocked to Beirut in search of more opportunities. Even singers and actors lavished in the city's liberal mood. Meanwhile, Palestinian exiles established a vast network of intellectual activity there. The writers Nabil Sulayman from Aleppo and Abu ʿAli Yasin from Damascus moved to Beirut in spring of 1979 to avoid a "tight job market" in Syria. In Beirut, the two began "timidly seeking for jobs in one of the multiple cultural institutions that Beirut featured." These intellectuals were seeking jobs at publishing houses, which were the main institutions for hiring ideological writers. They even went to the cafés that publishers and translators attended daily, like Havana, Rawdah, and Freddy Bar, where Tarabishi used to meet with novelists such as Zakariyya Tamer and Adeb Ghunim. When the "vague answers came in," they concluded that "every cultural institution belonged to or was [tied to] a different Palestinian revolutionary group." To find work, they had to be "affiliated to Palestinian factions."[94] In reality, not all the cultural institutions in Beirut were on the Palestinian financial payroll. New literary journals emerged as a generation of young and passionate scholars came of age.

In Beirut, Idris filled the role that Yasin al-Hafiz had played vis-à-vis Tarabishi back in Damascus. Tarabishi would have most of his translations of Camus, Sartre, and de Beauvoir published in his publishing house. Initially, his relations with Suhayl Idris were merely economic until Tarabishi embraced existentialism more thoroughly, a shared interest that brought them closer. Idris's writings were influenced by existentialism but fused the two intellectual currents of nationalism and modernity, two topics that informed Tarabishi.[95] It was through Idris and his broad network that young Tarabishi entered the field of Arab letters in Beirut. As a translator and lexicographer, Idris was keen to render into Arabic much-needed French literature on existentialism. During his sojourn in Paris, Idris witnessed firsthand the strength and perspicacity of the French intellectual idiom and discourse on existentialism. He realized that in order to bring this philosophy to mass Arab readers he needed to apprentice excellent, promising young people with a flair for intellectual engagement. It was through Idris that Bashir al-Da'uk reached out to Tarabishi.

In his memoir, Tarabishi acknowledged his close relations with Idris: "My connections to Dar al-Adab, its journal, and its owner began to grow stronger. I had achieved to its account the translation of Simone de Beauvoir's novel *The Makings of an Intellectual Woman*, which was, as far as I'm concerned, one of the linchpins in *iltizam* literature."[96] In fact, Idris wrote his French-Arabic dictionary, *al-Manhal*, to facilitate the introduction of existentialism to the Arabic logosphere. It was of immense help to Tarabishi, who used it for years as a reference in his translations from French to Arabic.

Tarabishi settled in the Al-Jadidah neighborhood in West Beirut, quite far from his work at Dar al-Taliah in East Beirut. The city's prime would not last long, however. In the spring of 1975, the entire structure in which an intellectual culture flourished began to crumble under the weight of a savage civil war that wrecked the foundations of its educated class. This war spooked writers, inhibiting them from meeting each other and from exchangings ideas in cafés and bookstores. In the thick of the Lebanese Civil War, as one of Tarabishi's acquaintances stated, "Tarabishi rarely took the risk to drive to his workplace in Dar al-Taliah."[97] This war signaled the end of Tarabishi's hopes for an Arab world where people from different ethnicities and religious backgrounds would live in harmony, side by side. Tarabishi would not leave Beirut until 1984, eight years into the war. In late 1983, the situation in Beirut had become unbearable for Tarabishi and his family. On October 23, 1983, the French and U.S. headquarters of the Multi-National Force was bombed. With 241 American troops and 40 French dead, the civil war took yet another dangerous turn. In February of the following year, the so-called Lebanese Army melted away due to numerous defections from among the ranks of the Muslim and Druze military personnel. One month later, in March 1984, U.S. Marines withdrew from Lebanon, leaving a scorched land with little hope of salvation. The war atrocities left no sense of security for Tarabishi, who fled to Paris to save his life. Besides Idris's *al-Manhal*, he took with him another book, *The Formation of Arab Thought* by the Moroccan writer Jabiri. This was the last book Tarabishi reviewed for publication before leaving his lifetime job at Dar al-Taliah. He recommended it strongly to Bashir al-Dauok, the owner and founder of this publication, before his departure to Paris.[98]

Postcolonial Syria, where a cadre of social critics like Tarabishi grew up, pitted the emergent politics of the young generation against those of the ancien regime. In the midst of the fight against old politics, young social critics were indoctrinated in cultural sensibilities that denounced values and norms that had originated in the past, traditions that seemed to inhibit social progress and preclude their political participation. Translation, knowledge of Western languages and the canon, and immersion in existentialist, Marxist, and positivist theories were necessary means for making this class of Arab writers and publishers. Tarabishi's career offers a perfect example of the way men and women climbed the social ladder through education.

Most of the existing literature on Syria offers numerous exemplary stories in which individuals broke with traditions and rose to leading positions through either an ideologically driven party,[99] or through the newly established military institution.[100] Very few works, however, account for the third channel—namely, the revolution in Syria's educational landscape, which, like the army and political parties, helped to mold new identities and sensibilities that were incongruent with old traditions. Tarabishi's life and intellectual journey from Aleppo, Damascus, and Beirut saw a young, ordinary middle-class translator turned into a fully fledged social critic.

Tarabishi's experience throughout these years converges with the broader experience of a broader generation of the Arab Left. Ever since the days of his religious studies, Tarabishi fostered a deep suspicion of religiously poised folks and developed a dissatisfaction with past traditions; this education framed his mind and informed his visions in future pursuits. His years in a religious school, the tragic encounter with his theology teacher, the constant displacements, and his translations of new Western ideologies shaped his long-running aesthetics and outlook.

These experiences, which he shared with his generation, embedded him in a certain tradtion that ultimately made him into a social critic. Though in subsequent years Tarabishi would harshly judge this ideological stage of his life, the main premises and principles that took shape in this time of tumultuous politics would remain with him. A revolutionary sentiment informed by a deep sense of antipathy toward traditional authorities runs deep in Tarabishi's later thought and writings.

Tarabishi's vision and politics all point to a scholar with an unmistakable admiration of Western thought. Educated by many scholars with great exposure to and appreciation of European intellectual traditions and theorizations, Tarabishi was weaned early in his career on a view that thought ill of local traditions in Arab society and conceived Western modernity as the only path for renewal and social progress. His radicalism was reflected in his writings on Arab women, ideology, and social classes. He employed the Marxist idiom, with its rigid categories and classification, to discredit the old guard, traditional parties, and conservatives. Though his progressive position walked him out of the religious domain, Tarabishi rarely thought of religion or the past as viable sources of knowledge. Like many of his generation of postcolonial writers, Tarabishi thought that progress means following European models.

6

A CRACK IN THE EDIFICE OF THE SOCIAL CRITIC

From Thawrah to Nahda

In April 1992, Tarabishi published an article entitled "The Intellectual and the Fall of Marxism," in which he confessed to having personally abandoned an intellectual tradition in the Arab world. In highly Freudian language, he wrote that "one of the [two] breasts that fed Arab ideology had dried up: the Marxist text. Evidently, the allure to switch to the other breast grew bigger: the Salafi text. Whoever got accustomed to the textual milk will find it harder to wean himself off." This is how Tarabishi thought about the postcolonial condition: either one feeds from Western texts or Salafi texts—nothing in between. This exemplifies Tarabishi in the post-Marxian age, as an intellectual whose main quest was to "liberate the Arab intellectual from the bondage of [traditional] texts."[1]

The main project that Tarabishi set himself to defend was the steady erosion of the social critic in order to stave off—or at least delay—his free fall. Tarabishi might well be considered the last social critic, since none of his disciples and followers seem to have risen to his stature after his death in March 2016. Moroccan Said Nashid, Tunisian Raja' Ben Slama, and Algerian Hamid Zinaz are promising young scholars with great potential to carry the torch, yet so far none of them, who now lead the Rabitat al-ʿAqlaniyin al-ʿArab (the Arab Rationalist Association), have garnered enough cultural capital to take on Tarabishi's mantle.

As he waged his last battle against the connected critic, Tarabishi was well aware that he was on the losing end, for the decline of the social critic was inevitable in the wake of the cultural changes in the 1970s. However, with the rise of a new guard of intellectuals from North Africa, Tarabishi was not willing to surrender without putting up a fight against Jabiri and the connected critics. Tarabishi realized that Jabiri had taken over the rank and file of Arab intellectuals when he took control of the Center for Arab Unity Studies, which banished Tarabishi and his followers. It is for good reason that Tarabishi devoted the last twenty years of his life to decanonizing Jabiri after having endorsing him earlier. While Tarabishi failed to reverse the cultural trends Jabiri had set loose, he was able to form and galvanize a group of dedicated writers to carry his legacy forward.

What strategies did Tarabishi devise to stand up against the connected critic? How did he manage to ward off the diminishing ground left to the social critic? Ironically, one of strategies for slowing down the march of the connected critic was to redeploy and reassert the nahda—ironic, since Tarabishi had derisively ignored and overlooked the nahda in the 1960s. Now, in the face of the rising power of the connected critic, he began to appreciate its historical role and relevance in the Arab world. He perceived it to be a valid framework of reference and saw in it a new beginning. This turnabout from a dismissal of the nahda to a new investment in its authors and principles captures one of the major shifts that the great cultural war in the Arab world has imposed on postcolonial Arab thought.

THE SOCIAL CRITIC: THE END OF HEGEMONY

Tarabishi's frank confessions of the impending dangers of authorizing the past reinforce the impression that when he writes about turath, he also writes about the diminishing lot of the revolutionary generation of social critics. At the beginning of the 1990s, in delving deeply into turath, Tarabishi conceded that most of his previous wagers on Pan-Arabism, existentialism, and Marxism "were all but misguiding."[2] These ideologies, it belatedly dawned on him, had steered him and many like-minded social critics away from addressing the main issue: people's biases, cultural assumptions, religious prejudices, and embedded sectarianism. Ideologically disenchanted, Tarabishi argued that genuine intellectuals in the Third World should not fail to fulfill their duty by avoiding the inevitable clash with "the masses"—namely, with people's beliefs, norms, values, and collective memory. Tarabishi saw no use for Third World intellectuals who fell short of disrupting entrenched cultural attitudes, unsettling conventional social norms, and dislocating public morality. Rather than caving in to an obsolete value system, which inflicted much pain on women and minorities, Tarabishi was bent on questioning the added value many intellectuals have placed on their heritage and inherited norms. What emotional and cultural possibilities are facilitated by the new focus on turath? he asked. For him the answer was clear: sectarianism, a force that ripped through the Arab social fabric and that, dormant for decades, was reawakened by a renewed focus on turath. When asked about the Arab Spring, which soon turned into a sectarian war, Tarabishi responded that it was a direct result of the newfound emphasis on turath, and that he saw it coming.[3]

Tarabishi arrived in Paris in the summer of 1984, to start a new life and embark on a new intellectual journey. He had tendered his resignation letter to Bashir al-Dauok, notifying him of his plans to quit the editorial board of Dar al-Taliah, on which he had served for twelve years. Tarabishi's resignation signaled that both the Arab social critic and its institutions had fallen on hard times, as the civil war in Beirut had taken its toll on them. In deep despair over the relentless, nonsensical sectarian conflict, Tarabishi had longed to leave the smoking city of Beirut.[4] But he had little choice, until he received an offer from the journal *al-Wihdah*, which had been launched in Paris. Tarabishi did not think twice; he picked up and left Beirut with his family.

He had a long but exciting flight. With him he brought Jabiri's recent work. Tarabishi was gripped by it, and "every now and then," recalled his wife, "he would confess how stunned he was by the brilliance of the work at hand."[5] In Paris, Tarabishi took a new place in Créteil, in the southeast. From his apartment he could see the scenic Créteil Lake, around which he and his wife walked daily. As he settled into Paris, Tarabishi's career began to take a turn: his literary criticism would give way to a new engagement in nonfiction. His interest with turath would supplant his interest in translation.

Tarabishi had always been bewildered by turath's magnificent treasures, its genuine poetry and philosophy, its bold music and brave art, its Islamic astronomy, and even its heretic expressions and bizarre sexual norms. This is the "forgotten tradition" of what his teacher Arkoun called medieval "Arab humanism," which includes numerous, diverse modes of unorthodox religiosity. Yet Arab intellectuals' fascination with this compendium of texts, and their approved attempts to pursue these medieval cultural models, left Tarabishi disconcerted. He eloquently described the "growing mania for turath" as a "collective neurosis."[6] For him the simple fact that the relatively progressive Arab intelligentsia of yesterday had begun looking past Europe and its modernity, turning to the Arab-Islamic past for original, authentic solutions to modern-day challenges, attests to a true cultural backwardness or regression (*ridda*). This angst with turath had far-reaching effects, not only with regard to the path Arab nations had taken, but also to the way young generations were trained and socialized and their school curricula was determined. As an intellectual who spent the better part of his career translating Western ideas and models into Arabic, Tarabishi felt betrayed, shunned, and ostracized as the value of his translation of existential and Marxist tomes began dwindling in the wake of the age of authenticity in the Arab world.

Nothing in Tarabishi's previous translations of the most progressive ideas in Europe anticipated the new trends in current Arab thought. Nothing in his writings of the 1960s seemed relevant in the new age of Arab authenticity. Firm in his adherence to the diffusion model, he had hoped of turning the Middle East around by exposing its people to genuine European ideas and ideologies. But this model proved vacuous and ineffective, increasingly losing its sway over people's minds. Within a couple of years after arriving in Paris, Tarabishi felt adrift, removed from everything except the armory of critique (*silāḥ al-naqd*). Calling on his colleagues for self-reflection, he turned to appreciate the advantageous value of critique, which he deemed as "the supreme mode of social thinking."[7]

Declaring war against turath, and in particular against connected critics like Jabiri and Hasan Hanafi, seemed inevitable to Tarabishi, who was now poised to subject their work to critique. He was convinced that his cultural war—which reminded him of the war Michael ʿAflq and other Baathists declared against the old guard of landowners—was winnable, but in it he was on the losing side, because he wanted to defend the status quo being challenged by connected critics like Jabiri. It is no surprise that the first book Tarabishi published in Paris addressed turns and shifts in contemporary Arab discourse. Entitled *Al-Muthaqqafūn al-ʿArab Wa-al-Turāth* (Arab intellectuals and turath), it subjected to analysis connected critics' exhileration with turath. More than a critique, it declared cultural war against Jabiri and Hanafi, the two leading connected critics in the Arab world. Tarabishi focused his analysis on the history of knowledge in Arab and Islamic societies. Conceding that different people organize their knowledge differently, Tarabishi's interest lay in exploring the ways in which knowledge is structured and ordered in different times within the Arab historical space.[8] Specifically, he was intrigued by the question of when and in what contexts Arab peoples were poised to revise their values and norms that for a long time held them together.[9] To this question, he offered the classical answer: Arab people's perceptions and "collective consciousness" are subjected to change by "external shocks" (like the shock Napoleon inflicted on the Arab world when he invaded Egypt in three days in 1798).[10] That event launched the Arab world into a new era of cultural and material awakening: the so-called nahda era.

Tarabishi proposed another context in which Arab people might be amenable to testing their cultural assumptions and inherited values, which had been taken for granted for a long time. When confronted with major historical events and unexpected, disruptive experiences, a perceptible change in Arab people's thought system can be noticed—for example, in the wake of the trauma in 1967, when Israel blew away three Arab armies in six days, a defeat that imprinted itself on peoples' minds and souls and informed their way of thinking and became a part of who they are. The event was traumatic because it disrupted the story many Arab peoples told themselves. Yet the overriding problematic that baffled Tarabishi was the challenge of explaining the dramatic change in the frame of reference in the contemporary Arab world—specifically, the increasing authority of cultural references like turath and the growing marginality of modern frameworks like European models. Tarabishi's inquiry into how modern Arab peoples shifted from one mode of knowledge production to another also sheds light on the decline of the social critic in the Arab world. Though Tarabishi never explicitly discussed the issue in terms of decline and ascent, his questions and comments left little doubt to the potency of this rise and fall narrative.

Al-Muthaqqafūn Al-ʿArab Wa-Al-Turath (Arab intellectuals and turath), a book that diagnoses the cultural pains of the postcolonial condition, advances this thesis, centering on the cultural defeat in 1967 that "left open a bleeding narcissistic wound" that set in motion a cultural trend of looking back to find better models for present-day ills.[11] He referred to this trend derisively as a "cultural recoil," or *nukus*, at the end of which Arabs were led to readopt medieval norms, values, and codes. It is this drift backward to the "imagined medieval past," or the revival of turath, that Tarabishi accounts for in this book, which unfolds as a gentle parable of a defeated world going astray. Reading Tarabishi's textual psychoanalysis of Arab intellectuals is to be immersed in an experience of falling. In this dense work, Tarabishi offers an example of how readily human beings fall prey to their own language and their hypotheses—namely, delusions about the solutions that turath could provide to social ailments. Tarabishi leaned heavily on Freud's notion of "collective neuroses" to elaborate on the trends that led up to the reawakening of a "glorious" medieval past, which a number of Arab intelligentsia were taken by. This resort to past traditions did not happen by accident. As far as Tarabishi was concerned, Arab intellectuals were affected by *ʿusāb jamaʿī* (collective neuroses): man's inability to free himself from the grip of the past and the burden of history. Tarabishi vividly demonstrated that the complex of the collective neurosis was embodied by the fixation on turath in order to heal the narcissistic wounds that the modern condition inflected on the Arab world.

The main strategy Tarabishi came up with was to readopt the nahda, or nineteenth-century Arab awakening, that he had previously rejected. Starting in the late 1980s, a period marked by cultural openness, Tarabishi called upon his colleagues to turn their "attention to nahda mechanisms."[12] Insisting on authorizing the nahda over turath, prioritizing its cultural spirit, he bestowed it with the prescriptive capacity to counter the "backslide toward turath." In one of his rare interviews, he maintained that "our hope [today] hinges upon the renewal of the nahda." For Tarabishi, the nahda provided the right antidote to the current erosion in what he called "Arab rationalism," implying that the perspective of the social critic was the only rational view, and that the rest were irrational. He wrote, "The renewal of the nahda means to accept [to submit before] reason again [by] making reason the supreme authority over religion."[13]

COUNTEROFFENSIVE: REVOKING THE NAHDA

What was so unique in the nahda era that Tarabishi was so eager to valorize? How does the nahda counteract the return to turath? Tarabishi was not alone in calling for a new engagement with it in the 1990s; in fact, scores of Arab social critics had to recourse to it in addressing the cultural challenges of the postcolonial condition. The turn to the nahda during the last decade of the twentieth century raises the following questions: Why did so many social critics and secular intellectuals embrace the nahda after having disowned it in earlier decades? How do we explain this shift in their attitudes? How did the nahda come to change from a relic of a "forgotten era" to a new and compelling framework of reference among social critics? To address these questions, one must come to understand the way the shifting cultural landscape since the 1970s had created a social "need" for many social critics, who saw their cultural capital slipping away with every passing day.

The renewed attention to the nahda had been extensive, reaching far beyond narrow academic circles and scholarly debates. The conversation echoed in public spaces: in dailies, cafés, and spontaneous political conversations. A few months before his tragic assassination in 2005, Lebanese journalist Samir Kassir had dedicated a book in which he lauded the nahda, extolling its optimistic spirit. Kassir proposed a return to it as a way to counter the mounting challenges of the postcolonial condition (what he called "Arab malaise"). The nahda, for Kassir, not only provided a healthy corrective path to the ubiquitous pessimism that pervaded Arab intellectual circles, but also reflected the first attempt in Arab thought to desacralize the past and depathologize its beginnings. Though he asserted that "it would be impossible to exaggerate the benefits of restoring this era to its proper place in Arab history," he continued that "it would allow one to reinterpret this malaise as a moment in history."[14] Kassir, a social critic with an immaculately future-oriented orientation, found that the optimism that characterized the nahda was sorely missing in his own day. He never lived to see how his book was received. While his eulogists took note of his insistence on the value of the nahda, no one seemed to have asked the question: Why the nahda now?

The renewed interest in the nahda met a cultural need that was not so obvious before the late 1980s: the clear victory of the connected critics. As soon as the social critic noticed that he had lost his grip on the intellectual conversation, he invoked the nahda primarily to fend against the return to turath. Branding the nahda as "recent past," which everyone should aspire to emulate, Tarabishi called to appropriate and deploy its spirit to stave off the drift toward the remote past of medieval age. At the beginning of the 1990s, the nahda was available for cultural appropriation, given the time that had lapsed since its completion in the late 1930s. Even though it lacked truly revolutionary ideas, the nahda now emerged as a powerful countering force that afforded the means to disarming the forces of turath.

Yet embracing the nahda was a partial solution to the stature and standing of the social critics as they faced a rising reading public taken with the significant writings on turath. The cultural indifference toward the writings and works of social critics signaled a low point for the social critics, who had been in steep decline since the beginning of 1970s, as many formerly keen Marxists began renouncing Marxism. For Tarabishi, however, the inherent weaknesses of this class of critics—whether Marxists, positivists, existentialists, or nationalists—stemmed from an excessive focus on politics at the expense of culture. This focus, he believed, had backfired: it limited the reach of the social critic, primarily due to the fact that he antagonized cautious Arab regimes that suffered from an extreme shortage of self-confidence and political legitimacy, as military coups were part of the political norm. These Arab regimes, taking extra measures to eliminate any perceived adversary, were in no position to condone the social critics' strident critique. In a letter to a former social critic, Tarabishi acknowledged that the works of Sadiq Jalal al-Azm—especially his *Critique of Theology*—generated a political and cultural backlash. He explained that what had initially looked like the social critic's swift victory became a protracted controversy over the book, the identity of the author, and its publisher, with the Lebanese court ruling against Azm. Before long, many of the publishing houses in the Arab world were subjected to diligent vetting, which curtailed the reach and scope of the writing of social critics.[15] Arab regimes, vigilant and weary, were watching what they published.

Azm's radical ideas were among the first bold responses to the cultural outrage stirred by the defeat in 1967.[16] He endeavored to undermine the structure of feeling and shake the "religious orthodoxy" and was applauded by many for setting in motion a new style of writing.[17] Many historians described Azm's ideas as launching a new era in Arab thought.[18] While many observers commended his audacity for the initial inroads he made, they rarely, if ever, attended to the politics his books generated. Focusing on the "revolutionary content of the book left the political fallouts of the book unattended [to]," Tarabishi stated. The effects of this work were devastating to the social critics, and the minor cultural changes Azm's works initially sparked (in questioning faith in particular) were soon reversed in the ensuing years, Tarabishi confided to his friend in a letter, "The public hysteria these books provoked" led many Arab regimes to enact and ratify a new set of strict policies on the publication of books on Arab leftist thought," which significantly exhausted the quality of their translations and dulled their critical drive.[19] This moratorium on free thinking suspended, if not derailed, the secular thrust that Azm's works had launched. In retrospect, Azm's attempt to counter Islamic thinking—to reconfigure the cultural view of Islam as a liability rather than an asset—proved premature and, Tarabishi concluded, harmful to the social critic in the long run.

With the ideological retreat of the social critic, the intellectual ground was cleared for the connected thinkers. Meanwhile, many readers could not hide their frustration with social critics' writings, which not only grew more ideological, but also engaged in dry topics that seemed far removed from the challenges of daily life and economic hardship. The focus of this writing gave the impression that they were in conversation with their Western leftist colleagues rather than addressing Arab affairs. The social critics had not only seen their ranks shrinking during the 1970s, but also the numbers of their publications dropped significantly. In the late 1970s, Bu ʿAli Yasin, an avid Marxist, noticed that most of the publishing houses of the Arab Left began losing their readership.[20] If, during the 1960s, these publishing houses printed two thousand copies of a book, starting in the late 1970s they reduced this number to only one thousand. Readers felt increasingly alienated by the writing on the Vietnamese guerilla war, Soviet labor unions, social classes, and Marxist theories of surplus and value. The more the works of the social critics estranged their readership, writings on more authentic issues like turath grew more appealing. Turath was also increasingly seen as a secure haven during times of accelerated change, especially with the unprecedented movement of populations from the country to cities, as a new set of cultural and literary tastes began to emerge. Though the deviation from literary norms was slow, the accumulated effects of these changes culminated in a dramatic shift by the beginning of the 1980s.

Minor changes in literary tastes triggered by restrictive laws on free thinking took their toll on the Arab social critic. Though Arab regimes had successfully muted the roaring Marxists, dispersing their major thinkers around the world, these intellectuals were able to regroup themselves in diaspora during the 1980s. The first step they took to lift the moratorium forced on them by Arab regimes was to ask uneasy questions about turath. Many of social critics who could not publish their works with Dar al-Adab or Dar al-Taliah turned to new publishing houses in London, Dar Riyyad al-Rayis and Dar al-Saqi. The attempts of the social critics to divert the cultural trends in the Arabic-speaking world were partially successful. To stand up to the connected critics, the social critics realized, they have to engage them in turath.

EMBRACING TURATH

Tarabishi's first and most serious engagement with turath came in the form of a book in 1996.[21] This work launched Tarabishi into a more expansive project on turath that would consume his intellectual attention in the last two decades of his life. Yet no one could have expected Tarabishi to take this turn in his career, much less to leave behind a corpus of translations and commentary on Sartre, Hegel, Freud, and Marx. This apparent shift in his intellectual concerns led many Arab readers and commentators to wonder at his seemingly incongruent move. How could Tarabishi, whose writings were essential to the dissemination of Western thinking in the Arab world, give up on his original intention? Did he surrender to the cultural trends around him? As one Arab commentator incredulously remarked, "No one could have imagined that the Syrian writer and literary critic, who demonstrated early on a mature sense of criticism, ingenuity in his theses, and developed a new analysis with distinctive tastes, would turn his back—without a return—on all of this literature and delve headlong into the taxonomies and references of the Arab and Islamic turath."[22]

What seems to have struck many observers as out of step is Tarabishi's "metamorphosis" from a revolutionary writer to a commentator on turath. In 1998, Tarabishi recognized the indispensability of addressing turath. The need to encounter it, Tarabishi maintained, arises from a widespread realization among social critics that "no revolution nor any [cultural] change would enable us to enter the modern age [*dukhūl al-ʿaṣr*] without relating it to the critique of turath."[23] Meaning, as long as Arab intellectuals are not done with turath, it is unlikely that any serious change would occur, much less take hold, in a society gripped by past traditions. In another article published in 2006, Tarabishi admitted (probably for the first time) the limited success of the diffusion model, writing that "all the defeats and the disillusionments" had beholden him to revise his "attitude toward cultural turath."[24] This led him to conclude that the previous consensus about turath as a declining tradition was no longer a guarantee of its comeback.

Tarabishi's turn toward turath marked not only a watershed in his personal life, but also a significant conjuncture in the annals of contemporary Arab thought. Scholars who steered away from turath, like Sadiq Jalal al-Azm, would lose their bearings and their readership; scholars who took on turath like Nasr Hamid abu Zayd would see a surge in popularity. The "rediscovery of Turath" (*Iʿādat Iktishāf al-Turath*) naturally offers a name to a new era in Arab thought. Coming to discover turath in Paris, Tarabishi wrote in 2006, "I found turath an alternative to the homeland [*watan*] I left behind."[25] Yet it is remarkable that Tarabishi conceived turath as an unmistakable threat that might unravel all the intellectual effort put forth by generations of Arab intellectuals since the nahda. His embrace of turath, as we will see below, was only the first step in his agenda to dismantle, disrupt, and disqualify it as a model for living in the modern Arab world.

Another reason that prompted Tarabishi to address turath was French Algerian writer Mohammad Arkoun, under whose guidance he worked as a doctoral student in Paris. Though Tarabishi never submitted his completed dissertation, which he published as a book in Arabic, Arkoun's ideas swayed him from his previous ideological thinking, which perceived turath as dangerous, a place to be avoided. Instead, Arkoun encouraged him to rethink his rigid attitude and partisanship, cajoling him to view turath the way Islamists in the Middle East viewed it, as more than Islamic fiqh. Arkoun, a historian, pushed Tarabishi in particular to adopt the tools of the Annales school, which influenced Arkoun immensely as a student in the late 1960s. The new emphases on social and daily practices of the Annales that downplayed the previous centrality of official narrative and political history appealed to him. Eager to apply the Annales school's approach to non-European spaces, Arkoun was the first native Middle Eastern scholar who sought to write a new history of Arab and Islamic history that appropriated the methods and terminology the school promoted. For instance, in his quest to undermine what he called the "official closed corpus" in the Arab and Islamic historical experience, Arkoun focused on "fringe movements" in Islam to open new horizons for modern-day Muslims to follow.[26] Arkoun's reading of medievalist Islamic philosophers and his reconstruction of a forgotten "humanistic tradition in Islam" prodded Tarabishi, along with many of his Arab students, to follow his path by offering an against-the-grain reading of turath. The new exploration of turath, informed by Arkoun's concepts, trickled down to Tarabishi, who began investigating the formative period of Islam by laying bare the ways in which social classes, political feuds, and economic and tribal rivalries played into the forging of the first interpretations of the holy book. Moving away from the mechanical reading of Islamic history, Arkoun taught Tarabishi to emphasize contingency in history and to examine the manners in which the set of Islamic beliefs came together.[27]

In what follows, I argue that Tarabishi's turn to turath marks no radical change in his approach, orientation, or historical outlook. I show that he remained firm in his modern beliefs, and that his supposed metamorphosis was unnecessarily exaggerated. It is important to ask not only why he ended up engaging turath, but also how he treated turath. I contend that his agenda was to convince readers that turath was neither redeemable nor salvageable the way connected critics presented and framed it. Put simply, for Tarabishi the most pressing issue on the Arab agenda was to demonstrate that turath was not a sure path for Arab modernity. In his interviews as well as in his writings, he reiterated the same notion: that no medieval rationality could provide the framework for being modern in the postcolonial era.

TURATH THROUGH CONTEMPORARY EYES

In 1993, Tarabishi published a terse survey of the different schools of thought on turath in the form of a short book with the inflammatory title *Madhbaḥat al-turath fī al-thaqāfah al-ʿArabīyah al-muʿāṣirah* (The massacre over turath).[28] The young Tarabishi of the 1960s is hardly recognizable in this sharp text. Except for his trenchant critique, nothing in this book evokes the thoughts and themes of his earlier writings on Hegel, Marx, social justice, total revolution, sovereignty, and imperialism. Unlike any previous work, this book is relatively free of Western theories or Marxist jargon. The main concern is not to authorize yet another European idea, but to examine the drift toward turath. After Tarabishi published this book, he did not translate a single Western work into Arabic again, suggesting that his intellectual priorities had fundamentally changed.

Taking his cues from Arkoun, Tarabishi could no longer afford to flout the heated intellectual debates around turath, nor address the subject from a materialist-Marxist approach. By writing this book, Tarabishi intended to question contemporary intellectuals who produced a skewed interpretation of turath. Emphasizing its evils, Tarabishi regarded the cultural turn toward turath with apprehension. Though he never fell short of providing historical evidence of the adverse effect of turath on the lives of modern Arab citizens, in *Madhbaḥat al-turath fī al-thaqāfah al-ʿArabīyah al-muʿāṣirah* he convincingly showed the ways in which Arab intellectuals failed to stand up to their initial, more advanced positions.

"Even if the subject of *judhūr* [roots, ancestors, or heritage] is a common theme among many nations," Tarabishi wrote in the opening of his book, "it has a particular bearing to contemporary Arab world." Since the defeat in 1967, Tarabishi rationalized, Arab intellectuals had taken refuge in turath and along the way turned it into their main ideology: "Educated Arabs lost their control over reality, so they looked for a discourse through which to control . . . and they found the discourse of turath." Tarabishi contended that Arab intellectuals—including former colleagues of his—had projected their preconceptions and biases onto turath and, as a result, offered ideological readings of turath, with little regard to historical truths. Tarabishi deployed two ideas in his analysis of the common readings of turath: *izāḥah* (dislocation) and *istibdāl* (transference). Whether contemporary Arab readers unconsciously fell prey to psychological transference or dislocation, they had made turath into an "absolute ideology" that bred only "absolute truths."[29]

Tarabishi subjected to critique four streams in contemporary Arab thought: the Marxist, nationalist, Islamic Left, and epistemological schools. Addressing each separately, he offered an analysis that delved deep into the mental mechanism that drives them, raising questions on the assumptions that guide their thinking and the frameworks that sustain their analysis. In one example, Tarabishi argued that Arab Marxists were inherently eclectic and unsystematic in their reading of turath; they were not interested in understanding turath's historical truth, he said, but in choosing the elements that fit into their preconceived ideological visions. The problem with this "instrumental reading," Tarabishi asserted, was that this selective use of turath ran contrary to the Marxists' claim of an "objective and scientific reading of the past." He wrote, "Arab Marxists, whose enemies had always dismissed them as turath-nihilists, responded by reviving turath following Lenin: insisting that turath is not a homogenous unity that is either taken or thrown away. The turath is a conflicting field . . . one part of which can be taken to confront the other part."[30] This bifurcation of turath seemed not to have bothered Arab Marxists, Tarabishi concluded, impeding any attempt to deconstruct it. Instead of invalidating turath, they ended up asserting its value.

Tarabishi resorted again to a thesis he developed in 1989 that defined the postcolonial age as an era marked by a narcissistic wound, an idea he attributed to the psychological blow of the defeat in 1967.[31] Tarabishi argued that Egyptian writer Mohammad Amarah, a Marxist who turned turathist, had idealized turath as rational, humanistic, and applicable to present-day life. This romanticizing of turath, which Tarabishi referred to as a psychological projection, not only made turath what it was not, but also deepened the bleeding wound of the Arab body. Rather than alleviating the pains of the present condition of failed postcolonialism, the comparison between the glorious past and debased present "accelerate[d] the feeling of impotence and disability," wrote Tarabishi.[32] This way of thinking, Tarabishi continued, only perpetuated the unmitigated sense of "a feeling of inferiority" and explained why Arab intellectuals were returning to turath. But, in their return, they did not make up for their dejected and incomprehensible realities, but, rather, further lowered their self-esteem.

The overriding idea that seems to have concerned Tarabishi in this work is what he called the "fragmentation [*tamzīq*] of turath." Tarabishi concluded that Arab scholars had failed to grasp turath on its own terms and still less within its holistic historical meaning; they borrowed certain aspects and neglected others in their ideological reading of it. These schools, and the individual scholars who worked within them, all presented turath as a solution to the host of problems that ail postcolonial Arab societies. Tarabishi believed that this was not the way turath should be approached and understood. Turath, the reader concludes, is neither salvageable nor redeemable; it is simply irrelevant. For Tarabishi, there was no way out of acknowledging that there is no option to pick and choose a more comfortable version of history.

SECULARIZING TURATH

When Tarabishi embarked on studying turath to contain its spread and to show its invalidity as a framework of reference in the postcolonial condition, he had no idea that turath might provide a genealogy for the idea of secularism. In the article "Buthūr al-Almaniyya fi al-Islām" (Secular seeds in Islam), Tarabishi expressed his rebellion against Arab and non-Arab scholars, naming, among others, Bernard Lewis, who had falsely argued that Islam had never differentiated between the spiritual and temporal domains.[33] Countering this ill-conceived idea, Tarabishi suggested that, by looking at daily historical experience, "Islam does not completely diverge from Christianity in separating between the here and now and the hereafter."[34] Bringing together moderate Islamists who categorically denounced secularism, along with Western scholars, who denied secularism as an available condition within Islamic historical space, Tarabishi's article debunked erroneous readings of Islamic experience as practiced throughout history. Promoting his thesis, Tarabishi wrote, "Whenever the dialectics of the sacred and profane played out under Islam, the second prevailed," Tarabishi asserted this conclusion by writing that "the state masked itself in Islam while it's true face was invariably Jāhilī [un-Islamic]."[35]

No other Arab scholar went as far as Tarabishi to entrench (*Ta'ṣīl*) the secular notion in Islamic historical experience. As one critic wrote, "Tarabishi wished his project not only to stave off a fading idea [secularism], but primarily to establish a forgotten genealogy [of the secular] in past Arab-Islamic historical experience."[36] Indeed, Tarabishi was the first to exhume the Arabic word *ʿālmaniyya*, or "secularism," from a book written in the tenth century that he'd encountered by accident. *Miṣbaḥ al ʿaql* (Reason's light) was written by an Arab Christian author in Egypt named Ibn al-Muqaffaʿ al-Masrri. The discovery of this word overwhelmed Tarabishi:

> My focus was to explore the [roots of the] word secularism [to give evidence that] it was not imported from the West as we have often been charged. Others have charged secularism [of being] a Western word. Secularism is an essential part of our heritage as it existed in the core of al-turath. Here is the place to point out that Ibn al-Muqaffaʿ al-Masrri of the fourth century [tenth-century AD] used this word without expounding on it in his *Miṣbaḥ al ʿaql*, which means that it was a familiar [concept]. Secularism, for Ibn al-Muqaffaʿ al- Masrri, meant "who he is not a priest"—namely, whoever is not a religious man.[37]

For Tarabishi, this was a conclusive verdict that Arabic employed the secular idea even before it emerged in the West.

With this revelation, Tarabishi believed that Arab thought was now poised to break through the misguided duality of turath versus contemporaneity. This unveiling of the secular idea undercut the claim of conservatives (the guardians of turath), who renounced secularism as a foreign idea that had failed to adapt to the Arab soil, or the contention that Arab historical experience is not conducive to secularism. Unearthing the idea of secularism in the Arab land, Tarabishi concluded, should help to "lubricate its assimilation," transforming it from a malicious term to a palatable notion easy to "digest," meaning embrace.[38] This finding did not move Arab intellectuals as Tarabishi had expected, but it left him with the conclusion that the most efficient way to change minds is by showing how Arab and Islamic turath was constructed and narrated.

MIRACLES IN ISLAM: CRITIQUING MODERATE ISLAM

At a time in which the Arab world had seen a sea of political change, Tarabishi was, ironically, carried away by turath. "His fascination with turath literature was insatiable," wrote his wife. "Tarabishi won't stop reading except for coffee." He dedicated little time to contemporary politics and didn't have much to say about the tumultuous events unfolding in the Middle East. One of his critics wondered, "How could Tarabishi write 3000 pages against medieval Sunni Islam and no more than two pages on the 250,000 Syrian mortalities?"[39] Tarabishi's critics made little effort to hide their contempt toward the social critics who clustered around him in Paris and elsewhere for steering clear of politics. Yasin Haj Salih, a Syrian intellectual, prisoner, and one of Tarabishi's prominent detractors, attacked him for being so "doggedly loyal" to the regime in Syria, accusing intellectuals like him of afflicting the Arab Left in Syria with its weakening scourge.[40] Al-Sayyid wrote, referring to Tarabishi and his group, "I have known no other intellectuals who let their people down as much as Arab intellectuals."[41]

Indeed, Tarabishi had never stood out as a brilliant political analyst. In fact, he went out of his way to disentangle himself from politics in order to avoid criticizing Asad's regimes before and after 2011. Yet the entire intellectual endeavor in which he had been engaged was not free from political repercussions. The existential threat to the current Arab order, Tarabishi asserted, came not only from the Baathist regime but political Islam. Specifically, Tarabishi argued that the challenge political Islam posed was supported in *texts*—namely, in the *way* texts are made sacred and then deployed, disseminated and put to political use. As a political activist in the 1960s, Tarabishi learned the hard way that changes in the conceptualization of these texts are the only guarantee to generate a ripple effect in the political sphere. With this working assumption in mind, he addressed the prophet Mohammad's status in the Islamic imagination. Tarabishi believed that political change in the Arab world hinges in part on a previous change in the image held of prophet Mohammad in contemporary Arab societies.

In *Al-Muʿjizah, aw, Subāt al-ʿaql fī al-Islām* (Miracle and the eclipse of reason in Islam), Tarabishi argued that among the founders of all religions, Mohammad stood out in owning up to no miracle but the writing of the Qurʾan. Remarkably, Tarabishi argued, the Holy Book of the Qurʾan denies Mohammad the status of a prophet (*nabī*) while insisted on calling him messenger (*rasūl*). Mohammad was sent with the clear mission to spread the word of God, the lawgiver. "Shorn of any capacity to issue laws," Mohammad's image in the Qurʾan is reinforced time and again as "no more than a messenger," deprived of any authority to legislate, still less to express any opinion or command any order with regard to heaven and life after death.[42] In a manner distinctive only to classical Orientalists and atypical of his writing from the 1970s, Tarabishi provided numerous verses from the Qurʾan in which God addresses Mohammad as his messenger, not only divested of any authority to express his opinion but also chastised for uttering "decrees" and "verdicts" independently. Overwhelming his reader with the citations of numerous Qurʾanic verses, Tarabishi not only enshrines the entire discussion with evidence that speaks voluminously to Muslims, but he also leaves the reader humbled and disenchanted with the truncated statue of Mohammad. All the holiness that once shrouded Mohammad slipped away as his human condition burst forth.

After establishing the status of Mohammad as a messenger of God in the Qurʾan, Tarabishi emphasized his findings of the unbridgeable disparity between this Qurʾanic portrayal and the ever-growing Hadith literature that refers to Mohammad as "the last prophet." The Hadith, a collection of Mohammad's sayings and deeds, not only explicitly contradicts the spirit of the Holy Book, Tarabishi demonstrated, but also confers on Mohammad legal authority and political clout that the Qur'an explicitly denies him. By revealing that the Hadith is at odds with the Qur'an, rather than completing it, Tarabishi provided a unique occasion to inveigh against the authenticity of the Hadith, facilitating the first point of entry for questioning the way normal texts were made into sacred texts.[43]

This method that sought to bring to the fore contradictions and disparities between the Qur'an and the Hadith/Sunna was and remains the most effective strategy embraced by Tarabishi and the rest of the social critics to make inroads for rational and secular thinking in contemporary Arab thought. Effecting small shocks in the mythical belief system, by overwhelming devout Muslims with more nuanced and subtle understandings of Islamic belief and digging up the earthly aspects in Mohammad's ordinary life, were among the rationalist strategies employed to question the moral certainties of turath. For Tarabishi, disenchanted with political activism in the wake of the failure of the postcolonial project, this kind of work made political interventions. This reinforces his conviction that changing minds preceeds any other change.

His most recent work, *Min Islām Al-Qur'ān Ilá Islām Al-Ḥadīth (*From Islam of the Qur'an to the Islam of the Hadith), which Tarabishi viewed as the pinnacle of his entire career, further defied the common conception of turath. In this book Tarabishi explained how the Sunna literature that began to develop around the figure of Mohammad hijacked the Qur'an and tweaked its meaning from its original aim. A florid narrative of the downgrading of the Qur'an through the deification of the Hadith, in over six hundred pages Tarabishi accounted for the lengthy but steady process in which ensuing generations of Muslim *'ulama* had eroded the edge the Qur'an had over the Hadith, until the thirteenth century, when many Muslims began subscribing equal value to the Hadith compendium. Intertwined in this process is the way in which Hadith literature was relocated from the domain of the temporal to the sacred. Once consecrated and canonized, Hadith was given equal status compared only to the Qur'an. Tarabishi pointed out that al-Shafiʿi, the preeminent jurist of the ninth century, set this process in motion, overseeing the pairing between the Qur'an and Hadith. The previous divergence between them, which many early Muslims strictly maintained, was erased, Tarabishi argued, to facilitate and legitimize religious people to intervene in politics.

Like a true modernist, Tarabishi clumped together connected critics with moderate Islam. Subjecting moderate Islam to a trenchant critique emanates from Tarabishi's belief that Islamists' sway over politics and culture cannot be easily contained, since their piety branches out into politics. To understand the bind in which Islamists have placed Arab societies, Tarabishi contended, it is useful to start with the specific fears that they are exploiting. Islamists, particularly in the wake of the 1967 war, rebooted the Islamic discourse to serve particular needs, uttering the same old quips with a radicalized tinge to position themselves as the only authentic alternative. According to Tarabishi, Islamists transformed Islam through a widespread network of publishing, funding, and mobilizing, giving rise to a new and unfamiliar mode of religiosity. Rather than asserting continuity, they broke with classical Islam in whose name they make (political) claims.

Against this bleak assessment of the postcolonial condition that give rise to irrational writings, Tarabishi reminded his readers of the rational way nahdawi writers dealt with turath. When it was time for Tarabishi to launch the Arab Rationalist Association in Paris in 2004, he reminded all members to think of the nahda as a new beginning, a period in which Arabs confronted their turath for the first time and reevaluated their medieval traditions while keeping their eyes fixed on Europe. Applauding nahdawis' fair-minded assessment of turath, Tarabishi marveled at how during the nahda past traditions were not seen as infringing on the concerns of the present. Under the conditions of the late nineteenth and early twentieth century, nahdawis acknowledged that the "time has truly changed, and the circumstances of the twentieth century are unlike those of the beginning of Islam."[44] The most committed nahdawis wrestled with the unfolding realities, not through a detour to the past, but by developing a new perspective on turath.[45] For Tarabishi, the nahda stood for the concept of a new beginning, rather than the medieval past.

Yet, in the postcolonial condition, Tarabishi noted regretfully, the present was disregarded in the name of the past. Haunted by the trauma of the defeat, postcolonial thinkers and Islamists emerged firmly committed to restoring a long-gone turath. In particular, Tarabishi decried the manner in which Arab readers and intellectual turned away from the concerns of the modern age, finding cures to their current social tribulations in turath. Therefore, Tarabishi questioned the assumptions, biases, and frameworks that define the movement of connected critics. For this movement the main concern is no more whether the changes in recent history are "deep enough to entail the replacement of the Shariʿa," but how to reappropriate it to the new reality.[46] This gap between nahdawi and current postcolonial scholars illustrated how far apart they were. In every aspect the postcolonial scholars emerged to have fallen behind their nahdawi predecessors. While nahdawis acknowledged the deep changes that forced fundamental adaptations to their understanding of the sacred texts, "the community of current Muslim jurists claimed that the modification of the manifested decrees in the Qurʾan and Hadiths are illegal except with necessity." Here, Tarabishi wondered, "does this necessity exist?" Do the radical changes that the postcolonial state brought about amount to the necessity? For Tarabishi, this only indicates that current postcolonial thinkers and Islamists are in the grasp of the "certainties of the text."[47]

THE FINAL TURN TOWARD THE NAHDA

Tarabishi's notion to start with cultural revolution rather than political reforms—like his advocacy for a culture of democracy over mechanical democracy—led many critics to charge that he risked advocating a culturist approach. Indeed, his countryman Burhan Ghalyun, a political scientist at the Sorbonne, was among the first to argue that Tarabishi attributed many of the challenges and problems facing Arab societies to cultural characteristics rather than political conditions.[48] Tarabishi considered it impossible to address the challenges of postolonial societies by ignoring the cultural record of these societies; to him the recorded textuality forbid Arab populations from assimilating and adopting modern capacities smoothly. To counter the "culturalist" allegation, Tarabishi established a genealogy of a culturist attitude that prevailed in the writing of the nahda period. For Tarabishi, the principal mindset that defined the nahda was most obvious in its intellectuals' propensity to borrow from the "other" (West). This awe-inspiring willingness to embrace the other was reflected in their eagerness to revise their history rather than repeat it, and, more important, in their ability to acknowledge that something was wrong. This disposition and capacity to open up to new models can be found in the acknowledgment of many nineteenth-century reformers that "there is no second civilization, civilization means European civilization."[49] Learning from other cultures, therefore, was not alien to Arab intellectual discourse, but constitutive of it.

Curiously, Tarabishi's attitude toward the nineteenth-century nahda was ambiguous until the beginning of the 1980s. During his time as a revolutionary, Tarabishi assailed nahdawi reformists for their timid criticism. The absence of an ideological critique was conspicuous during the nahda, he argued. The nahdawis' tendency to graft modern practices onto Islam was, he thought, most outrageous. He chafed at the reconciliation model of the nineteenth century and was disappointed that that the nahdawis took an earnest look at the sacred text only to reconcile it with modernity. And though Arab feminists of the nahda such as Qassim Amin, Jamil Bayhum, and others advocated for more rights for women, they eventually fell short of providing a compelling ground for their arguments. Nineteenth-century "Arab feminists evaded critiquing religion," he complained, since they "searched in religion itself" for verses that "support their arguments to legitimize women rights."[50]

Tarabishi's criticism of nahda pioneers was not limited to the issue of women's rights, however. He railed against their constrained epistemological scope, which failed to differentiate between social and natural conditions. For the most part, nahdawi writers took the socially constructed, "subordinate status of women as natural," Tarabishi lamented, a "God-given order or simply a natural way of life." For these writers, "what generated from social conditions was attributed to natural order." They failed to see that "the gap between men and women was engraved in society, rather than in nature, but it was viewed as if this gap was inscribed in nature not society, to justify its continuity in the name of natural instinct."[51] Muhammad Jamil Bayhum, one of the most ardent advocates of women's rights in the nahda and a writer whom Tarabishi venerated yet criticized,[52] wrote that "social orders are the result of laws of nature," and that "any attempt that aims at disrupting it by replacing the social order, according to individuals' desire, is damaging and considered against natural laws."[53]

This essential shortsightedness of nahdawi scholars guarantees some criticism, yet, given the intellectual space and time of these writings, it must be forgiven. The nineteenth century took the social to be natural, a view that wasn't particular to Arab intellectuals only. French intellectuals, from whom many Arab nahdawis took inspiration, considered many social phenomena natural. As historian Joan Scott has recently shown, the idea of nature was essential in nineteenth-century thought regarding "women, cultural hierarchies, and social ordering. In the discourse of secularism, the existence of separate spheres for women and men was no longer attributed to God, it was taken as a natural fact. The insistence on nature's mandate was a distinctive aspect of nineteenth-century secularism. Human biology was the ultimate source of the unequal and distinctive roles for women and men."[54]

In 1980, Tarabishi's misgivings began to give way to an unambiguous admiration of nahdawi writers. Despite Bayhum's view that women are less than men by nature, he nonetheless was credited by Tarabishi for his eagerness and willingness to learn from the West. In the first line of the introduction to *Al-Mar'ah Fī al-Islām Wa-Fī al-Ḥaḍārah al-Gharbīyah* (Women in modernity), published in 1927, Bayhum writes: "The East today exists in a learning and developing [stage], and his teacher is the West."[55] This struck Tarabishi as a genuine idea that captured the cultural mood of the nahdawi: "Contrary to subsequent generations of the postcolonial era, who desired to assert their identity not through borrowing from the West but against it, Jamil Bayhum did not feel uncomfortable asserting the imperative and indispensability of the West being the teacher of the East."[56]

Tarabishi clearly did not make a profound turnabout; his approach and intellectual views remained consistent. Although he turned to address new topics and themes, this turn did not entail a new positioning or a profound shift in his intellectual outlook. His defense of the nahda served one purpose: to counteract the connected thinkers and the partisans of turath. For Tarabishi, the spirit of the nahda provided the antidote against a growing public demand to go against modernity in the name of cultural authenticity and turath. This rejection of European modernity imperiled the entire intellectual project Arab scholars had pursued since the beginning of the nineteenth century. Taking his cues from the nahdawis, who demonstrated a rational mind unencumbered by the dead hand of turath, Tarabishi wondered how turath at the end of the twentieth century became increasingly prescriptive, when its hold had lost its cohesive force in previous generations. For Tarabishi, the nahda should be seen as a new beginning and the only framework of reference for the postcolonial subject.

The undoing of revolutionary Tarabishi and the emergence of the neo-nahdawi Tarabishi is probably the shortest way to summarize the intellectual career of the Arab social critic. Few other narratives capture Tarabishi's passage from utopia to dystopia as the transition from thawrah to nahda and his urge to renew the positions and cultural attitudes valorized by nineteenth-century intellectuals. Retrieving the spirit of the nahda in the late twentieth century addressed many challenges faced by the social critic: the rise of turath as a central question in Arab thought, the dismantling of the social critic and his cultural institutions during the 1970s, and the failure of the postcolonial project. The constellation of these events forced the hand of the social critic to readopt the nahda.

The engagement of the social critic with turath did not mark the end of the grinding cultural war among Arab intellectuals, nor the final victory of the connected critic. This cultural war has reconfigured the Arab intellectual landscape, forcing intellectuals to take a journey they had never imagined. Most important, it compelled the social critic to let go of the diffusion model through which he believed the Arab world could be modernized. He had to concede that there is more than one way to achieve change in the postcolonial world. He came to the conclusion that in ex-colonized societies change can begin by reordering the past rather than following the modernist perception of breaking with the past. To acknowledge this, as many Arab intellectuals did, is to accept the multiplicity and diversity of world cultures and histories; to accept this means questioning the assumptions of European modernity, which creates more unrest than social cohesion in the non-Western world—a modernity that has enshrined the expectation that the future is superior to the past and made the sharp break in historical continuity a precondition for social betterment. But this prescription stirred a prolonged cultural war in the Arabic-speaking world, precluding its organic emergence from its past. The major divergence in contemporary Arab thought is due, in great part, to this European idea or prescription: to break with the past in order to be modern.

CONCLUSION

Many of the new cultural concerns and questions that gripped Arab intellectuals and political activists in the wake of the 1970s were defined by the collapse of the postcolonial project. This project, which instilled the belief that a changing world order was within reach, had promised to establish just, free, and democratic societies. It even went so far as to promise to give birth to a free Arab subject—a decolonized Arab self that is sovereign, liberated, and authentic. The project's breakdown, however, launched the Arab world into a new age of authenticity, which, in many ways, was marked by a categorical rebuke of the predominant intellectual conversations and political visions of the 1950s and 1960s.

The defeat of the postcolonial project in the Arab world signaled, first and foremost, the loss of the story Arab peoples had told themselves and held dearly for many years. Because this narrative gave their identity coherence, its disintegration and collapse constituted a great loss. As Andrew Sullivan writes, "No one is untouched by loss. Human beings live by narrative; and we get saddened when a familiar character disappears. . . . Loss imprints itself on our minds and souls and forms us. It is part of what we are."[1] The loss of the postcolonial project, its stunning collapse, confirmed and amplified by a tragic sequence of events that culminated in the Arab defeat in the war against Israel in 1967, was the harbinger of a new structure of feeling that gave shape and content to the politics of authenticity.

For a short period of time, in the two decades that followed World War II, the postcolonial vision appeared to have materialized. The end of colonialism heralded the rise of a new world order in which ex-colonized peoples reclaimed their voices, freedom, and political sovereignty. The new countries that emerged in places like Latin America, Asia, and Africa would soon revel in their hard-won freedoms, vowing to create new citizens and democratic countries. During this time, ex-colonized regions appeared to be vital places, cities bustling with new intellectual movements, whirring printers and publishing houses, new bureaucracies that devised new fiscal policies, land reforms, and health systems that ensured their subjects' well-being. This project, which came to erase what Arabs often refer to as the "traces of colonialism," meant to remake the world order. It cultivated the feeling that a better future was awaiting the peoples of the Global South. The same wave of the future that swept over Europe in the nineteenth century seemed, for a fleeting moment, to frame thought and discourse in the postcolonial world, with one marked difference: while decolonized nations welcomed the wave of the future with high expectations, Europe—a long-invincible continent—awakened to a post–World War II reality humiliated, bruised, and badly wounded.

From 1945 until 1970, a new generation of activists emerged to design their project. They took the lead in the effort to "confront the legacies of imperial hierarchies with a demand for the radical reconstitution of the international order."[2] Coming from a recently constituted middle class, this cohort was educated in and exposed and attuned to the latest intellectual trends and political ideas in the metropole. Thanks to their frequent travels and studies abroad, they were marked as "the generation of broad expectations."[3] While some historians refer to them simply as "postcolonial intellectuals" or "anticolonial nationalists," throughout this book I have referred to them as "social critics." Intent on bringing about social change to their peripheral societies, this generation inaugurated radical political parties, launched cultural institutions, and developed educational initiatives to create a new social order starkly different from the one that former colonial powers left behind. Politically aware and highly sensitive to social injustices, this generation of social critics realized that the social order in ex-colonized nations was shaped by colonial powers to make it governable and amenable for economic exploitation. They rejected this order and called to revolutionize it, questioning the local norms, shared values, and past traditions that undergirded the social structure. Their insistence on the necessity of transforming reality by changing people's perspectives was only possible by replacing the social order altogether. Defying colonialists' biases and the prejudices of a stagnant, moribund ex-colonized world populated by compliant and passive people, social critics popularized a spirit of social change as a solution to all colonial woes.

Times of sweeping change, however, are unsettling, and these social and political transformations invoked fear and cultural anxiety. As local populations were pushed too hard to let go of old habits, to look forward to a better future, to fully live their new freedom, they responded with skepticism. Formerly, before the beginning of the postcolonial era, Arab leaders had prepared their people for a measured and gradual change. But under the postcolonial condition this model of slow change was rejected. With the rise of the postcolonial generation of social critics, the gradual change—now associated with the old bourgeoisie—gave way to radical change, whose main idea was revolution. As young and worldly political activists, the social critics balked at the idea of steady, measured, step-by-step change. The postcolonial condition, they thought, called for a thorough, all-encompassing social reconstruction of the Arab world, lest things change but remain the same. Unfortunately, not all Arab populations were willing to follow through with the agenda of these educated, middle-class social critics. To a significant swathe of Arab society, the eagerness to redesign the social order appeared risky, untested, and hazardous.

During the 1950s, more than half of the Arab population in the Middle East and North Africa lived outside of big cities. They led a rural lifestyle, with many settled into their accustomed ways and expectations. They took the social order as natural, the only normal way of living. The sudden and abrupt changes that the righteous social critics were calling for seemed pretentious, foreign, unfamiliar, and even patronizing. Their claim to shepherd a population in the grip of tradition was reminiscent of the British or French lords of the colonial period. While the local population was not recalcitrant or averse to change, the high-handed demands of the middle-class social critics made them look as such. In fact, the Arab population acknowledged the need for change and was open to accept social and even cultural transformation—but it would resist and push back against forced radical demands overseen by the postcolonial social critics.

As this book demonstrates, the collapse of the postcolonial project in the Middle East was and remains the main event in the making and remaking of the contemporary Arab world. Yet, despite the failure of the postcolonial architects—most prominently, their inability to quell the profound sense of skepticism among recently decolonized populations—political and demographic changes were nonetheless unfolding in the Middle East. With the beginning of the 1970s, mass emigration and urbanization would transform Arab cities, which were swelling into enormous municipalities. For the first time in modern Arab history, more than 70 percent of the Arab population dwelled in urban rather than rural settings, where the differences between classes, between the haves and have-nots, was as clear as the differences between shantytown and downtown. Like nineteenth-century Europe, the transition from rural to urban was accompanied by rising anxiety and restlessness. Not everything the Arab city had to offer was palatable to the cultural tastes of the newcomers. In fact, more than searching for social mobility and a better future, country people were goaded to move to cities, as they felt that their old world was fading away from them. Arriving with a profound sense of loss, they mostly looked for the familiar but were met instead by a radical generation of social critics impatient to remake their social and cultural DNA.

Modern Arab cities like Cairo, Alexandria, Beirut, Baghdad, Tunis, Fes, Marakesh, Damascus, and Aleppo were not simply homes to the new class of social critics. As I have shown, these cities furnished a set of cultural institutions that courted the social critics and fostered their modern taste, sensibility, and aesthetic. Unlike former generations, the postcolonial generation of social critics looked contemptuously at the past as they began to admire the foreign and look excitedly to the future. While for centuries Muslims looked at the past with admiration, struggling to live up to the examples set by past generations, the postcolonial generation would turn away from it and its exemplars with disgust. Enthralled with new ideas, they were the first generation who dared to act without the guidance of any past authority. It is indeed fascinating to notice that while this generation was obsessed with political decolonization and highly sensitive to its political sovereignty, it nonetheless consecrated Europe as the model for replacing the vanished past, which had provided traditions for the Arab people for centuries.

This intense fascination with the West, paralleled only by an equally intense disdain for the past, was not a sustainable situation or even a healthy way of living—first, because it did not provide a solution to the split self of the decolonized subject, nor to his struggle to live peacefully with his past and cultural heritage. Second, the continued insistence on breaking with the past had magnified, rather than assuaged, the cultural anxiety around the postcolonial subject. Third, the neocolonial economic exploitation of the postcolonial era bore an eerie resemblance to colonial rule. With the beginning of the 1970s, as these social and cultural grievances bubbled up to the surface, the Arab world stood on the brink of an abyss, poised to fall victim to its own makers—the postcolonial social critics. It was a painful ending to a wonderful and truly ambitious project.

Ironically, the social critics who came into power in order to decolonize the Arab self from colonial modernity ended up deploying the same "modernist" prescriptions under a different guise—or so it appeared to the connected critics. The connected critics fashioned a different agenda of decolonization, one that valorized cultural decolonization over political decolonization. Opposed to the revolutionary sensibility that animated the social critic, the connected critics claimed that social critics (their adversaries) rejected the European man in *politics* but followed and imitated him in *culture*—or in everything else. In this book I have showed how this phenomenon of the rise of a new breed of Arab intellectuals is central for understanding of the Arab world in particular and the postcolonial world in general.

Historically speaking, the end of colonialism should have put an end to the visions and ideas of colonial modernity. But it did not. The longevity of colonial modernity, the endurance of its concepts and perspectives, is mystifying, since it resisted an easy death. Long after many Arab countries in Asia and Africa gained political independence, the main ideas of colonial modernity (i.e., theology of progress, cultural imitation, catching up with the West, the diffusion model, and overcoming narratives) were still at work, influencing intellectuals and political activists. The two decades that had passed since the last European soldier evacuated the Middle East in 1945 did not appear to have loosened the grip of European ideas over the ex-colonized. They continued to work until well into the 1970s.

A noticeable change in cultural and intellectual visions of local political activists began to take place as the political turmoil in Arab societies settled down in the 1970s. With the passing of Egyptian leader Nasser and the vicious end to a two-decade-long scramble for power in Syria, among other events, a new era of relative stability prevailed in the Arab world. In this political climate, in which new autocrats tightened their grasp on power, the social critics—who admired Nasser—were on the losing side. The new regimes would censor their writings, doctor their publications, and shut down their publishing houses. The social and political configuration that began to constrain the activities of social critics was an opportune time for a new breed of intellectuals to emerge. Disillusioned with social critics and their opponents the Islamists, the connected critics suggested a third way, claiming that both sides of the political aisle have distorted the past, disfigured the present, and left the postcolonial subject naked, unprotected from the vagaries of state tyranny. Assailing Islamists on the right, they also questioned the epistemological underpinnings that sustained social critics. As they subjected their colleagues to criticism, they discovered that turning the modern hierarchy upside down by questioning the validity of the European system of classification opened up wholly new possibilities in the decolonized world.

Indeed, one of the major goals of this book is to establish the connected critic as a valid persona and category in understanding Arab political thought. The birth of this persona amounts to one of the most remarkable consequences of the collapse of the postcolonial project in the Middle East. The connected critics parted ways with their progressive leftist colleagues, not in order to join the Islamic Right, as many historians tend to think, but to form a separate front against both Islamic conservatism and the secular Left. The connected critics argued that for many decades colonized Arab nations in Asia and Africa meekly followed the instructions of colonial modernity, which called on colonized peoples to dispense with their cultural heritage and past traditions in order to be modern. Many writers and intellectuals in the ex-colonies seem to have condoned or abided by the recommendations of colonial modernity; they held firm to the belief that colonial modernity secured a better way for a better future. Rejecting colonial modernity, however, implied in part a disavowal of modernity itself and many of the intellectual and cultural assumptions upon which the social critic based his thought, ideology, and perspective. The break in the ranks of Arab intellectuals that led to the emergence of the connected critic was profound, and it presaged the great cultural war in the Arabic-speaking world.

Exploring the cultural war between the social and connected critics affords a new way of looking at cultural debates since the end of World War II and the rise of the sovereign Arab state. Contemporary Arab thought has long confounded intellectual historians and political theorists of the region, many of whom found these endless polemics and intrigues among Arab writers and activists bewildering. Thinking of the debate in terms of cultural war offers order and direction in navigating their voluminous writings. Like all wars, cultural wars organize adversaries into clearly defined camps. The feuds among Arab intellectuals were a secret to no one. Intellectuals who lined up behind the social critic Tarabishi did not respond to their opponents, nor did they publish the works of the other side. Conferences and publishing houses, too, were embroiled in this cultural war, sometimes even feeding it. This war—the scale of which had been unparalleled in the annals of Arab thought since the 1920s—provides a greatly unexploited vantage point from which to consider the intellectual movements of the contemporary Arab world.

Moving from considering past traditions of turath as standing in the way of progress to seeing them as an indispensable source of social and cultural progress kindled the first spark of the cultural war. This might look too trivial of an issue to set a cultural war in motion, but the rearrangement of relations with turath emerged as a transformative act in the ex-colonized world, revealing the uncalculated damage inflicted on the colonized by making him overlook his heritage. Few things could be more humiliating to the new Arab sensibilities than making them see the world like their colonizers. This realization provided the ground upon which they launched their politics of authenticity. Engaging turath, as it were, was not only a clear rebuke to the (now discredited) politics of social critics, but also a rejection of Europeans' misleading idiom and vocabulary as applied in the Global South. Europe's ideas and paradigms had never before lost the ability to shape the lives and tastes of the Arab peoples as powerfully as they did at the beginning of the engagement with turath in the 1970s, though Arab anticolonial critique dates back to the early nineteenth century. Turath provided an alternative canon, a different framework of reference that assured ex-colonized Arabs cultural freedom from the European perspective. For millions of Arab peoples in Asia and Africa who lived in the shadow of European modernity, the newfound cultural connections with a presumably "dark" past amounted to the first act of *cultural* independence.

When European categories and cultural taxonomies began to lose their hold on the Arab mind, ex-colonized intellectuals recognized the constraints of these categories. No matter how revolutionary and progressive these ideas appeared to be, once European ideas were imported to the Global South, they lost much of their critical edge along the way. The decline of class analysis, which was preceded by a break with *wujudiyya* (existentialism), left Arab intellectuals to their own devices. If

Sartre and Marx fell short of mentoring Arab intelligentsia "in finding the way out of colonialism," the new cultural orientation turned to Ibn Rushd and Al-Shatibi, Ibn Khaldun and Ibn Tufil, Ibn Sina and Ibn a-Haytham. Turath featured rationalist groups like al-Muʿtazila and Ikhwan al-Safa, whose intellectual potential had never been realized since Napoleon arrived in Egypt in 1798.[4] In the 1970s, however, it dawned on Arab intellectuals that what was missing was more than a way of overcoming the past; it was a reordering of the relation between present and past that would bring closure to the undefined relations with the past. Regulating the emotional links that inexorably tied the new Arab man to turath became an urgent task on the intellectual agenda.

It would have been impossible to make sense of the great cultural war along the old vocabulary of Right and Left. This cultural war began when a perceptive cluster of thinkers recognized the cultural challenges facing Arab society, which the rise of the connected critic came to meet. His advent, however, amounted to an unmistakable acknowledgment that the social critic had failed his first mission: to heal the psychological wounds colonialism had inflicted on the Arab subject. The two decades of early decolonization (1950–1970), it turned out, did not put a definite end to the misery of the ex-colonized, but rather magnified his deep sense of helplessness and cultural estrangement, political depression, and social alienation. Political independence did not restore the lost dignity of the Arab subject, either. After taking control of their destiny—that is, owning their world—Arab people continued, against all odds, to lean on Europe, taking from it their cues and cultural references. In fact, during the peak of Arab decolonization in the 1950s and 1960s, the Arab world was as Europeanized as it had ever been, with its citizens seeing their cultural heritage and religion through European eyes.

The cultural agenda unfurled by the connected critic stirred the ire of the social critics as well as the Islamists. The insistence on reconnecting the Arab subject to his heritage—turath—in order to create a sense of historical continuity, which colonialism had severed, not only drove a wedge between the connected critic and the social critic, but also sparked the suspicions of the Islamists. The refunctioning of turath, which allowed the connected critic to lay claim to more authentic traditions, placed the Islamist under fire for two reasons. First, reclaiming the past from Islamists, who for centuries conceived of themselves as the gatekeepers and guardians of the heritage of the *umma*, was a humbling task. Second, the new reading of turath was an affront to the Islamists whose "readings" had deformed and disfigured the canon. With the intervention of the connected critic, Islamists emerged as highly politicized figures who for a long time had sacralized turath in order to maintain their social status.

The story this book tells about the fall of the postcolonial project and its consequences could have been told in different ways. But central to this story, I thought, is the rise of scholars like Jabiri, who have gone unnamed in the current historiography. It is no longer possible to write about the Arab Left, because within it there are many groups and associations. The connected critic is an apt term for the group that Jabiri represents, due to the fact that his idea of refunctioning turath was less of an intellectual pursuit of purity than an attempt to demonstrate that if the original elements of turath could be reassembled and seen again, they would raise questions about the political and partisan instrumentalizations that had distorted the past. For the connected critic, turath, as a cultural canon, is foreign to the modern world, and its epistemological power stems from this foreignness. As historian David Gross has argued, "The power of a tradition text is not only that it was handed down from one age to the next," but, rather, that it "unavoidably carries with it traces of historical otherness."[5] Turath's main power derives not only from its "historical otherness" but from the fact that it is seen as a framework of reference that contests modern frameworks of reference. As such, it is impossible not to appreciate its power to shape the ways in which Arabic speakers experience life, indulge in social and intellectual interactions, savor new ideas, make sense of the world, and remember the past. The postcolonial Arab subject, like any human being, is incapable of thinking or remembering without owning cultural references that the framework of reference provides. As Hannah Arendt argues in the context of her defense of past traditions, the "human mind is only on the rarest occasions capable of retaining something which is altogether unconnected."[6] The ex-colonized subject knew that idea by instinct. For him to fully experience life, he must do so through connecting to his framework of reference.

NOTES

PREFACE AND ACKNOWLEDGMENTS

1. Thomas Friedman, "A Geopolitical Earthquake Just Hit the Middle East," *New York Times*, August 13, 2020, https://www.nytimes.com/2020/08/13/opinion/israel-uae.html.
2. Andrew Sullivan, *The Conservative Soul: Fundamentalism, Freedom, and the Future of the Right* (New York, NY: Harper Perennial, 2007), 10. "Today's conservatives support the idea of limited government, but they have increased government's size and power to new heights. They believe in balanced budgets, but they have boosted government spending, debt, and pork to record levels. They believe in national security but launched a reckless, ideological occupation in Iraq that has made us tangibly less safe. They have substituted religion for politics and damaged both. In *The Conservative Soul*, one of the nation's leading political commentators makes an impassioned call to rescue conservatism from the excesses of the Republican far right, which has tried to make the GOP the first fundamentally religious party in American history. In this bold and powerful book, Andrew Sullivan makes a provocative, prescient, and heartfelt case for a revived conservatism at peace with the modern world, and dedicated to restraining government and empowering individuals to live rich and fulfilling lives."

INTRODUCTION

1. I borrow the term "roaring 1960s" from Kamāl Dīb, *Tārīkh Lubnān al-Thaqāfī: Min ʿAṣr al-Nahḍah Ilá al-Qarn al-Ḥādī Wa-al-ʿishshrīn* (Beirut: al-Maktabah al-Sharqīyah, 2016).

2. Since the idea of a framework of reference is foundational to this work, it entails a precise and accurate definition. According to Karl Popper, a framework is "a set of basic assumptions, or fundamental principles—that is to say, an intellectual framework." An intellectual framework, he writes, "can be thought of as consisting not only of a 'dominant theory,' but also as being, in part, a psychological and sociological entity. It consists of a dominant theory together with what one might call a way of viewing things in tune with the dominant theory, including sometimes even a way of viewing the world and a way of life. Accordingly, such a framework constitutes a social bond between its devotees: it binds them together, very much as a church does, or political or artistic creed, or an ideology." See Karl Raimund Popper and Mark Amadeus Notturno, *The Myth of the Framework: In Defence of Science and Rationality* (New York: Routledge, 1994), 33, 55.
3. Samira Haj, *Reconfiguring Islamic Tradition: Reform, Rationality, and Modernity* (Stanford, CA: Stanford University Press, 2011), 5.
4. Joseph Massad, *Desiring Arabs* (Chicago: University of Chicago Press, 2007), 53. Massad asserts that the term *turath* is "first and foremost a product of twentieth-century modernity where, or more precisely, when it is located as an epistemological anchor of the present in the past" (16).
5. Cited in Robyn Creswell, *City of Beginnings: Poetic Modernism in Beirut (Translation/Transnation)* (Princeton, NJ: Princeton University Press, 2019), Kindle, loc. 1257.
6. Creswell, *City of Beginnings*, 537–38.
7. Elizabeth Suzanne Kassab, *Contemporary Arab Thought: Cultural Critique in Comparative Perspective* (New York: Columbia University Press, 2010), 121–71.
8. Aziz al-Azmeh referred to the new engagement with turath as the "rise of irrationalism as a central conceptual sensibility of the age." Aziz al-Azmeh, *Secularism in the Arab World: Contexts, Ideas and Consequence*, trans. David Bond (Edinburgh: Edinburgh University Press, 2020), 322.
8. I adopt the terms "connected" and "social" critics from Michael Walzer and develop them in chapter 2. See Walzer, *The Company of Critics: Social Criticism and Political Commitment in the Twentieth Century* (New York: Basic Books, 2002); and *Interpretation and Social Criticism* (Cambridge, MA: Harvard University Press, 1988.
10. Jeremy Bowen, *Six Days: How the 1967 War Shaped the Middle East* (New York: Simon & Schuster, 2013). See also Nasser's speech to the Egyptian Parliament on November 23, 1967 ("The road was open to Israeli forces"). For the entire three-hour speech, see https://www.youtube.com/results?search_query=1967+نوفمبر+22+الناصر+عبد+جمال+خطاب.
11. For English works that discuss Arab responses to the defeat, see Ibrahim M. Abu-Rabiʿ, *Contemporary Arab Thought* (London: Pluto, 2004); Elizabeth Suzanne Kassab, *Contemporary Arab Thought: Cultural Critique in Comparative Perspective* (New York: Columbia University Press, 2010); Issa J. Boullata, *Trends and Issues in Contemporary Arab Thought* (Albany: State University of New York Press, 1990); and Hisham Sharabi, *Neopatriarchy: A Theory of Distorted Change in Arab Society* (New York: Oxford University Press, 1988).

12. Adom Getachew, *Worldmaking After Empire: The Rise and Fall of Self-Determination* (Princeton, NJ: Princeton University Press, 2019), 23.
13. Getachew, *Worldmaking After Empire*, 2.
14. Yoav Di-Capua, *No Exit: Arab Existentialism, Jean-Paul Sartre, and Decolonization* (Chicago: University of Chicago Press, 2018), 2.
15. Samir Kassir, *Being Arab* (London: Verso, 2013).
16. Jeffrey James Byrne, *Mecca of Revolution: Algeria, Decolonization, and the Third World Order* (Oxford: Oxford University Press, 2019), 3.
17. Byrne, *Mecca of Revolution*, 3.
18. Kassab, *Contemporary Arab Thought*, 7.
19. Samir Amin, *Imperialism and Unequal Development* (New York: Monthly Review, 1977).
20. Samir Amin, *The Long Revolution of the Global South: Towards a New Anti-Imperialist International* (New York: Monthly Review, 2019), 45.
21. Charles Taylor, *A Secular Age* (Cambridge, MA: Belknap Press of Harvard University Press, 2007), 475.
22. Wael B. Hallaq, *Reforming Modernity* (New York: Columbia University Press, 2019), 4.
23. Wael B. Hallaq, *Restating Orientalism: A Critique of Modern Knowledge* (New York: Columbia University Press, 2018).
24. Hallaq, *Reforming Modernity*, 5–6.
25. Kassab, *Contemporary Arab Thought*, 15.
26. Moḥammad ʻĀbid al-Jābirī, *Al-Turath Wal-Hadatha: Dirāsāt Wa-Munāqashāt* (Beirut: Markaz Dirāsāt al-Waḥdah al-ʻArabīyah, 1991), 10.
27. Ahmad Amin, "Turathunā al-Kadīm," *al-Risālah*, no. 5 (1933): 7–8.
28. Albert Memmi, *Decolonization and the Decolonized* (Minneapolis: University of Minnesota Press, 2006), 4.
29. Getachew, *Worldmaking After Empire*, 17.
30. Wael B. Hallaq, *The Impossible State: Islam, Politics, and Modernity's Moral Predicament* (New York: Columbia University Press, 2012), 12–13.
31. Peter Gordon, "Contextualism and Criticism in the History of Ideas," in *Rethinking Modern European Intellectual History*, ed. Darrin McMahon and Samuel Moyn (Oxford: Oxford University Press, 2014), 44.
32. Moḥammad ʻĀbid al-Jābirī, *Fikr Ibn Khaldūn: Al-ʻAṣabīyah Wa-al-Dawlah: Maʻālim Naẓarīyah Khaldūnīyah Fī al-Tārīkh al-Islāmī*, al-Ṭabʻah 2 (Casablanca: Nashr al-Maghribīyah, 1979). The committee was made up of two French scholars and three Arabs: Henry Laust and Roger Arnaldez, and Arab researchers Najeed Baladi, Amjad Tarablusi, and Ibrahim Boutaleb.
33. For a discussion of Jabiri's ideas and his many critics, see Zaid Eyadat, Francesca M. Corrao, and Mohammed Hashas, eds., *Islam, State, and Modernity: Mohammed Abed al-Jabiri and the Future of the Arab World* (London: Palgrave Macmillan, 2017); and Wael B. Hallaq, *Reforming Modernity* (New York: Columbia University Press, 2019).

34. Jūrj Ṭarābīshī, *Sārtar Wa-Al-Mārksīyah* (Beirut: Dār al-Ṭalī'a, 1964), 8.
35. Ṭarābīshī, *Sārtar Wa-Al-Mārksīyah*, 13.
36. Ṭarābīshī, 13.
37. Constantine Zuriq, *Nahnu wal-Tarikh* (Beirut: Dār al-'Ilm lil-Malayyīn, 1959), n.p.
38. In an article that seeks to problematize canonical intellectual histories and genealogies of modern Arabic cultural production, Hoda El-Shakry defines "the Maghreb" as a "site framed by its relational geography visa-a-vis the Arab East or 'Mashriq.' Etymologically, it denotes 'the place where the sun sets,' . . . while 'al-Mashriq' refers to 'the place where the sun rises,' . . . the terms emerged around the seventh century to indicate the westernmost territories to be occupied as part of the expansion of the Arabo-Islamic empire, but continues to be used to distinguish the 'Middle East' from 'North Africa.'" See Hoda El Shakry, "Lessons from the Maghreb," in *Arabic Literature for the Classroom: Teaching Methods, Theories, Themes and Texts*, ed. Muhsin Mussawi (New York: Routledge, 2017), 111.
39. Zahiya Salhi, *Occidentalism: Literary Representions of the Meghrebi Experience of the East-West Encounter* (Edinburgh: Edinburgh University Press, 2019).
40. Ahmad Issa, "Thawrat al-Kitāb," *Al-Kitāb al-Arabī*, January 1971, 3–4.
41. "For reasons difficult briefly to pin down, the new interpretive approach was undertaken with particular effectiveness by North African intellectuals and scholars, particularly in Morocco, where the movement found its strongest and clearest expression." See Hisham Sharabi, "Cultural Critics of Contemporary Arab Society," *Arab Studies Quarterly* 9, no. 1 (1987): 5.
42. Zaki Najib Maḥmūd, *Tajdid Al-Fikr al-Arabi* (Beirut: Dār al-Shourooq, 1971).
43. Ilham Khuri-Makdisi, *The Eastern Mediterranean and the Making of Global Radicalism, 1860–1914* (Berkeley: University of California Press, 2010); Fawaz A. A. Gerges, *Making the Arab World: Nasser, Qutb, and the Clash That Shaped the Middle East* (Princeton, NJ: Princeton University Press, 2018); Charles Kurzman, ed., *Liberal Islam: A Sourcebook* (New York: Oxford University Press, 1998); Christoph Schumann, ed., *Nationalism and Liberal Thought in the Arab East: Ideology and Practice* (New York: Routledge, 2010); Albert Hourani, *Arabic Thought in the Liberal Age, 1798–1939* (Cambridge: Cambridge University Press, 1983).
44. Many Middle Eastern historians subscribe to this model: see Michaelle Browers, *Political Ideology in the Arab World: Accommodation and Transformation* (Cambridge: Cambridge University Press, 2009); R. Stephen Humphreys, *Between Memory and Desire: The Middle East in a Troubled Age* (Berkeley: University of California Press, 1999); Fouad Ajami, *The Dream Palace of the Arabs: A Generation's Odyssey* (New York: Pantheon, 1998); and Meir Hatina and Christoph Schumann, eds., *Arab Liberal Thought After 1967: Old Dilemmas, New Perceptions* (New York: Palgrave Macmillan, 2015).
45. Recent scholarship has doubted the certitude with which the defeat in 1967 marked a new stage in Arab intellectual thought. See Omnia El Shakry, "'History Without Documents': The Vexed Archives of Decolonization in the Middle East," *American Historical Review* 120, no. 3 (June 1, 2015): 920–34; Jeffrey Sacks, *Iterations of Loss:*

Mutilation and Aesthetic Form, al-Shidyaq to Darwish (New York: Fordham University Press, 2015); and Samah Selim, "Literature and Revolution," *International Journal of Middle East Studies* 43 (2011), 385–86.

46. Kurzman, *Liberal Islam*.
47. One of the authors who translated the reemergence of the cultural turath to a mere "return of Islam" is Bernard Lewis. See Bernard Lewis, "The Return of Islam," *Commentary Magazine*, January 1, 1976, https://www.commentary.org/articles/bernard-lewis/the-return-of-islam/.
48. Cited by Joan Wallach Scott in *Sex and Secularism* (Princeton, NJ: Princeton University Press, 2017), 18–19.
49. Saba Mahmood, "Secularism, Sovereignty, and Religious Difference: A Global Genealogy?," *Environment and Planning D: Society and Space* 35, no. 2 (April 1, 2017): 197–209.

1. THE EMERGENCE OF A NEW FIELD

1. Zaki Najib Maḥmūd, *Tajdīd Al-Fikr Al-ʿArabi* (Beirut: Dār al-Shirūq, 1971), 5.
2. Ibrahim El-Ariss, "Hiwar Maʿ Ṭarābīshī," *Al-Hayyat*, January 30, 2006, http://www.arabphilosophers.com/Arabic/aphilosophers/acontemporary/acontemporary-names/Ṭarābīshī/D_Alhayat.htm.
3. On the liberal moment in Egypt, see I. Gershoni and James P. Jankowski, *Egypt, Islam, and the Arabs: The Search for Egyptian Nationhood, 1900–1930* (New York: Oxford University Press, 1986), h; I. Gershoni and James P. Jankowski, *Redefining the Egyptian Nation*, 1930–1945 (Cambridge: Cambridge University Press, 2002).
4. Henry Osborn Taylor, *The Classical Heritage of the Middle Ages* (New York: Columbia University Press, 1901).
5. The best-known example of the diffusion model is Hourani's classical work. See Albert Hourani, *Arabic Thought in the Liberal Age, 1798–1939* (New York: Cambridge University Press, 1983).
6. Walīd Mahmud Khāliṣ, *Law kāna Fūltīr ʿArabīyan?* (Masqaṭ: Bayt al-Ghashshām lil-Nashr wa-al-Tarjamah, 2015).
7. Yoav Di-Capua, *No Exit: Arab Existentialism, Jean-Paul Sartre, and Decolonization* (Chicago: University of Chicago Press, 2018), 163.
8. Rasheed El-Enany, "Tawfiq Al-Hakim and the West: A New Assessment of the Relationship," *British Journal of Middle Eastern Studies* 27, no. 2 (November 1, 2000): 165–75.
9. Jurj Ṭarābīshī, "Bisabab Ismi Fashiltu Ann Akun Munadilan 'Arabiyyan," accessed July 8, 2015, http://www.alriyadh.com/161158.
10. Fouad Ajami, *The Dream Palace of the Arabs: A Generation's Odyssey* (New York: Pantheon, 1998); Judith Miller, "The Embattled Arab Intellectual," *New York Times*, June 9, 1985, https://www.nytimes.com/1985/06/09/magazine/the-embattled-arab-intellectual.html; Robert F. Worth, "The Arab Intellectuals Who Didn't Roar," *New*

York Times, October 30, 2011, https://www.nytimes.com/2011/10/30/sunday-review/the-arab-intellectuals-who-didnt-roar.html.

11. Carool Kersten, *Contemporary Thought in the Muslim World* (New York: Routledge, 2019), 4.
12. Ḥasan Ḥanafī, *Al-Turath Wa-Al-Tajdīd* (Cairo: al-Markaz al-ʻArabī lil-Baḥth wa-al-Nashr, 1980); ʻAbd al-Ilāh Balqaziz, *Naqd Al-Turath*, Al-ʻArab Wa-Al-ḥadāthah 3 (Beirut: Markaz Dirāsāt al-Waḥdah al-ʻArabīyah, 2014); Muḥammad ʻĀbid Jābirī, *Naḥnu Wa-Al-Turath: Qirāʼāt Muʻāṣirah Fī Turathinā Al-Falsafī*, al-Ṭabʻah 1 (Beirut: Dār al-Ṭalīʻah, 1980); Jūrj Ṭarābīshī, *Min Al-Nahḍah Ilá Al-Riddah: Tamazzuqāt Al-Thaqāfah Al-ʻArabīyah Fī ʻaṣr Al-ʻawlamah*, al-Ṭabʻah 1 (Beirut: Dār al-Sāqī, 2000).
13. Ahmed El Shamsy, *Rediscovering the Islamic Classics: How Editors and Print Culture Transformed an Intellectual Tradition* (Princeton, NJ: Princeton University Press, 2020).
14. Ibrahim A. Abu-Lughod, *Arab Rediscovery of Europe: A Study in Cultural Encounters* (Princeton, NJ: Princeton University Press, 1963).
15. Yusif Zaydan, *Al-Turath al-Majhūl: Itlālah ala Ālam al-Makhtutāt* (Cairo: Dar al-Amin, 1997), introduction.
16. For a work that commends Orientalists' work in defining, mapping, and thematizing the classical history of the Arabs, see Mohammed Arkoun, *Al-Istishrāq Bayna duʻātihi wa Maʻāriḍīh*, al-Ṭabʻah al-ʻArabīyah (Beirut: Dār al-Sāqī, 1994).
17. Joseph Massad, *Desiring Arabs* (Chicago: University of Chicago Press, 2007).
18. Zaki Najib Maḥmūd, *Tajdid al-Fikr al-Arabi* (Beirut: Dar al-Shourooq, 1971), 12; see also chap. 2.
19. Stéphane Lacroix and George Holoch, *Awakening Islam: The Politics of Religious Dissent in Contemporary Saudi Arabia* (Cambridge, MA: Harvard University Press, 2011), 24.
20. Marwa Elshakry, *Reading Darwin in Arabic, 1860–1950* (Chicago: University of Chicago Press, 2013), 17.
21. Ussama Makdisi, *Age of Coexistence: The Ecumenical Frame and the Making of the Middle East* (Oakland: University of California Press, 2019), 206.
22. Samir Amin, *The Long Revolution of the Global South* (New York: Monthly Review, 2019), 52–53.
23. Aziz al-Azmeh, *Secularism in the Arab World: Contexts, Ideas, and Consequences*, trans. David Bond (Edinburgh: Edinburgh University Press, 2020), 423.
24. Wael B. Hallaq, *Reforming Modernity* (New York: Columbia University Press, 2019), 125.
25. One of the intellectuals to develop this attitude is Yassin al-Hafiz. See Yāsīn Ḥāfiẓ, *Hazīmah Wa-Al-īdyūlūjiyā Al-Mahzūmah* (Beirut: Dār al-Ṭalīʻah lil-Ṭibāʻah wa-al-Nashr, 1979), chap. 5.
26. Nadav Safran, *Egypt in Search of Political Community: An Analysis of the Intellectual and Political Evolution of Egypt, 1804–1952* (Cambridge: Harvard University Press, 1961), 151–64.
27. Stephan Shaheen, *Foundations of Modern Arab Identity* (Gainesville: University Press of Florida, 2004), 35–37.

28. Amin, *Long Revolution*, 53–54.
29. David Gross, *Lost Time: On Remembering and Forgetting in Late Modern Culture*, (Amherst: University of Massachusetts Press, 2000), 144.
30. Adonis, *Mawaqif*, vol. 1. N.p.: n.p., 1968.
31. Adonis reiterated these ideas in his later works. See Adonis, *Al-Kitāb Al-Khiṭāb Al-ḥijāb: Dirāsah* (Beirut: Dār al-Ādāb, 2009).
32. Rula Abisaab, "Deconstructing the Modular and the Authentic: Husayn Muroeh's Early Islamic History," *Critique: Critical Middle Eastern Studies* 17, no. 3 (2008): 239–59.
33. Adonis, *Al-Thābit Wa-Al-Mutaḥaūil: Baḥth Fī Al-Ittibāʿ Wa-Al-Ibdāʿ ʿinda Al-ʿArab* (Beirut: Dār al-Fikr, 1986); Ṭayyib Tīzīnī, *Min Al-Turath Ilá Al-Thawrah: ḥawla Naẓarīyah Muqtaraḥah Fī Qaḍīyat Al-Turath Al-ʿArabī*, Mashrūʿ Ruʿyah Jadīdah Lil-Fikr Al-ʿArabī Mundhu Bidāyatihi ḥattá Al-Marḥalah Al-Muʿāṣirah (Beirut: Dār al-Jīl, 1976); Ghali Shukri, *Al-Turath wal-Thawra* (Beirut: Dār al-Taliʿah, 1979); Ḥusayn Murūwah, *Al-Nuzʿāt Al-Māddīyah Fī Al-Falsafah Al-ʿArabīyah Al-Islāmīyah* (Beirut: Dār al-Farābī, 1978); Zaki Najib Maḥmūd, *Al-Maʿqūl Wa-Al-Lā-Maʿqūl Fī Turathinā Al-Fikrī* (Al-Qāhirah: Dār al-Shurūq, 1975). See also Jabiri, *Naḥnu Wa-Al-Turath*.
34. In Egypt, Ḥanafī's project took the lead with titles like *Al-Turath Wa-Al-Tajdīd*; see also Yasmeen Daifallah, "Turath as Critique: Hassan Ḥanafī on the Modern Arab Subject," in Jens Hanssen and Max Weiss, *Arabic Thought Against the Authoritarian Age* (Cambridge: Cambridge University Press, 2017), 308.
35. Al-Hashimi Bashir, "Wāqiʿ Al-Kitāb Al-ʿArabī Fī Al-Sabʿīnāt Wa-Afāqihi Fī Al-Thamanīnāt," *Majalat Al-Bayan al-kuwītiyah*, March 1, 1983, http://archive.sakhrit.co.
36. al-Azmeh, *Secularism in the Arab World*, 419.
37. Tarif Khalidi, *Arabic Historical Thought in the Classical Period* (Cambridge: Cambridge University Press, 1994), 234.
38. ʿAbd al-Ilāh Balqaziz, *Naqd Al-Turath* (Beirut: Markaz Dirāsāt al-Waḥdah al-ʿArabīyah, 2014), 97–134.
39. Balqaziz, *Naqd Al-Turath*, 78–84.
40. For a discussion of Badawi's teachers and intellectual career, see Yoav Di-Capua, "Arab Existentialism: An Invisible Chapter in the Intellectual History of Decolonization," *American Historical Review* 117, no. 4 (October 1, 2012): 1061–91. On the faculty of Cairo University, see Donald M. Reid, *Cairo University and the Making of Modern Egypt* (Cambridge: Cambridge University Press, 1990).
41. On the list of works Badawi edited, see Balqaziz, *Naqd Al-Turath*, 97.
42. Farah Antun has complained as late as 1903 that while Ibn Rushd's medical books are available in Arabic, his "philosophical works are rare." He expressed a bafflement with the irony that it is impossible "to attain a copy of Ibn Rushd's philosophical works in Arabic," whereas "if you seek them in Latin or Hebrew, European big libraries rarely lacked them." See Faraḥ Anṭūn and Muḥammad ʿAbduh, *Ibn Rushd Wa-Falsafatuhu* (Alexandria: n.p., 1903), 85–86.
43. Ahmad Khan and Elisabeth Kendall, eds., *Reclaiming Islamic Tradition: Modern Interpretations of the Classical Heritage* (Edinburgh: Edinburgh University Press, 2016), 54.

44. ʿAbd al-Majīd Sharafi, *Taḥdīth Al-Fikr Al-Islāmī*, Munāẓarāt (Casablanca: Nashr al-Fanak, 1998), 26.
45. Sharafī, *Taḥdīth Al-Fikr Al-Islāmī*, 26.
46. On the ethical commitments that guided Arab scholars in editing turath texts, see Joseph Massad, *Desiring Arabs* (New York: Columbia University Press, 2007).
47. Yasīn Sayyid, *Al-Turath Wa-Taḥadiyyat Al-Aṣr Fī Al-Waṭan Al-ʿArabī* (Beirut: Markiz Dirāsāt al-Waḥdah al-ʿArabīya, 1984), 11.
48. Khair El-Din Haseeb, "The Centre for Arab Unity Studies (CAUS) Has Passed Its 35th Anniversary: 'Where There Is a Will, There Is a Way!,'" *Contemporary Arab Affairs* 6, no. 2 (April 1, 2013): 159–63.
49. Ziyād al-Hafiz, "Baḥth Fī Ta'thīr Markiz Dirasāt al-Wiḥada al-ʿArabiyya," *Issam Fares Institute for Public Policy and International Affairs*, no. 6 (February 2012): 9.
50. Al-Hafiz, "Baḥth Fī Ta'thīr Markiz Dirasāt al-Wiḥada al-ʿArabiyya."
51. Shibley Telhami, "Power, Legitimacy, and Peace-Making in the Arab Coalitions: The New Arabism," in *Ethnic Conflicts and International Politics in the Middle East*, ed. Leonard Binder (Gainesville: University Press of Florida, 1999), 61-77.
52. "The Center for Arab Unity Studies," *Middle East Studies Association Bulletin* 21, no. 1 (1987): 22–24. In 1999 the center established a unit for translation.
53. Ahmad Tayyīb, *Al-Turāh wal-Tajdīd: Munāqashat wa-Rudūd* (Cairo: Sharikat al-Quds, n.d.), 131.
54. Kassab points out that the center presided over one of the most important conferences to take place in the last few decades: "Heritage and the Challenges of the Age in the Arab Homeland" in 1984. See Kassab, *Contemporary Arab Thought*, 150–51.
55. Sayyid, *Al-Turath Wa-Taḥadiyyat Al-Aṣr Fī Al-Waṭan Al-ʿArabī*, 22.
56. Georges Corm, *Arab Political Thought: Past and Present* (London: Hurst, 2020), 170.
57. Philip Hitti, *History of the Arabs* (London: Palgrave Macmillan, 2002), 757.
58. "Fearing that such an outcome would prompt an Israeli intervention, Syria's president Assad won tacit US approval to send his troops across the border to prevent a Christian defeat." See Kamāl Dīb *Tārīkh Lubnān Al-Thaqāfī: Min ʿaṣr al-Nahḍah Ilá al-Qarn al-Ḥādī Wa-al-ʿishshrīn* (Beirut: al-Maktabah al-Sharqīyah, 2016), n.p.
59. H. E. Chehabi, '"The Paris of the Middle East': Iranians in Cosmopolitan Beirut," in *Iran in the Middle East: Transnational Encounters and Social History*, ed. E. Chehabi (New York: I. B. Tauris, 2015), 120.
60. Thomas L. Friedman, *From Beirut to Jerusalem* (New York: Farrar, Straus & Giroux, 1989), 49–76.
61. Some estimations go as high as 150,000. See R. Stephen Humphreys, *Between Memory and Desire* (Berkeley: University of California Press, 1999), 75–76.
62. Eric Pace, "Malcolm Kerr, Expert on the Arabs," *New York Times*, January 19, 1984, https://www.nytimes.com/1984/01/19/obituaries/malcolm-kerr-expert-on-the-arabs.html.
63. Malcolm H. Kerr, *The Arab Cold War, 1958–1964: A Study of Ideology in Politics* (London: Oxford University Press, 1965), 1.
64. Fouad Ajami, "The Arab Inheritance," *Foreign Affairs*, January 28, 2009, https://www.foreignaffairs.com/articles/middle-east/1997-09-01/arab-inheritance.

65. Lebanon had to yet again restore its established tradition of immigration since the mid-nineteenth century, when its first civil war, in the 1860s, between Christians and Druze set off intermittent communal feuds. But the civil war that started in the spring of 1975 presented many Lebanese with existential threats, increasing their urge to leave the country altogether. In 2014, Lebanon was ranked the highest migration population in the world; close to eighty-four out of every one thousand citizens would flee the country; "World Factbook—Lebanon," https://www.cia.gov/library/publications/the-world-factbook/geos/print/country/countrypdf_le.pdf (no longer available).

2. THE GREAT CULTURAL WAR

1. Samira Haj, *Reconfiguring Islamic Tradition: Reform, Rationality, and Modernity* (Stanford, CA: Stanford University Press, 2011), 29.
2. Muḥammad ʿĀbid Jābirī, *Naḥnu Wa-al-Turath: Qirā'āt Mu'āṣirah Fī Turathinā al-Falsafī* (Beirut: Dār al-Ṭalīʿah, 1980); Ḥasan Ḥanafī, *Al-Turath Wa-al-Tajdīd: Mawqifunā Min al-Turath al-Qadīm* (Cairo: al-Markaz al-ʿArabī lil-Baḥth wa-al-Nashr, 1980).
3. Exceptions are: Wael B. Hallaq, *Reforming Modernity* (New York: Columbia University Press, 2019); Ahmad Khan and Elizabeth Kendall, *Reclaiming Islamic Tradition: Modern Interpretations of the Classical Heritage* (Edinburgh: Edinburgh University Press, 2016); Ahmed El Shamsy, *Rediscovering the Islamic Classics: How Editors and Print Culture Transformed an Intellectual Tradition* (Princeton, NJ: Princeton University Press, 2020); and Elizabeth Suzanne Kassab, *Contemporary Arab Thought: Cultural Critique in Comparative Perspective* (New York: Columbia University Press, 2010).
4. "Authenticity, the central cultural quality expressed through a particular type of individuality, has come to overshadow all other forms of authority." Michael Wilkinson, "The Transformation of Religion and the Self in the Age of Authenticity," *Pneuma* 40, nos. 1–2 (2014): 93.
5. Omnia El Shakry, "'History Without Documents': The Vexed Archives of Decolonization in the Middle East," *American Historical Review* 120, no. 3 (June 1, 2015): 924.
6. The debate was later published in a book. See Ḥasan Ḥanafī and Muḥammad ʿĀbid Jābirī, *Ḥiwār Al-Mashriq Wa-al-Maghrib: Talīhi Silsilat al-Rudūd Wa-al-Munāqashāt*, al-Ṭabʿah 1 (Al-Qāhirah: Maktabat Madbūlī, 1990). The topics were: dialogue, fundamentalism, secularism, Arab unity, liberalism, modernism, Nasserism, dialogue revised, Arabs and the French Revolution, and the Palestinian question.
7. The extensive intellectual exchanges between Egypt and the Levant unified these two spheres into what Khuri-Makdisi called "geography of contestation." See Ilham Khuri-Makdisi, *The Eastern Mediterranean and the Making of Global Radicalism, 1860–1914* (Berkeley: University of California Press, 2010).
8. On the transition of Arab intellectuals to screens in the late 1980s after Najīb Maḥfouz's Nobel Prize, see Franck Mermier and Firidrīk Maʿtūq, eds., *al-Faḍā'*

al-'Arabī: al-faḍā'īyāt wa-al-intirnit wa-al-i'lān wa-al-nashr, al-Ṭab'ah 1 (Dimashq: Qadmus lil-Nashr wa-al-Tawzī', 2003), 477–79.

9. Ḥasan Ḥanafī and Muḥammad 'Ābid Jābirī, *Ḥiwār Al-Mashriq Wa-al-Maghrib: Talīhi Silsilat al-Rudūd Wa-al-Munāqashāt*, Al-Ṭab'ah 1 (Al-Qāhirah: Maktabat Madbūlī, 1990), 71–83.
10. While the secular idea appeared on the Arab intellectual horizon in the late nineteenth century, the new debates around this Western idea in the late 1980s recreated it anew. See Shākir Nābulusī, *Al-Fikr al-'Arabī Fī al-Qarn al-'ishrīn, 1950–2000: Dirāsah Naqdīyah Taḥlīlīyah Fī Thalāthat Ajzā'*, vol. 2 (Beirut: al-Mu'assasah al-'Arabīyah lil-Dirāsāt wa-al-Nashr; Dār al-Fāris lil-Nashr wa-al-Tawzī', 2001), chap. 2.
11. Though many historians and observers of Arab debates latch onto the idea that Arab Marxists turned to Islam in the wake of the decline in class analysis, the evidence they provide is limited in scope. More and more ex-Marxists took a secular path. See Fouad Ajami, *The Arab Predicament: Arab Political Thought and Practice since 1967* (Cambridge: Cambridge University Press, 1981); Michaelle Browers, *Political Ideology in the Arab World: Accommodation and Transformation* (Leiden: Cambridge University Press, 2009); and Emmanuel Sivan, *Radical Islam: Medieval Theology and Modern Politics* (New Haven, CT: Yale University Press, 1985).
12. Jābirī and Ḥanafī, *Ḥiwār*, 77.
13. Hisham Shirabi, "Cultural Critics of Contemporary Arab Society," *Arab Studies Quarterly* 9, no. 1 (1987): 1–19; Issa J. Boullata, *Trends and Issues in Contemporary Arab Thought* (Albany: State University of New York Press, 1990); Kassab, *Contemporary Arab Thought*.
14. Ibrahim M. Abu-Rabi', *Contemporary Arab Thought: Studies in Post-1967 Arab Intellectual History* (London: Pluto, 2004).
15. Abu-Rabi', *Contemporary Arab Thought*. See, in particular, chap. 5.
16. Saba Mahmood, *Religious Difference in a Secular Age: A Minority Report* (Princeton, NJ: Princeton University Press, 2015).
17. Talal Asad, *Formations of the Secular: Christianity, Islam, Modernity* (Stanford, CA: Stanford University Press, 2003).
18. Joseph Andoni Massad, *Islam in Liberalism* (Chicago: University of Chicago Press, 2015).
19. Jūrj Ṭarābīshī, *Harṭaqāt*, al-Ṭab'ah 1 (Beirut: Rābiṭat al-'Aqlānīyīn al-'Arab; Dār al-Sāqī, 2006), 65–66.
20. It is remarkable that this argument fits well with French writer Marcel Gauchet's vision of the secular as a genuinely Western European idea. See Marcel Gauchet, *The Disenchantment of the World: A Political History of Religion* (Princeton, NJ: Princeton University Press, 1997).
21. Talal Asad rules out such a misleading comparison that stresses "*absenceness*": "There is a widespread conviction that Christian doctrine has been receptive" to democracy, secularism, human rights "because in Christendom (unlike Islam) church and state began as separate entities." See Talal Asad, *Is Critique Secular?*

Blasphemy, Injury, and Free Speech (New York: Fordham University Press, 2013), Kindle, loc. 452–53.

22. For a trenchant critique of Jabiri's reliance on Ibn Rush, see Hallaq, *Reforming Modernity*, 74–76.
23. On the emerging Mashreq-Maghreb divide, see Idriss Jebari, "An Intellectual Between the Meghreb and the Meshreq: Mohammed Abed al-Jabiri and the Location of Thought," in *Islam, State, and Modernity: Mohammed Abed al-Jabiri and the Future of the Arab World*, ed. Zaid Eyadat, Francesca M. Corrao, and Mohammed Hashas (New York: Palgrave Macmillan, 2017), 79–109.
24. Haj, *Reconfiguring Islamic Tradition*, 31–67.
25. Samah Selim, "Literature and Revolution," *IJMES* 43, no. 3 (August 2011): 385–86; El Shakry, "History Without Documents."
26. The classical typology of the Arab intellectual field in the wake of World War II features three groups: Islamists, reformists, and revolutionists. See Albert Hourani, *Arabic Thought in the Liberal Age, 1798–1939* (Cambridge: Cambridge University Press, 1983); Abu-Rabi', *Contemporary Arab Thought*; Michael Hudson, *Arab Politics: The Search for Legitimacy* (New Haven, CT: Yale University Press); Azzam Tamimi and John L. Esposito, eds., *Islam and Secularism in the Middle East* (London: Hurst, 2000); Jens Hanssen and Max Weiss, eds., *Arabic Thought Against the Authoritarian Age: Towards an Intellectual History of the Present* (Cambridge: Cambridge University Press, 2018); and Sadek Jalal al-ʿAẓm and Abu Fakhr, "Trends in Arab Thought: An Interview with Sadek Jalal al-ʿAẓm," *Journal of Palestine Studies* 27, no. 2 (1998): 68–80.
27. Gadi Algazi, "Exemplum and Wundertier: Three Concepts of the Scholarly Persona," *BMGN—Low Countries Historical Review* 131, no. 4 (2016): 8.
28. Yoav Di-Capua, "The Intellectual Revolt of the 1950s and 'The Fall of the Udabā'," in *Commitment and Beyond: Reflections on/of the Political in Arabic Literature Since the 1940s*, ed. Friederike Pannewick and George Khalil (Wiesbaden: Ludwing, 2015), 89–104.
29. Cited by Maya Kesrouany in *Prophetic Translation: The Making of Modern Egyptian Literature* (Edinburgh: Edinburgh University Press, 2019), 1. Haqqi did not hesitate to "admit" that the social critics were "pioneering individuals who had been influenced by European, especially French literature."
30. Verena Klemm, "Different Notions of Commitment (Iltizam) and Committed Literature (Al-adab Al-multazim) in the Literary Circles of the Mashriq," in *Middle Eastern Literatures* 3, no. 1 (2000): 51–68, 52.
31. Sharabi, "Cultural Critics of Contemporary Arab Society," 3.
32. Sharabi, 11.
33. See Michael Walzer, *The Company of Critics: Social Criticism And Political Commitment in the Twentieth Century* (New York: Basic Books, 2002); and Michael Walzer, *Interpretation and Social Criticism* (Cambridge, MA: Harvard University Press, 1987). For a critical take on Walzer's connected critic, see Mark Krupnick, "The Critic and His Connections: The Case of Michael Walzer," *American Literary History* 1, no. 3 (1989): 689–98.

34. Abu-Rabi', *Contemporary Arab Thought.*
35. El Shakry, "History Without Documents," 928.
36. David Scott, *Conscripts of Modernity: The Tragedy of Colonial Enlightenment* (Durham, NC: Duke University Press, 2004). On the utopian narrative of the anticolonialists, Scott writes, "They have tended to be narratives of overcoming, often narratives of vindication; they have tended to enact a distinctive rhythm and pacing, a distinctive direction, and to tell stories of salvation and redemption. They have largely depended upon a certain (utopia) horizon toward which the emancipationist history is imagined to be moving" (8).
37. Eric Foner, "Students for a Democratic Society: The Port Huron Statement, 1964," in *Voices of Freedon: A Documentary History*, ed. Eric Foner, vol. 2 (New York: Norton, 2017), 292.
38. Haydar Haydar, *Awrāq Al-Manfa* (Damascus: Dār Ward, 2008).
39. Hallaq, *Reforming Modernity*, 11.
40. Keith David Watenpaugh, *Being Modern in the Middle East: Revolution, Nationalism, Colonialism, and the Arab Middle Class* (Princeton, NJ: Princeton University Press, 2006), 8.
41. Michael Walzer, *Interpretation and Social Criticism* (Cambridge, MA: Harvard University Press, 1987), 36.
42. On the persona of Mihyar that Adonis promotes as an ideal type of a figure of extreme solitude, see Robyn Creswell, *City of Beginnings: Poetic Modernism in Beirut (Translation/Transnation)* (Princeton, NJ: Princeton University Press, 2019), Kindle, loc. 2212–13.
43. Haydar, *Awrāq Al-Manfa*, 9.
44. Haydar, 8–9.
45. Walzer, *Company of Critics*, 37.
46. Andrew Arsan, "Under the Influence? Translations and Transgressions in Late Ottoman Imperial Thought," *Modern Intellectual History* 10, no. 2 (2014): 375–97.
47. Previous generations of Arab writers were defined by an Islah-interpretive framework, as writers who valorized an interpretive mode of thinking, which the social critic deemed insufficient and incapable of rising to the challenges of the moment. The Islah-reform movement launched by Mohammad Abduh offers an example of scholars bent on bringing cultural change from *within*. Their criticism took inspiration from the multivalent modes of religiosity that characterized Islam. Tarabishi and his comrades, on the other hand, proposed a Western-oriented critique that went beyond undercutting the social standing of religion and tradition in society to delegitimize the Adeb as a social player. See John O. Voll, "Renewal and Reform in Islamic History: Tajdid and Islah," in *Voices of Resurgent Islam*, ed. John Esposito (Oxford: Oxford University Press, 1983), 32–45.
48. Cited by Max Weiss, "Genealogies of Ba'thism: Michel 'Aflaq Between Personalism and Arabic Nationalism," in *Modern Intellectual History* 17, no. 4 (2019): 22.
49. These publications "supported new literary trends and innovative work, and perceived literature as a vehicle for change, reform, and progress. It transformed the language of criticism and developed new critical approaches to literature from

psychoanalytical to Marxist and existential criticism." Sabry Hafez, "Cultural Journals and Modern Arabic Literature: A Historical Overview,"Alif 37 (2017,) 20.

50. Kesrouany, *Prophetic Translation*, 2.
51. Watenpaugh, *Being Modern in the Middle East*, 8.
52. Burhān Ghalyūn and Raḍwān Ziyādah, *Al-ʿArab Wa-Taḥawwulāt al-ʿālam Min Suqūṭ Jidār Birlīn Ilá Suqūṭ Baghdād* (Beirut: al-Markaz al-Thaqāfī al-ʿArabī, 2003).
53. ʿAlī Harb, *Ās'lat al-Haqīqa Wa-Rihānāt al-Fiqr* (Beirut: Dār al-Ṭalīʿah, 1994).
54. Yāsīn Ḥājj Ṣāliḥ, *Al-Thaqāfah Ka-Siyāsah: Al-Muthaqqafūn Wa-Mas'ūlīyatuhum al-Ijtimāʿīyah Fī Zaman al-Ghīlān*, al-Ṭabʿah al-ūlá (Beirut: al-Muʿassasah al-ʿArabīyah lil-Dirāsāt wa-al-Nashr, 2016).
55. Walzer, *Company of Critics*, 38.
56. Ḥājj Ṣāliḥ, *Al-Thaqāfah Ka-Siyāsah*.
57. Haydar, *Awrāq Al-Manfa*, 64–65.
58. "The central idea of a revolutionary movement that addresses itself to change the course of life of a nation is to undo the common values. No doubt the prevalent and embedded values are in harmony with and nurturing the current order, thus it makes no sense to have these values common among us while we are revolutionaries." Michel ʿAflaq, *Fī Sabīl Al-Baʿth*, (Beirut: Dār al-Ṭalīʿah, 1970): 30.
59. Muḥammad ʿĀbid Jābirī, *Al-Turath Wal-Hadatha: Dirāsāt Wa-Munāqashāt* (Beirut: Markaz Dirāsāt al-Waḥdah al-ʿArabīyah, 1991), 33.
60. Jābirī, *Naḥnu wal-Turath*, 21.
61. "Political nostalgia," writes Mark Lilla, "reflects a kind of magical thinking about history. The sufferer believes that a discrete Golden Age existed and that he possesses esoteric knowledge of why it ended." See Mark Lilla, *The Shipwrecked Mind: On Political Reaction* (New York: New York Review Books, 2016), 21.
62. Yasmeen Daifallah, "Turath as Critique," in Hanssen and Weiss, *Arabic Thought Against the Authoritarian Age*, 292.
63. On the cultural differencs between borrowing and imitation, see Holmes and Krastev, *The Light That Failed*.
64. Jābirī, *Al-Turath Wal-Hadatha*, 33.
65. Jābirī, *Al-Khiṭāb al-ʿArabī al-Muʿāṣir*.
66. Muḥammad ʿĀbid Jābirī, *Binyat Al-ʿaql al-ʿArabī: Dirāsah Taḥlīlīyah Naqdīyah Li-Nuẓum al-Maʿrifah Fī al-Thaqāfah al-ʿArabīyah* (Beirut: al-Markaz al-Thaqāfī al-ʿArabī, 1986), 568.
67. Jābirī, *Al-Khiṭāb al-ʿArabī al-Muʿāṣir*, 205.
68. Walzer, *Interpretation and Social Criticism*, 39.
69. Walzer, 39.

PART 2: CURATORS

1. Zaid Eyadat, Francesca M. Corrao, and Mohammed Hashas, eds., *Islam, State, and Modernity: Mohammed Abed al-Jabiri and the Future of the Arab World* (New York: Palgrave Macmillan, 2017), xii.

2. Sonja Hegasy, "'Dare to be Wise!' On the Reception of al-Jabiri Post-2011," in Eyadat, Corrao, and Hashas, *Islam, State, and Modernity*, 186.
3. Hegasy, "Dare to be Wise!," 187.

3. JABIRI AS A THINKER OF (INTERNAL) DECOLONIZATION

1. Moḥammad ʿĀbid al-Jābirī, *Naḥnu Wa-al-Turath: Qirā'āt Mu'āṣirah Fī Turathinā al-Falsafī*, al-Ṭabʿah 1 (Berut: Dār al-Ṭalīʿah, 1980), 56.
2. Jābirī, *Naḥnu Wa-al-Turath*, 56.
3. Moḥammad ʿĀbid al-Jabirī, *Al-Turath Wal Hadātha: Dirāsāt Wa-Munāqshāt* (Beirut: Markaz Dirāsāt al-Wiḥdah al-ʿArabīyah, 1991), 94.
4. See also Yūsef Zaydān, *Al-Turath al-Majhūl: Iṭalālah ʿala ʿAlam al-Makhṭūṭāt* (Cairo: Dār al-Amin, 1997); and Zaki Najib Maḥmūd, *Tajdid Al-Fikr al-Arabi* (Beirut: Dār al-Shirūq, 1971).
5. Carl Schorske, *Fin-de-Siècle Vienna: Politics and Culture* (New York: Vintage, 1981), 1.
6. Jābirī, *Al-Turath Wal-Hadatha*, 256.
7. Jūrj Ṭarābīshī, *Madhbaḥat al-Turath Ffī al-Thaqāfah al-ʿArabīyah al-Muʿāṣirah* (Beirut: Dār al-Sāqī, 1993); Wael B. Hallaq, *Reforming Modernity* (New York: Columbia University Press, 2019); Joseph Massad, *Desiring Arabs* (Chicago: University of Chicago Press, 2007).
8. David Carr, review of *Futures Past: On the Semantics of Historical Time*, by Reinhart Koselleck and Keith Tribe, *History and Theory* 26, no. 2 (1987): 197–204.
9. Moḥammad ʿĀbid al-Jābirī, *Ḥafriyat Fi Al-Dhākira Min Ba'īd* (Beirut: Markaz Dirāsāt al-Waḥdah al-ʿArabīyah, 1996), 19.
10. Zaid Eyadat, Francesca M. Corrao, and Mohammed Hashas, eds., *Islam, State, and Modernity: Mohammed Abed al-Jabiri and the Future of the Arab World* (New York: Palgrave Macmillan, 2017), 130. Italics in original.
11. Jābirī, *Ḥafriyat Fi Al-Dhākira Min Ba'īd*, 140.
12. David Stenner, "On the Margins of the Arab World?," *International Journal of Middle East Studies* 52, no. 1 (February 2020): 154–60; David Stenner, *Globalizing Morocco: Transnational Activism and the Postcolonial State* (Stanford, CA: Stanford University Press, 2019).
13. Jūrj Ṭarābīshī, interview with the author, Paris, May 22, 2015. Jabiri addresses his unsuccessful experiments with girls in his memoir; see in particular *Ḥafriyat Fi Al-Dhākira Min Ba'īd*, 129–33.
14. On Jabiri's journey in Syria, see Mohamed Amine Brahimi, "The International Becoming of an Arab Philosopher: An Analysis of the Non-reception of Mohammed Abed al-Jabiri in Euro-American Scholarship," in Eyadat, Corrao, and Hashas, *Islam, State, and Modernity*, 127–48.
15. Jābirī, *Fi Ghimār Al-Siyāsah*, vol. 3 (Beirut: Al-Shabaka al-Arabiya, 2010), 93–94.

16. Jābirī, *Fi Ghimār Al-Siyāsah*, vol. 1, 25–52.
17. Jābirī, *Naḥnu Wa-al-Turath*, 80.
18. Jābirī, *Al-Turath Wal-Hadatha*, 33.
19. Jābirī, *Naḥnu Wa-al-Turath*, 134.
20. "Fi al-Baḥth ʿan Rūʾya Jadīdah: al-Turath wal-Fikr al-Alʿālami al-Muʿāsir," reproduced in Jābirī, *Al-Turath Wal-Hadatha*. All citations in this section are taken from this article.
21. Moḥammad ʿĀbid al-Jābirī, *Al-Khiṭāb al-ʿArabī al-Muʿāṣir*, al-Ṭabʿah 2 (Beirut: Dār al-Ṭalīʿah, 1985), 197–98.
22. Moḥammad ʿĀbid al-Jābirī, *Masʾālat al-Hawiya: Al-ʾUrūba Wal-Islām Wal-Gharb* (Beirut: Markaz Dirāsāt al-Waḥdah al-ʿArabīyah, 1991), 22.
23. Jābirī, *Masʾālat al-Hawiya*, 28.
24. Jābirī, *Al-Turath Wal-Hadatha*, 37.
25. Jābirī, *Al-Khiṭāb al-ʿArabī al-Muʿāṣir*, 61.
26. Jābirī, *Naḥnu Wa-al-Turath*, 47.
27. Jābirī, *Al-Khiṭāb al-ʿArabī al-Muʿāṣir*, 38.
28. Jābirī, 204.
29. Jābirī, 204.
30. Massad, *Desiring Arabs*, 36–38.
31. Patrick Deneen, *Why Liberalism Failed* (New Haven, CT: Yale University Press, 2019), 73.
32. Zaki Najib Maḥmūd, *Ḥaṣād Al-Sinīn* (Cairo: Dār al-Shurūq, 1991), 34.
33. Zaki Najib Maḥmūd, *Ḥaṣād Al-Sinīn*, 39.
34. Zaki Najib Maḥmūd, 35.
35. Moḥammad ʿĀbid al-Jābirī, *Al-Mashrūʿ al-Nahḍawi al-ʿArabi* (Beirut: Markaz Dirāsāt al-Waḥdah al-ʿArabīyah, 1996), 118.
36. Deneen, *Why Liberalism Failed*, 84. "Communities maintain standards and patterns of life that encourage responsible and communally sanctioned forms of erotic bonds, with the aim of fostering the strong family ties and commitments that constitute the backbone of communal health and the conduit of culture and tradition" (79).
37. Salama Musa, *Mā Hiya al-Nahḍa* (Cairo: Hindawi Foundation for Education and Culture, 2011), 108.
38. Yoav Di-Capua, *No Exit: Arab Existentialism, Jean-Paul Sartre, and Decolonization* (Chicago, University of Chicago Press, 2018); Robyn Creswell, *City of Beginnings: Poetic Modernism in Beirut* (Princeton, NJ: Princeton University Press, 2019).

4. RESTATING TURATH IN THE POSTCOLONIAL AGE

1. Muḥammad ʿĀbid Jābirī, "Lʾanna al- ʿAqlaniya Darūrah," in *Al-Thaqāfa al-Jadīdah*, 21 (1981), reproduced in *Al-Turath Wal-Hadatha: Dirāsāt Wa-Munāqashāt* (Beirut: Markaz Dirāsāt al-Waḥdah al-ʿArabīyah, 1991), 257.

2. Stephen Holmes and Ivan Krastev, *The Light That Failed: Why the West Is Losing the Fight for Democracy* (New York: Pegasus, 2020), 13.
3. Nasr Hamid Abu Zayd and Carool Kersten, *Critique of Religious Discourse*, trans. Jonathan Wright (New Haven, CT: Yale University Press, 2018), 19.
4. Zayd and Kersten, *Critique of Religious Discourse*, 21.
5. Zayd and Kersten, 9.
6. Muḥammad ʿĀbid Jābirī, *Al-Mashrūʿ al-Nahḍawī al-ʿArabī* (Beirut: Markaz Dirāsāt al-Waḥdah al-ʿArabīyah, 1996), 122.
7. Muḥammad ʿĀbid Jābirī, *Al-Turath Wal-Hadatha: Dirāsāt Wa-Munāqashāt* (Beirut: Markaz Dirāsāt al-Waḥdah al-ʿArabīyah, 1991), 15–16.
8. Jābirī, *Al-Turath Wal-Hadatha*, 350.
9. Muḥammad ʿĀbid Jābirī, *Naḥnu Wa-al-Turath: Qirā'āt Muʿāṣirah Fī Turathinā al-Falsafī*, al-Ṭabʿah 1 (Beirut: Dār al-Ṭalīʿah, 1980), 134.
10. Jābirī, *Al-Mashrūʿ al-Nahḍawi al-ʿArabi*, 19.
11. Jābirī, *Al-Turath Wal-Hadatha*, 11.
12. Jābirī , *Al-Mashrūʿ al-Nahḍawi al-ʿArabi*, 20.
13. Jābirī, *Al-Turath Wal-Hadatha*, 11.
14. Jābirī, 257–58.
15. Jābirī, 350.
16. Jābirī, *Naḥnu Wa-al-Turath*, 55.
17. Muḥammad ʿĀbid Jābirī, *Faṣl Al-Maqāl* (Beirut: Markaz Dirāsāt al-Waḥdah al-ʿArabīyah, 1997), 43–44.
18. Jabiri, *Naḥnu Wa-al-Turath*, 43.
19. Muḥammad ʿĀbid Jābirī, *Naḥnu Wa-al-Turāth: Qirā'āt Muʿāṣirah Fī Turāthinā al-Falsafī*, al-Ṭabʿah 1 (Beirut: Dār al-Ṭalīʿah, 1980); Muḥammad ʿĀbid Jābirī, *Al-Turāth Wal-Hadatha: Dirāsāt Wa-Munāqashāt* (Beirut: Markaz Dirāsāt al-Waḥdah al-ʿArabīyah, 1991, 1991), 8–13.
20. Jābirī, *Al-Turath Wal-Hadatha*, 168.
21. Jābirī, 84.
22. Jābirī, *Takwīn al-ʿaql al-ʿArabī* (Beirut: Bayrūt : Dār al-Ṭalīʿah., 1984), 22–24.
23. Jābirī, 75.
24. Jābirī, *Al-Turath Wal-Hadatha*, 168.
25. Jābirī, 72.
26. Jābirī, 256.
27. Muḥammad ʿĀbid Jābirī, *Ishkāliyāt Al-Fikr al-ʿArabī al-Muʿāsir* (Beirut: Markaz Dirāsāt al-Waḥdah al-ʿArabīyah, 1989), 69.
28. Jābirī, *Naḥnu Wa-al-Turath*, 182.
29. Jābirī, 183.
30. Jābirī, *Al-Mashrūʿ al-Nahḍawi al-ʿArabi*, 58.
31. Jābirī, 137.
32. Jābirī, *Ishkāliyāt Al-Fikr al-ʿArabī al-Muʿāsir*, 62.
33. Jābirī, 67.
34. Jābirī, 67.

35. Jābirī, *Al-Khiṭāb al-ʿArabī al-Muʿāṣir*, 59.
36. Jābirī, *Al-Turath Wal-Hadatha*, 33.
37. Jābirī, *Al-Turāth Wal-Hadathat*, 33.
38. Michaelle Browers, "From 'New Partisans of the Heritage' to Post-Secularism: Mohammed Abed al-Jabri and the Development of Arab Liberal Communitarian Thought in the 1980s," in Meir Hatina and Christoph Schumann, eds., *Arab Liberal Thought After 1967* (New York: Palgrave Macmillan, 2015), 143.
39. Muḥammad ʿĀbid Jābirī, *Fi Ghimār Al-Siyāsah*, vol. 1 (Beirut: al-Shabaka al-Arabiya, 2010), 306.
40. Jābirī, *Naḥnu Wa-al-Turath*, 43.
41. Jābirī, *Ishkāliyāt Al-Fikr al-ʿArabī al-Muʿāsir*, 63.
42. Ahmad Agbaria, "The Arab Rationalist Association and the Turn to Nahḍah in Contemporary Arab Thought," *British Journal of Middle Eastern Studies* (July 2020): 1–18.
43. Jābirī, *Fi Ghimār Al-Siyāsah*, vol. 1, 306.
44. Jābirī, *Al-Turath Wal-Hadatha*, 256.
45. Jābirī, *A* 33.
46. Jābirī, *Fi Ghimār Al-Siyāsah*, vol. 3, 195.
47. Jābirī, *Al-Turath Wal-Hadatha*, 43.
48. Jābirī, *Ishkāliyāt Al-Fikr al-ʿArabī al-Muʿāsir*, 169.
49. Peter E. Gordon, "Contextualism and Criticism in the History of Ideas," in *Rethinking Modern European Intellectual History*, ed. Darrin McMahon and Samuel Moyn (Oxford: Oxford University Press, 2014), 44.
50. Jābirī, *Al-Turath Wal-Hadatha*, 199.

PART 3: BACKLASH

1. Jūrj Ṭarābīshī, *Al-Wiḥdah*, vol. 1 (n.p., 1984), 80.
2. Jūrj Ṭarābīshī, *Min Al-Nahḍah Ilá al-Riddah: Tamazzuqāt al-Thaqāfah al-ʿArabīyah Fī ʿaṣr al-ʿawlamah*, al-Ṭabʿah 1 (Beirut: Dār al-Sāqī, 2000).
3. Yoav Di-Capua, *No Exit: Arab Existentialism, Jean-Paul Sartre, and Decolonization* (Chicago: University of Chicago Press, 2018), 163.
4. This was one of the most recurring ideas that Tarabishi employed against Jabiri and his followers. See, for example, Jūrj Ṭarābīshī, *Madhbaḥat al-turāth fī al-thaqāfah al-ʿArabīyah al-muʿāṣirah* (Beirut: Dār al-Sāqī, 1993), 12–13.

5. THE MAKING OF A SOCIAL CRITIC

1. One of the main voices to propagate this agenda was Syrian Marxist Yasin al-Hafiz. See Yāsīn Ḥāfiẓ, Al-*Hazīmah Wa-Al-Īdyūlūjiyā Al-Mahzūmah* (Beirut: Dār al-Ṭalīʿah, 1977).

2. An early work that was innovative in its discussion of this group was written in Hebrew; see Yehoshafat Harkabi, *'Emdat Ha-'Aravim Be-Sikhsukh Yiśra'el-'Arav* (Tel Aviv: Devir, 1968).
3. Jūrj Ṭarābīshī, "Al-Tarjama Bayn al-Khiyāna Wal-Ijtihād," *Al-Awan*, December 17, 2014, https://www.alawan.org/2014/09/17/الترجمة-بين-الخيانة-والاجتهاد/.
4. It bears recalling that, although during World War I France held out against the German forces for four years, during World War II French resistance lasted only two weeks. Tarabishi, who was highly attuned to French philosophical debates, thought of the Arab defeat in 1967 as a scourge in a similar manner as his French philosophers thought of France surrender during the war.
5. Jūrj Ṭarābīshī, *Sārtar Wa-Al-Mārksīyah* (Beirut: Dār al-Ṭalī'ah, 1964).
6. Jūrj Ṭarābīshī, *Al-Muthaqqafūn al-'Arab Wa-al-Turath: Al-Taḥlīl al-Nafsī Li-'iṣābin Jamā'ī* (London: Riyad el-Rayyes li-l-Kutub wa-al-Nashr, 1991).
7. Jūrj Ṭarābīshī, *Sharq Wa-Gharb* (Beirut: Dār al-Ṭalī'ah, 1979); Jūrj Ṭarābīshī, *Al-Rujūlah Wa-Aydiyūlūjiyā Al-Rujūlah Fī Al-Riwāyah Al-'Arabīyah* (Beirut: Dār al-Ṭalī'ah, 1983; Jūrj Ṭarābīshī, *Woman Against Her Sex* (London, Saqi, 1988); Jūrj Ṭarābīshī, *Al-Adab Min Al-Dākhil* (Beirut: Dār al-Ṭalī'ah, 1977).
8. Joseph Massad, *Desiring Arabs* (Chicago: University of Chicago Press, 2007), 20. Massad flatly accuses Tarabishi's analysis of being "implicated in an evolutionary narrative," and "colonial evolutionary schema."
9. Jūrj Ṭarābīshī, *Al-Mar'ah Fī Al-Islām Wa-Fī Al-ḥaḍārah Al-Gharbīyah* (Beirut: Dār al-Ṭalī'ah, 1980), 8.
10. Keith David Watenpaugh, *Being Modern in the Middle East: Revolution, Nationalism, Colonialism, and the Arab Middle Class* (Princeton, NJ: Princeton University Press, 2006).
11. On the prevailing pessimistic mood among Arab intellectuals, see Samir Kassir, *Being Arab* (London: Verso, 2013).
12. James Jankowski, *Nasser's Egypt, Arab Nationalism, and the United Arab Republic* (Boulder, CO: Lynne Rienner, 2001); Joel Gordon, *Nasser's Blessed Movement: Egypt's Free Officers and the July Revolution* (New York: Oxford University Press, 1992). These intellectuals' and actors' belief in their historical role was affirmed and endorsed one year prior in the Bandung Conference of 1955, in which postcolonial nations were seen as independent and colonialism was seen as the ultimate enemy.
13. On the cultural trauma, see Ṭarābīshī, *Al-Muthaqqafūn al-'Arab Wa-al-Turāth*, chap. 1. Later Tarabishi published this chapter in a separate book.
14. 'Amer Hassan, "Tasīl Al-Hazima," *Al-Akhbar*, June 8, 2015, https://al-akhbar.com/Opinion/22160.
15. Charless Issawi saw this generation as the first generation to truly break away with medieval Arab traditional society See Charles Philip Issawi, *The Arab World's Legacy: Essays* (Princeton, NJ: Darwin, 1981), 231–32.
16. Jūrj Ṭarābīshī, *Min Al-Nahḍah Ilá Al-Riddah: Tamazzuqāt al-Thaqāfah al-'Arabīyah Fī 'aṣr al-'awlamah*, al-Ṭab'ah 1 (Beirut: Dār al-Sāqī, 2000), 114.
17. Watenpaugh, *Being Modern in the Middle East*, 32–33.

18. Watenpaugh, 32–33.
19. Abraham Marcus, *The Middle East on the Eve of Modernity: Aleppo in the Eighteenth Century* (New York: Columbia University Press, 1989).
20. Patrick Seale and Maureen McConville, *Asad of Syria: The Struggle for the Middle East* (London: I. B. Taurus, 1988), 44.
21. Jeremy Bowen, *Six Days: How the 1967 War Shaped the Middle East* (New York: Simon & Schuster, 2003), 14–15.
22. Seale and McConville, *Asad of Syria*, 39.
23. Seale and McConville, 38.
24. Jūrj Ṭarābīshī, *Min Al-Nahḍah Ilá Al-Riddah: Tamazzuqāt Al-Thaqāfah Al-ʿArabīyah Fī ʿaṣr Al-ʿawlamah*. (Beirut: Dār al-Sāqī, 2000), 122.
25. Jūrj Ṭarābīshī, "Sitat Maḥatāt Fi Ḥayātti," *Al-Awan*, February 23, 2015, https://www.alawan.org/2016/03/11/ست-محطات-في-حياتي-جورج-طرابيشي/.
26. Jūrj Ṭarābīshī, "Bisabab Ismi Fashiltu Ann Akun Munadilan ʿArabiyyan," accessed July 8, 2015, https://samisalah.wordpress.com/2012/03/16.
27. Ṭarābīshī, "Bisabab Ismi Fashiltu."
28. Seale and McConville, 7.
29. Seale and McConville, 14.
30. Seale and McConville, *Asad of Syria*, 12.
31. Syrian writer and ex-Baathist Muta Safadi conveys a bleak picture of the educational system in Syria after independence. He argues that very few intellectuals were in Syria at mid-century. Most of the founding fathers of the Baath Party, he claims, were no more than high school teachers. See Muṭāʿ Ṣafadī, *Ḥizb Al-Baʿth, Maʾsāt al-Mawlid, Maʾsāt al-Nihāyah*, Al-Ṭabʿah al-Ūlā (Beirut: Dār al-Ādāb, 1964). Seale mentions that "in Zabadani, west of Damascus, only eight boys were admitted to secondary school in 1941 out of a population of some 40,000" (Seale and McConville, *Asad of Syria*, 25). In a footnote he continues: "In 1946 there were only 8000 places in Syrian secondary schools; by 1953 this had risen to 50,000" (479n2).
32. Ṭarābīshī, "Sitat Mahatat Fi Hayyati."
33. Ṭarābīshī.
34. Ṭarābīshī. Literarily "ceased to be Christian."
35. Tarabishi writes 1955, but he meant the coup that took place on February 24–25, 1954, when Shishikli was forced out of office because of the looming threats. He fled the country to Brazil, where he was assassinated by a Druze fellow, Nawāf Ghazāleh, to revenge the killing of his family. Hānī Khayyir, *Adīb Al-Shīshaklī: ṣāḥib Al-Inqilāb Al-Thālith Fī Sūriyā, Al-Bidāya . . . Wa-Al-Nihāya*, al-Ṭabʿah 1 (Damascus: H. al-Khayyir, 1994).
36. Khayyir, *Adīb Al-Shīshaklī*.
37. Writing from memory, Tarabishi had a tendency to confuse dates and events. Damascus University created a Faculty of Sharia in 1954 in the wake of the coup in which Mutafa al-Sibaʿi was appointed its first dean, a position he held while remaining secretary-general of the Syrian Muslim Brotherhood.
38. Ṭarābīshī, "Sitat Maḥaṭāt Fi Ḥayyati."

39. See the autobiography of Rayyis, one of Tarabishi's contemporaries. Riyāḍ Najīb Rayyis, *Ākhir Al-Khawārij: Ashyā' Min Sīrah ṣiḥāfīyah*, al-Ṭab'ah 1 (Beirut: Riyāḍ al-Rayyis lil-Kutub wa-al-Nashr, 2004), 74.
40. Damascus University was still a small—but growing—campus when Tarabishi joined the Arabic department. Between 1947 and 1948 the number of female students at Damascus University were just 284; by 1952 the tally had quadrupled to a total of 501 out of 2404 students. See Tarabishi's introduction in Jamel Bayhum, *Al-Mar'ah Fī Al-Islām Wa-Fī Al-ḥaḍārah Al-Gharbīyah* (Beirut: Dār al-Ṭalī'ah, 1982), 33.
41. R. Stephen Humphreys, *Between Memory and Desire: The Middle East in a Troubled Age* (Berkeley: University of California Press, 1999), 71.
42. Seale and McConville, *Asad of Syria*, 26.
43. Ṣafadī, *Ḥizb Al-Ba'th, Mā'sāt Al-Mawlid, Mā'sāt Al-Nihāyah*, 57.
44. "By the mid-twentieth-century, 1 percent of the population of Syria owned about 50 percent of the land." Quoted in by James Galvin, *The Modern Middle East*, 3rd ed. (Oxford: Oxford University Press, 2011), 243.
45. Bowen, *Six Days*, 13–15.
46. Ṭarābīshī, *Sārtar Wa-al-Mārksīyah*, 187.
47. In Damascus, Tarabishi met an outstanding student, Henriette 'Abūd, who would accompany him as a wife and a translator partner. Henriette, who came from the famous 'Abud family, brought order and discipline into Tarabishi's life. Most prominently, she transformed his literary taste in favor of writing on women. She became a well-known novelist and translator of classical modernity literature. They would have three daughters together. See Henriette 'Abūd, *Ayyāmi ma' Jûrj Tarabishi* (Beirut: Dār Madarek, 2020).
48. Jūrj Ṭarābīshī, interview with the author, Paris, May 22, 2015.
49. The best accounts in Arabic of the history of the Baath are Ṣafadī, *Ḥizb Al-Ba'th, Ma'sāt al-Mawlid, Ma'sāt al-Nihāyah*; and Nabīl Shuwayrī and Ṣaqr Abū Fakhr, *Sūrīyah Wa-Ḥuṭām al-Marākib al-Muba'tharah: Ḥiwār Ma'a Nabīl al-Shuwayrī: 'Aflaq Wa-al-Ba'th Wa-al-Mu'āmarāt Wa-al-'askar*, Ḥiwārāt (Beirut: al-Mu'assasah al-'Arabīyah lil-Dirāsātwa-al-Nashr, 2005).
50. Suhayl Idrīs, *Mawāqif Wa-Qaḍāyā Adabīyah*, Āfāq Al-Ādāb 2 (Beirut: Dār al-Ādāb, 1977), 27–28.
51. David Keith Watenpaugh, " 'Creating Phantoms': Zaki al-Arsuzi, the Alexandretta Crisis, and the Formation of Modern Arab Nationalism in Syria," *International Journal of Middle East Studies* 28, no. 3 (1996): 363–89.
52. Cyrus Schayegh, *The Middle East and the Making of the Modern World* (Cambridge, MA: Harvard University Press, 2017), 48.
53. Seale and McConville, *Asad of Syria*, 16.
54. Ṣafadī, *Ḥizb Al-Ba'th, Ma'sāt al-Mawlid, Ma'sāt al-Nihāyah*, 71–91.
55. Bowen, *Six Days*, 14.
56. Jūrj Ṭarābīshī, "Qisatti ma' Al-'Afif Al-Akhdar," Hakaekonline, July 7, 2013, https://www.turess.com/hakaek/20045.

57. In 1955, three leading parties in Syria were forcefully disbanded, leaving the Baath to fill the vacuum. Al-Hizb al-Watani, Hizb al-Shab, and al-Hizb al-Suri al-Qawmi al-Ijtima'ī were eliminated under Syrian tyrant Shishikli. Shuwayrī and Abū Fakhr, *Sūrīyah Wa-Ḥuṭām al-Marākib al-MuBa'tharah*, 170.
58. Bowen, *Six Days*, 14.
59. Ṣafadī, *Ḥizb Al-Ba'th, Ma'sāt al-Mawlid, Ma'sāt al-Nihāyah*.
60. Ṭarābīshī, "Sitat Mahatat Fi Hayyati."
61. Ṭarābīshī.
62. Ṭarābīshī.
63. Samer Frangie, "Historicism, Socialism, and Liberalism After the Defeat: On the Political Thought of Yasin al-Hafiz," *Modern Intellectual History* 12, no. 2 (August 2015): 325–52.
64. Ḥāfiẓ, *Hazīmah Wa-al-Īdyūlūjiyā al-Mahzūmah*, n.p.
65. Karam Nashar, "On Yassin Al-Hafiz: The Man and His Revolutionary Time," *Al-Jumhuriya*, accessed November 1, 2015, http://aljumhuriya.net/32545.
66. Ḥāfiẓ, *Hazīmah Wa-al-Īdyūlūjiyā al-Mahzūmah*, 5.
67. On the differences between critique and Marxist critique, see Wendy Brown, "The Sacred, the Secular, and the Profane: Charles Taylor and Karl Marx," In *Varieties of Secularism in a Secular Age*, ed. Michael Warner, Jonathan VanAntwerpen, and Craig Calhoun (Cambridge, MA: Harvard University Press, 2010), 83–105.
68. Yāsīn Ḥāfiẓ, *Al-Tajribah al-Tārīkhīyah al-Fiyitnāmīyah: Taqyīm Naqdī Muqārin Ma'a al-Tajribah al-Tārīkhīyah al-'Arabīyah*, al-Ṭab'ah 2 (Beirut: Dār al-Ṭalī'ah, 1979), 7.
69. Ḥāfiẓ, *Al-Tajribah*, 6.
70. Ḥāfiẓ, 12.
71. Ḥāfiẓ, *Hazīmah Wa-al-Īdyūlūjiyā al-Mahzūmah*, 14.
72. Ṭarābīshī, *Sārtar Wa-al-Mārksīyah*, 9.
73. Suhayl Idrīs, *Mawāqif Wa-Qaḍāyā Adabīyah* (Beirut: Dār al-Ādāb, 1977), 29.
74. Tahtawi was the first to oversee one of the innovative translation projects in nineteenth century that made more than two thousand (!) Western books to Arabic. According to some historians, the translations had no method, lacked any systematic style, and were for the most part random. Ibraham A. Abu-Lughod, *Arab Rediscovery of Europe: A Study in Cultural Encounters* (Princeton, NJ: Princeton University Press, 1963), 46–52.
75. This article reproduced in Idrīs, *Mawāqif Wa-Qaḍāyā Adabīyah*, 28–41.
76. Idrīs, 32.
77. Idrīs, 33.
78. Suhayl Idrīs, *Dikrayāt al-adab wa-al-ḥubb* (Beirut: Dār al-Ādāb, 2001), 106. He earned a PhD in Arabic literature after his adviser, the well-known historian of Islam Levi-Provencal, turned him down. Idris turned to Gegis Blachere to supervise him through his dissertation, "Foreign Influences on Arabic Fiction from 1900 to 1940."

79. In an obituary to Idris, *Al-Sharq al-Awsat* said that he was the first to publish Najib Mahfouz's " 'Awlad Haritna," as Nassir banned it in Egypt. See Susan Abtah, "Al-Adib wal-Nashit al-Mutamrid," *Al-Sharq Al-Awsat*, February 20, 2008, https://archive.aawsat.com/details.asp?issueno=10626&article=459255#.Yb Oudy1h2gQ
80. Idrīs, *Dikrayāt al-adab wa-al-ḥubb.*
81. Ṭarābīshī, "Qisatti Maʿ Al-ʿAfif Al-Akhdar."
82. Orit Bashkin, *The Other Iraq: Pluralism and Culture in Hashemite Iraq* (Stanford, CA: Stanford University Press, 2009), 91.
83. Cited in Robyn Creswell, *City of Beginnings: Poetic Modernism in Beirut* (*Translation/Transnation*) (Princeton, NJ: Princeton University Press, 2019), Kindle, loc. 1957–58.
84. One historian of Iraq writes, "One of the major catalysts that affected the thinking of Iraqi and indeed all Arab intellectuals was the writings of Jean-Paul Sartre. . . . Intellectuals were greatly attracted to Sarter's view of a committed writer as a man reflecting on the events of his age and society." See Bashkin, *Other Iraq*, 89–90.
85. Mamduh al-Mihini, "Hiwar Ma' Tarabishi," *Jasad Al-Thaqafa*, November 19, 2009, n.p.
86. Idrīs, *Mawāqif Wa-Qaḍāyā Adabīyah*, 64.
87. Walid Muhmod Khalis, *Law kāna Fūltīr 'Arabīyan?* (Yemen: Bayt al-Ghusham, 2015), 14–15.
88. "U.S. News Releases 2015 Best Arab Region Universities Rankings—U.S. News," U.S. News & World Report, http://www.usnews.com/education/arab-region-universities /articles/us-news-ranks-best-arab-region-universities (accessed May 29, 2015).
89. Jūrj Ṭarābīshī, *Harṭaqāt* (Beirut: Rābiṭat al-ʿAqlānīyīn al-ʿArab 2006), 149.
90. ʿAbūd, *Ayyāmi maʿ Jûrj Tarabishi*, 124–26.
91. Fouad Ajami, *The Dream Palace of the Arabs: A Generation's Odyssey* (New York: Pantheon, 1998), 16.
92. Beth Baron, *The Women's Awakening in Egypt: Culture, Society, and the Press*, rev. ed. (New Haven, CT: Yale University Press, 1997).
93. Fawwāz Ṭarābulsī, *Qaḍiyat Lubnān Al-Waṭanīyah Wa-Al-Dimuqrāṭīyah*, al-Ṭabʿah 1 (Beirut: Dār al-Ṭalīʿah, 1978), 11–12.
94. Nabil Sulayman, "Abu Ali Yassin: Ahad Wujuh Al-Fikr Al-Naqdi," *Alawan*, April 19, 2009, http://www.alawan.org/article4794.html.
95. Farouq Maussi, "A Reading into the Biography of Suhayl Idriss," *Rabitat Adaba' Al-Sham*, October 22, 2005, http://www.odabasham.net/61469-قرا61469-/نقد-أدبي.
96. Ṭarābīshī, *Harṭaqāt*, 151.
97. Sulayman, "Abu Ali Yassin."
98. Ṭarābīshī, interview with the author.
99. Itamar Rabinovich, *Syria Under the Baʿth, 1963–66: The Army Party Symbiosis* (Jerusalem: Israel Universities Press, 1972).
100. Seale and McConville, *Asad of Syria.*

6. A CRACK IN THE EDIFICE OF THE SOCIAL CRITIC

1. Jūrj Ṭarābīshī, "Al-Muthaqaf w-Siqūṭ al-Mārkisiyyah," *Al-Nāqid*, no. 46 (1992): 13.
2. Jūrj Ṭarābīshī, *Min Al-Nahḍah Ilá Al-Riddah: Tamazzuqāt Al-Thaqāfah Al-ʿArabīyah Fī ʿAṣr Al-ʿawlamah* (Beirut: Dār al-Sāqī, 2000), 7.
3. Jūrj Ṭarābīshī, interview with the author, Paris, May 22, 2015.
4. Ṭarābīshī, interview with the author.
5. Henriette ʿAbūd, *Ayyāmi Maʿ Jūrj Tarabishi* (Beirut: Dār Madarek, 2020), 136.
6. Jūrj Ṭarābīshī, *Al-Marad bil-Gharb: Al-Taḥlīl al-Nafsī Li-ʿiṣābin Jamāʿī* (Damascus: Dār Batra, 2005), 11–12.
7. Tarabishi's ideas against the turn to the past were informed by his previous readings and translations of Marx. "The struggle against the political present of the Germans," Marx wrote, "is a struggle against the past of the modern nations, who are still continually importuned by the reminiscences of this past." Robert C. Tucker, Karl Marx, and Friedrich Engels, eds., *The Marx-Engels Reader*, 2nd. ed. (New York: Norton, 1978), 56.
8. Jūrj Ṭarābīshī, *Al-Muthaqqafūn al-ʿArab Wa-al-Turath: Al-Taḥlīl al-Nafsī Li-ʿiṣābin Jamāʿī* (London: Riyāḍ al-Rayyis lil-Kutub wa-al-Nashr, 1991).
9. See, for example, Tarabishi's article "Who Murdered the Translation Movement in Islam," in *Harṭaqāt* (Beirut: Rābiṭat al-ʿAqlānīyīn al-ʿArab; Dār al-Sāqī, 2006), 39–59; on the modes of knowledge production, see also Jūrj Ṭarābīshī, *Min Al-Nahḍah Ilá Al-Riddah* (Beirut: Dār al-Sāqī 2000); and Jūrj Ṭarābīshī, *Min Islām Al-Qur'ān Ilá Islām Al-Ḥadīth: Al-Nash'ah Al-Musta'nafah* (Beirut: Dār al-Sāqī : Rābiṭat al-ʿAqlānīyīn al-ʿArab, 2010).
10. Ṭarābīshī, *Al-Muthaqqafūn al-ʿArab Wa-al-Turāth*, 13–21.
11. Ṭarābīshī , *Al-Muthaqqafūn Al-ʿArab Wa-Al-Turath*, 19–26.
12. Ṭarābīshī, *Min Al-Nahḍah Ilá Al-Riddah*, 7.
13. Tarabishi in an interview with *al-Riyyad* newspaper. See Ibrahim ʿAbdi, "Anā Usami Nafsi Mashruʿan Democratiyyan,'" *Thaqafat Al-Yaum*, June 8, 2006, http://www.alriyadh.com/161158.
14. Samir Kassir, *Being Arab* (London: Verso, 2013), 40–41.
15. Jūrj Ṭarābīshī , "Qisatī Maʿ Al-ʿAfīf al-Akhdar," Hakaekonline, July 7, 2013, https://www.turess.com/hakaek/20045.
16. Emmanuel Sivan, *Interpretations of Islam: Past and Present* (Princeton, NJ: Darwin, 1985).
17. Issa J. Boullata, *Trends and Issues in Contemporary Arab Thought* (Albany: State University of New York Press, 1990).
18. Ibrahim M. Abu-Rabiʿ, *Contemporary Arab Thought: Studies in Post-1967 Arab Intellectual History* (London: Pluto, 2004).
19. Ṭarābīshī, "Qisatī Maʿ Al-ʿAfīf al-Akhdar."
20. Bū ʿAlī Yāsīn *Ahl al-Qalam Wa-Mā Yasṭurūn: al-Mashhad al-Thaqāfī al-ʿArabī Fī Nihāyat al-Qarn al-ʿIshrīn*. (Beirut: Dār al-Kunūz al-Adabīyah, 2001).
21. Jūrj Ṭarābīshī , *Nathariyat al-ʿAql* (London: Dār al-Sāqī, 1996

22. Hussain Ben Hamzah, "Jurj Tarabishi: Qa'id Fi Harb Al-Mi'at ʿAmm," *Al-Akhbar*, May 20, 2009, http://al-akhbar.com/node/82403.
23. Zakariyya Jawad, "Interview with Tarabishi," *Al-Arabi*, 1998, http://www.arabphilosophers.com/Arabic/aphilosophers/acontemporary/acontemporary-names/Tarabishi/Ahmad_Abuzaid_and_George_Tarabish.htm (accessed December 20, 2021).
24. One must note that secular Arabs refuse to equalize turath with Islam, but they talk about *al-Turath al-Thaqqafi*, or "cultural turath." In Ḥasan Ḥanafī, *Al-Turath Wa-al-Tajdīd: mawqifunā min al-turāth al-qadīm* (Al-Qāhirah: al-Markaz al-ʿArabī lil-Baḥth wa-al-Nashr, 1980), 23–24. "Religion is part of the Turath, but the Turath is not part of religion."
25. Ibrahim El-Ariss, "Hiwar Ma' Tarabishi," *Al-Hayyat*, January 30, 2006.
26. Mohammed Arkoun and Hāshim Ṣāliḥ, *Qaḍāyā Fī Naqd al-ʿAql al-Dīnī Kayfa Nafham al-Islām al-Yawm* (Beirut: Dār al-Ṭalīʿah, 2004).
27. Susanne Olsson, *Alternative Islamic Discourses and Religious Authority*, ed. Carool Kersten, rev. ed. (New York: Routledge, 2016).
28. Jūrj Ṭarābīshī, *Madhbaḥat al-Turath Ffī al-Thaqāfah al-ʿArabīyah al-Muʿāṣirah* (London: Dār al-Sāqī, 1993).
29. Ṭarābīshī, *Madhbaḥat al-Turath Ffī al-Thaqāfah al-ʿArabīyah al-Muʿāṣirah*, 11–16. Here Tarabishi refers to Mohammad Arkoun's call to read the Turath by using the historical method not by emphasizing aspects and overlooking others.
30. Ṭarābīshī, 12.
31. Ṭarābīshī , 33.
32. Ṭarābīshī, 33–34.
33. Ṭarābīshī, *Harṭaqāt* (Beirut: Rābiṭat al-ʿAqlānīyīn al-ʿArab, 2006), 19–39.
34. Ṭarābīshī , *Harṭaqāt*, 21.
35. Ṭarābīshī, 29.
36. Hadi Yahmid, "Jurj Tarabishi: Al-'ilmaniyya Matlab Islami," Islam Online, June 2, 2008, http://www.arabphilosophers.com/Arabic/aphilosophers/acontemporary/acontemporary-names/Tarabishi /D_Islamonline.htm.
37. Ṭarābīshī, *Harṭaqāt*, 34–35; Yahmid, "Interview with Jurj Tarabishi."
38. Ṭarābīshī, 19–36.
39. Radwan Sayyid, "Limadha Hamaltu ʿAla Al-ʿAqallaniyyin Al-ʿArab," *Al-Sharq Al-Awsat*, May 3, 2014, https://archive.aawsat.com/leader.asp?section=3&issueno=12939&article=770501#.YbOppy1h2gQ.
40. Yāsīn Ḥājj Ṣāliḥ, *Al-Thaqāfah Ka-Siyāsah: Al-Muthaqqafūn Wa-Masʾūlīyatuhum Al-Ijtimāʿīyah Fī Zaman Al-Ghīlān*, al-Ṭabʿah al-ūlá (Beirut: al-Muʿassasah al-ʿArabīyah lil-Dirāsāt wa-al-Nashr, 2016).
41. Sayyid, "Limadha Hamaltu ʿAla Al-ʿAqallaniyyin Al-ʿArab."
42. Jūrj Ṭarābīshī, *Al-Muʿjizah, aw, Subāt al-ʿaql fī al-Islām* (Beirut: Dār al-Sāqī, 2008), 46–53.
43. Ṭarābīshī, *Al-Muʿjizah*.
44. Jūrj Ṭarābīshī and Muḥammad Jamīl Bayhum, *Al-Marʾah Fī Al-Islām Wa-Fī Al-ḥaḍārah Al-Gharbīyah* (Beirut: Dār al-Ṭalīʿah 1980), 24.

45. Ṭarābīshī, *Min Al-Nahḍah Ilá al-Riddah*. See chap. 1, on Qassim Amin, whose conception and worldview fundamentally transformed in a matter of two years, from a defender of Arab traditions to a harsh critic of it.
46. Ṭarābīshī and Bayhum, *Al-Mar'ah Fī al-Islām Wa-Fī al-Ḥaḍārah al-Gharbīyah*.
47. For a critical assessment of Tarabishi's ideas that conceives the Sharia as a humanly text like any text subject to all "Western" methods of textual analysis and hermeneutics, see Saba Mahmood, "Secularism, Hermeneutics, and Empire: The Politics of Islamic Reformation," *Public Culture* 18, no. 2 (March 20, 2006): 323–47; and Saba Mahmood, *Politics of Piety: The Islamic Revival and the Feminist Subject* (Princeton, NJ: Princeton University Press, 2005).
48. Burhān Ghalyūn and Raḍwān Ziyādah, *Al-ʿArab Wa-Taḥawwulāt Al-ʿālam Min Suqūṭ Jidār Birlīn Ilá Suqūṭ Baghdād* (Beirut: al-Markaz al-Thaqāfī al-ʿArabī, 2003).
49. Mohammed Arkoun, *Rethinking Islam: Common Questions, Uncommon Answers* (Boulder, CO: Westview, 1994), 25.
50. Ṭarābīshī and Bayhum, *Al-Mar'ah Fī Al-Islām Wa-Fī Al-ḥaḍārah Al-Gharbīyah*, 14.
51. Ṭarābīshī and Bayhum, 12.
52. Fruma Zachs, "Muḥammad Jamīl Bayhum and the Woman Question," *Die Welt Des Islams* 53, no. 1 (January 1, 2013): 50–75.
53. Ṭarābīshī and Bayhum, *Al-Mar'ah Fī al-Islām Wa-Fī al-Ḥaḍārah al-Gharbīyah*, 10.
54. Joan Wallach Scott, *Sex and Secularism* (Princeton, NJ: Princeton University Press, 2017), 60.
55. Ṭarābīshī and Bayhum, *Al-Mar'ah Fī al-Islām Wa-Fī al-Ḥaḍārah al-Gharbīyah*, 39.
56. Ṭarābīshī and Bayhum, 39–41.

CONCLUSION

1. Andrew Sullivan, *The Conservative Soul: Fundamentalism, Freedom, and the Future of the Right* (New York: Harper Perennial, 2007), 10.
2. Adom Getachew, *Worldmaking After Empire: The Rise and Fall of Self-Determination* (Princeton, NJ: Princeton University Press, 2019), 5.
3. Christoph Schumann, "The Generation of Broad Expectations: Nationalism, Education and Autobiography in Syria and Lebanon, 1930–58," *Die Welt Des Islams*, 2, 41 (2001): 174–205.
4. Yoav Di-Capua, *No Exit: Arab Existentialism, Jean-Paul Sartre, and Decolonization* (Chicago: University of Chicago Press, 2018), 3.
5. David Gross, *The Past in Ruins: Tradition and the Critique of Modernity* (Amherst: University of Massachusetts Press, 1992), 102.
6. Hannah Arendt, *Between Past and Future* (New York: Viking, 1961) 6. She wrote, "Remembrance, which is only one, though one of the most important, modes of thought, is helpless outside a pre-established framework of reference."

BIBLIOGRAPHY

ʿAbdi, Ibrahim. "Anā Usami Nafsi Mashruʿan Democratiyyan.'" *Thaqafat Al-Yaum*, June 8, 2006, http://www.alriyadh.com/161158.

Abisaab, Rula. "Deconstructing the Modular and the Authentic: Husayn Muroeh's Early Islamic History." *Critique: Critical Middle Eastern Studies* 17, no. 3 (2008): 239–59.

Abtah, Susan. "Al-Adib wal-Nashit al-Mutamrid," *Al-Sharq Al-Awsat*, February 20, 2008, https://archive.aawsat.com/details.asp?issueno=10626&article=459255#.YbOudy1h2gQ.

ʿAbūd, Henriette. *Ayyāmi Maʿ Jūrj Tarabishi*. Beirut: Dār Madarek, 2020.

Abu-Lughod, Ibrahim A. *Arab Rediscovery of Europe: A Study in Cultural Encounters*. Princeton, NJ: Princeton University Press, 1963.

Abu-Rabi', Ibrahim M. *Contemporary Arab Thought: Studies in Post-1967 Arab Intellectual History*. London: Pluto, 2004.

Adonis. *Al-Kitāb al-Khiṭāb al-Ḥijāb: Dirāsah*. Al-Ṭabʿah 1. Beirut: Dār al-Ādāb, 2009.

——. *Al-Thābit Wa-al-Mutaḥawwil: Baḥth Fī al-Ittibāʿ Wa-al-Ibdāʿ ʿinda al-ʿArab*. Al-Ṭabʿah 5. Beirut: Dār al-Fikr, 1986.

ʿAflaq, Michel. *Fī Sabīl Al-Baʿth*. Al-Ṭabʿah 4. Beirut: Dār al-Ṭalīʿah, 1970.

Agbaria, Ahmad. "The Arab Rationalist Association and the Turn to Nahḍah in Contemporary Arab Thought." *British Journal of Middle Eastern Studies* (July 2, 2020): 1–18.

Ajami, Fouad. "The Arab Inheritance." *Foreign Affairs*, January 28, 2009. https://www.foreignaffairs.com/articles/middle-east/1997-09-01/arab-inheritance.

——. *The Arab Predicament: Arab Political Thought and Practice Since 1967*. New York: Cambridge University Press, 1981.

——. *The Dream Palace of the Arabs: A Generation's Odyssey*. New York: Pantheon, 1998.

Algazi, Gadi. "Exemplum and Wundertier: Three Concepts of the Scholarly Persona." *BMGN—Low Countries Historical Review* 131, no. 4 (2016): 8–32.

ʿAmer, Hassan. "Tasīl Al-Hazima." *Al-Akhbar*, June 8, 2015. https://al-akhbar.com/Opinion/22160.

Amin, Ahmad. "Turathunā al-Kadīm." *Al-Risālah*, no. 5 (1933): 7–8.

Amin, Samir. *Imperialism and Unequal Development.* New York: Monthly Review, 1977.

Anṭūn, Faraḥ, and Muḥammad ʿAbduh. *Ibn Rushd Wa-Falsafatuhu.* Alexandria: n.p., 1903.

Arendt, Hannah. *Between Past and Future.* New York: Viking, 1961.

Arkoun, Mohammed. *Al-Istishrāq Bayna duʿātihi wa Maʿāriḍīh.* al-Ṭabʿah al-ʿArabīyah. Beirut: Dār al-Sāqī, 1994.

——. *Rethinking Islam: Common Questions, Uncommon Answers.* Boulder, CO: Westview, 1994.

Arkoun, Mohammed, and Hāšim Ṣāliḥ. *Qaḍāyā Fī Naqd al-ʿAql al-Dīnī Kayfa Nafham al-Islām al-Yawm.* Beirut: Dār al-Ṭalīʿat, 2004.

Arkoun, Mohammed, Maxime Rodinson, Alain Roussillon, Bernard Lewis, Francesco Gabrieli, Claude Cahen, and Hāshim Ṣāliḥ, eds. *Al-Istishrāq Bayna DuʿĀtihi Wa MaʿĀriḍīh.* Al-Ṭabʿah al-ʿArabīyah. Beirut: Dār al-Sāqī, 1994.

Arsan, Andrew. "Under the Influence? Translations and Transgressions in Late Ottoman Imperial Thought." *Modern Intellectual History* 10, no. 2 (2013): 375–97.

Asad, Talal. *Formations of the Secular: Christianity, Islam, Modernity.* Stanford, CA: Stanford University Press, 2003.

ʿAẓm, Ṣādik Jalāl, and Abu Fakhr. "Trends in Arab Thought: An Interview with Sadek Jalal al-Azm." *Journal of Palestine Studies* 27, no. 2 (1998): 68–80.

al-Azmeh, Aziz. *Secularism in the Arab World: Contexts, Ideas and Consequences.* Translated by David Bond. Edinburgh: Edinburgh University Press, 2020.

Balqaziz, ʿAbd al-Ilāh. *Naqd Al-Turath.* Al-ʿArab Wa-al-Ḥadāthah 3. Beirut: Markaz Dirāsāt al-Waḥdah al-ʿArabīyah, 2014.

——. *Nihāyat Al-Dāʿiyah: Al-Mumkin Wa-al-Mumtaniʿ Fī Adwār al-Muthaqqafīn.* Al-Ṭabʿah 1. Beirut: al-Markaz al-Thaqāfī al-ʿArabī, 2000.

Bardawil, Fadi A. "When All This Revolution Melts into Air: The Disenchantment of Levantine Marxist Intellectuals." PhD diss., Columbia University, 2010.

Baron, Beth. *The Women's Awakening in Egypt: Culture, Society, and the Press.* Rev. ed. New Haven, CT: Yale University Press, 1997.

Bashir, al-Hashimi. "Wāqiʿ Al-Kitāb al-ʿArabī Fī al-Sabʿīnāt Wa-Afāqihi Fī al-Thamanīnāt." Al-Bayan al-kuwītiyah, March 1, 1983. http://archive.sakhrit.co.

Bashkin, Orit. *The Other Iraq: Pluralism and Culture in Hashemite Iraq.* Stanford, CA: Stanford University Press, 2009.

Bayhum, Muḥammad Jamīl. *Al-Mar'ah Fī al-Islām Wa-Fī al-Ḥaḍārah al-Gharbīyah.* Al-Ṭabʿah 1. Beirut: Dār al-Ṭalīʿah, 1980.

Ben Hamzah, Hussain. "Jurj Tarabishi: Qā'id Fi Harb al-Mi'at 'Amm." Al-Akhbar, May 20, 2009. http://al-akhbar.com/node/82403.

Ben Slama, Manhal Sarraj, and Muhammad Saddam. *Al-Mar'ah Wa-Ḥijābuhā.* Damascus: Dār Bitra lil-Nashir, 2009.

Boullata, Issa J. *Trends and Issues in Contemporary Arab Thought.* Albany: State University of New York Press, 1990.

Bowen, Jeremy. *Six Days: How the 1967 War Shaped the Middle East.* New York: Simon & Schuster, 2003.

Browers, Michaelle. *Political Ideology in the Arab World: Accommodation and Transformation*. Cambridge: Cambridge University Press, 2009.

Bū, ʿAlī Yāsīn. *Ahl al-Qalam Wa-Mā Yasṭurūn: al-Mashhad al-Thaqāfī al-ʿArabī Fī Nihāyat al-Qarn al-ʿIshrīn*. Beirut: Dār al-Kunūz al-Adabīyah, 2001.

Byrne, Jeffrey. *Mecca of Revolution: Algeria, Decolonization, and the Third World Order*. Oxford: Oxford University Press, 2015.

Carr, David. Review of *Futures Past: On the Semantics of Historical Time*, by Reinhart Koselleck and Keith Tribe. *History and Theory* 26, no. 2 (1987): 197–204.

Chehabi, H. E. "'The Paris of the Middle East': Iranians in Cosmopolitan Beirut." In *Iran in the Middle East: Transnational Encounters and Social History*, edited by. H. E. Chehabi, 120–36. New York: I. B. Tauris, 2015.

Corm, Georges. *Arab Political Thought: Past and Present*. London: Hurst, 2020.

Creswell, Robyn. *City of Beginnings: Poetic Modernism in Beirut*. Princeton, NJ: Princeton University Press, 2019.

Deneen, Patrick. *Why Liberalism Failed*. New Haven, CT: Yale University Press, 2019.

Dīb, Kamāl. *Tārīkh Lubnān Al-Thaqāfī: Min ʿaṣr al-Nahḍah Ilá al-Qarn al-Ḥādī Wa-al-ʿishshrīn*. Beirut: al-Maktabah al-Sharqīyah, 2016.

Di-Capua, Yoav. "Arab Existentialism: An Invisible Chapter in the Intellectual History of Decolonization." *American Historical Review* 117, no. 4 (October 1, 2012): 1061–91.

——. "Changing the Arab Intellectual Guard." In *Arabic Thought Against the Authoritarian Age: Towards an Intellectual History of the Present*, edited by Jens Hanssen and Max Weiss, 41–61. Cambridge: Cambridge University Press, 2018.

——. "The Intellectual Revolt of the 1950s and 'The Fall of the Udabāʾ.'" In *Commitment and Beyond: Reflections on/of the Political in Arabic Literature Since the 1940s*, edited by Friederike Pannewick and George Khalil, 89–104. Wiesbaden: Reichert Verlag, 2015.

——. *No Exit: Arab Existentialism, Jean-Paul Sartre, and Decolonization*. Chicago: University of Chicago Press, 2018.

El-Ariss, Ibrahim. "Hiwar." *Al-Hayyat*, January 30, 2006. http://www.arabphilosophers.com/Arabic/aphilosophers/acontemporary/acontemporary-names/Tarabishi/D_Alhayat.htm.

El-Enany, Rasheed. "Tawfīq Al-Hakīm and the West: A New Assessment of the Relationship." *British Journal of Middle Eastern Studies* 27, no. 2 (November 1, 2000): 165–75.

Elshakry, Marwa. *Reading Darwin in Arabic, 1860–1950*. Chicago: University of Chicago Press, 2013.

El Shakry, Omnia. "'History Without Documents': The Vexed Archives of Decolonization in the Middle East." *American Historical Review* 120, no. 3 (June 1, 2015): 920–34.

Eyadat, Zaid, Francesca M. Corrao, and Mohammed Hashas, eds. *Islam, State, and Modernity: Mohammed Abed al-Jabri and the Future of the Arab World*. New York: Palgrave Macmillan, 2018.

Foner, Eric. "Students for a Democratic Society: The Port Huron Statement, 1964." In *Voices of Freedom: A Documentary History*, 292. Vol. 2. New York: Norton, 2017.

Frangie, Samer. "Historicism, Socialism, and Liberalism After the Defeat: On the Political Thought of Yasin al-Hafiz." *Modern Intellectual History* 12, no. 2 (August 2015): 325–52.

Friedman, Thomas L. *From Beirut to Jerusalem*. New York: Farrar, Straus & Giroux, 1989.

Galvin, James. *The Modern Middle East*. 3rd ed. Oxford: Oxford University Press, 2011.

Gauchet, Marcel. *The Disenchantment of the World: A Political History of Religion*. Princeton, NJ: Princeton University Press, 1997.

Gauchet, Marcel, and Charles Taylor. *The Disenchantment of the World*. Translated by Oscar Burge. Princeton, NJ: Princeton University Press, 1999.

Gerges, Fawaz A. A. *Making the Arab World: Nasser, Qutb, and the Clash That Shaped the Middle East*. Princeton, NJ: Princeton University Press, 2018.

Getachew, Adom. *Worldmaking After Empire: The Rise and Fall of Self-Determination*. Princeton, NJ: Princeton University Press, 2019.

Ghali, Shukri. *Al-Turath wal-Thawra*. Beirut: Dār al-Ṭalīʿah, 1979.

Ghalyūn, Burhān, and Raḍwān Ziyādah. *Al-'Arab Wa-Taḥawwulāt al-'ālam Min Suqūṭ Jidār Birlīn Ilá Suqūṭ Baghdād*. Al-Ṭabʿah 1. al-Dār al-Bayḍā'. Beirut: al-Markaz al-Thaqāfī al-ʿArabī, 2003.

——. *Al-ʿArab Wa-Taḥawwulāt al-ʿālam Min Suqūṭ Jidār Birlīn Ilá Suqūṭ Baghdād*. Al-Ṭabʿah 1. Beirut: al-Markaz al-Thaqāfī al-ʿArabī, 2003.

Gordon, Joel. *Nasser's Blessed Movement: Egypt's Free Officers and the July Revolution*. New York: Oxford University Press, 1992.

Gross, David. *Lost Time: On Remembering and Forgetting in Late Modern Culture*. Amherst: University of Massachusetts Press, 2000.

——. *The Past in Ruins: Tradition and the Critique of Modernity*. Amherst: University of Massachusetts Press, 1992.

Hafez, Sabry. "Cultural Journals and Modern Arabic Literature: A Historical Overview." *Alif* 37 (2017): 9–49.

——. *The Genesis of Arabic Narrative Discourse*. London: Saqi, 1993.

Ḥāfiẓ, Yāsīn. *Al-Tajribah al-Tārīkhīyah al-Fiyitnāmīyah: Taqyīm Naqdī Muqārin Maʿa al-Tajribah al-Tārīkhīyah al-ʿArabīyah*. Al-Ṭabʿah 2. Beirut: Dār al-Ṭalīʿah, 1979.

——. *Hazīmah Wa-al-Īdyūlūjiyā al-Mahzūmah*. Al-Ṭabʿah 1. Beirut: Dār al-Ṭalīʿah, 1979.

Haj, Samira. *Reconfiguring Islamic Tradition: Reform, Rationality, and Modernity*. Stanford, CA: Stanford University Press, 2011.

Ḥājj Ṣāliḥ, Yāsīn. *Al-Thaqāfah Ka-Siyāsah: Al-Muthaqqafūn Wa-Mas'ūlīyatuhum al-Ijtimāʿīyah Fī Zaman al-Ghīlān*. Beirut: al-Muʾassasah al-ʿArabīyah lil-Dirāsāt wa-al-Nashr, 2016.

Hallaq, Wael B. *The Impossible State: Islam, Politics, and Modernity's Moral Predicament*. New York: Columbia University Press, 2012.

——. *Reforming Modernity*. New York: Columbia University Press, 2019.

——. *Restating Orientalism: A Critique of Modern Knowledge*. New York: Columbia University Press, 2018.

Ḥanafī, Ḥasan. *Al-Turath Wa-al-Tajdīd: Mawqifunā Min al-Turath al-Qadīm*. Al-Ṭabʿah 1. Al-Qāhirah: al-Markaz al-ʿArabī lil-Baḥth wa-al-Nashr, 1980.

Ḥanafī, Ḥasan, and Muḥammad ʿĀbid Jābirī. *Ḥiwār Al-Mashriq Wa-al-Maghrib: Talīhi Silsilat al-Rudūd Wa-al-Munāqashāt*. Al-Ṭabʿah 1. Al-Qāhirah: Maktabat Madbūlī, 1990.

Hanssen, Jens, and Max Weiss, eds. *Arabic Thought Against the Authoritarian Age: Towards an Intellectual History of the Present.* Cambridge: Cambridge University Press, 2018.

Harb, Alī. *Ās'lat al-Haqīqa Wa-Rihānāt al-Fiqr.* Beirut: Dār al-Ṭalīʿah, 1994.

Harkabi, Yehoshafat. *'Emdat Ha-'Aravim Be-Sikhsukh Yiśra'el-'Arav.* Tel Aviv: Devir, 1968.

Haseeb, Khair El-Din. "The Centre for Arab Unity Studies (CAUS) Has Passed Its 35th Anniversary: 'Where There Is a Will, There Is a Way!'" *Contemporary Arab Affairs* 6, no. 2 (April 1, 2013): 159–63.

Hatina, Meir, and Christoph Schumann, eds. *Arab Liberal Thought After 1967: Old Dilemmas, New Perceptions.* New York: Palgrave Macmillan, 2015.

Haydar, Haydar. *Awrāq Al-Manfa.* Damascus: Dār Ward, 2008.

Hitti, Philip. *History of the Arabs.* London: Palgrave Macmillan, 2002.

Holmes, Stephen, and Ivan Krastev. *The Light That Failed: Why the West Is Losing the Fight for Democracy.* New York: Pegasus, 2020.

Hourani, Albert. *Arabic Thought in the Liberal Age, 1798–1939.* Cambridge: Cambridge University Press, 1983.

Hudson, Michael. *Arab Politics: The Search for Legitimacy.* New Haven, CT: Yale University Press.

Humphreys, R. Stephen. *Between Memory and Desire: The Middle East in a Troubled Age.* Berkeley: University of California Press, 1999.

Hussain, Ben Hamzah. "Jurj Tarabishi: Qa'id Fi Harb Al-Mi'at 'Amm." *Al-Akhbar,* May 20, 2009. http://al-akhbar.com/node/82403.

Laroui, Abdallah. *The Crisis of the Arab Intellectual: Traditionalism or Historicism?* Berkeley: University of California Press, 1976.

Idrīs, Suhayl. *Mawāqif Wa-Qaḍāyā Adabīyah.* Al-Ṭabʿah 1. Āfāq Al-Ādāb 2. Beirut: Dār al-Ādāb, 1977.

——. *Dikrayāt al-adab wa-al-ḥubb.* Beirut: Dār al-Ādāb, 2001.

Issa, Ahmad. "Thawrat al-Kitāb." *Al-Kitāb al-Arabī,* January 1971, 3–4.

Issawi, Charles Philip. *The Arab World's Legacy: Essays.* Princeton, NJ: Darwin, 1981.

Jābirī, Muḥammad ʿĀbid. *Al-Mashrūʿ al-Nahḍawi al-'Arabi.* Beirut: Markaz Dirāsāt al-Waḥdah al-ʿArabīyah, 1996.

——. *Binyat Al-ʿaql al-'Arabī: Dirāsah Taḥlīlīyah Naqdīyah Li-Nuẓum al-Maʿrifah Fī al-Thaqāfah al-'Arabīyah.* Al-Ṭabʿah 1, Ṭabʿah khāṣah bi-Al-Maghrib. Naqd Al-ʿaql al-'Arabī 2. Al-Dār al-Bayḍā': al-Markaz al-Thaqāfī al-ʿArabī, 1986.

——. *Faṣl Al-Maqāl.* Beirut: Markaz Dirāsāt al-Waḥdah al-ʿArabīyah, 1997.

——. *Fi Ghimār Al-Siyāsah: Fikran Wa-Mumārasah.* Vol. 1. Beirut: al-Shabakah al-ʿArabiya lilbaḥth wal-Nashir, 2009.

——. *Fikr Ibn Khaldūn: Al-'Aṣabīyah Wa-al-Dawlah: Maʿālim Naẓarīyah Khaldūnīyah Fī al-Tārīkh al-Islāmī.* Al-Ṭabʿah 2. Dār al-Bayḍā': Nashr al-Maghribīyah, 1979.

——. *Ḥafriyat Fi Al-Dhākira Min Baʿīd.* Beirut: Markaz Dirāsāt al-Waḥdah al-ʿArabīyah, 1996.

——. *Ishkāliyāt Al-Fikr al-'Arabī al-Muʿāsir.* Beirut: Markaz Dirāsāt al-Waḥdah al-ʿArabīyah, 1989.

——. *Al-Khiṭāb al-'Arabī al-Muʿāṣir.* Al-Ṭabʿah 2. Beirut: Dār al-Ṭalīʿah, 1985.

——. *Ma'ālat al-Hawiya: Al-'Urūba Wal-Islām Wal-Gharb*. Beirut: Markaz Dirāsāt al-Waḥdah al-ʿArabīyah, 1995.

——. *Naḥnu Wa-al-Turath: Qirā'āt Muʿāṣirah Fī Turathinā al-Falsafī*. Al-Ṭabʿah 1. Beirut: Dār al-Ṭalīʿah, 1980.

——. *Al-Turath Wal-Hadatha: Dirāsāt Wa-Munāqashāt*. Beirut: Markaz Dirāsāt al-Waḥdah al-ʿArabīyah, 1991.

Jacquemond, Richard. "Translation Policies in the Arab World. Representations, Discourses, Realities." *Translator* 15, no. 1 (2009): https://www.academia.edu/8162756/Translation_Policies_in_the_Arab_World_Representations_Discourses_Realities (accessed December 22, 2021).

Jaggi, Maya. "Profile: Amin Maalouf." *Guardian*, November 16, 2002. https://www.theguardian.com/music/2002/nov/16/classicalmusicandopera.fiction.

Jankowski, James. *Nasser's Egypt, Arab Nationalism, and the United Arab Republic*. Boulder, CO: Lynne Rienner, 2001.

Jawad, Zakariyya. "Interview with Tarabishi." *Al-Arabi*. Accessed December 20, 2021. http://www.arabphilosophers.com/Arabic/aphilosophers/acontemporary/acontemporary-names/Tarabishi/Ahmad_Abuzaid_and_George_Tarabish.htm.

Kassab, Elizabeth Suzanne. *Contemporary Arab Thought: Cultural Critique in Comparative Perspective*. New York: Columbia University Press, 2010.

Kassir, Samir. *Being Arab*. London: Verso, 2013.

Kerr, Malcolm H. *The Arab Cold War, 1958–1964: A Study of Ideology in Politics*. New York: Oxford University Press, 1965.

Kersten, Carool. *Contemporary Thought in the Muslim World*. New York: Routledge, 2019.

Kesrouany, Maya. *Prophetic Translation: The Making of Modern Egyptian Literature*. Edinburgh: Edinburgh University Press, 2019.

Khalidi, Tarif. *Arabic Historical Thought in the Classical Period*. Cambridge: Cambridge University Press, 1994.

Khalis, Walid Muhmod. *Law kāna Fūltīr 'Arabīyan?* Yemen: Bayt al-Ghusham, 2015.

Khan, Ahmad, and Elisabeth Kendall, eds. *Reclaiming Islamic Tradition: Modern Interpretations of the Classical Heritage*. Edinburgh: Edinburgh University Press, 2016.

Khayyir, Hānī. *Adīb Al-Shīshaklī: Ṣāḥib al-Inqilāb al-Thālith Fī Sūriyā, al-Bidāya . . . Wa-al-Nihāya*. Al-Ṭabʿah 1. Dimashq: H. al-Khayyir, 1994.

Khuri-Makdisi, Ilham. *The Eastern Mediterranean and the Making of Global Radicalism, 1860–1914*. Berkeley: University of California Press, 2010.

Klemm, Verena. "Different Notions of Commitment (Iltizam) and Committed Literature (Al-adab Al-multazim) in the Literary Circles of the Mashriq." *Middle Eastern Literatures* 3, no. 1 (2000): 51–63.

Krupnick, Mark. "The Critic and His Connections: The Case of Michael Walzer." *American Literary History* 1, no. 3 (1989): 689–98.

Kurzman, Charles, ed. *Liberal Islam: A Sourcebook*. New York: Oxford University Press, 1998.

Lacroix, Stéphane, and George Holoch. *Awakening Islam: The Politics of Religious Dissent in Contemporary Saudi Arabia*. Cambridge, MA: Harvard University Press, 2011.

Lewis, Bernard. "The Return of Islam." *Commentary Magazine*, January 1, 1976. https://www.commentarymagazine.com/print-page/.

Lilla, Mark. *The Shipwrecked Mind: On Political Reaction*. New York: New York Review, 2016.

Mahmood, Saba. *Politics of Piety: The Islamic Revival and the Feminist Subject*. Princeton, NJ: Princeton University Press, 2005.

——. *Religious Difference in a Secular Age: A Minority Report*. Princeton, NJ: Princeton University Press, 2015.

——. "Secularism, Hermeneutics, and Empire: The Politics of Islamic Reformation." *Public Culture* 18, no. 2 (March 20, 2006): 323–47.

——. "Secularism, Sovereignty, and Religious Difference: A Global Genealogy?" *Environment and Planning D: Society and Space* 35, no. 2 (April 1, 2017): 197–209.

Maḥmūd, Zaki Najib. *Tajdid Al-Fikr al-Arabi*. Beirut: Dar al-Shoruq, 1971.

Makdisi, Ussama. *Age of Coexistence: The Ecumenical Frame and the Making of the Middle East*. Oakland: University of California Press, 2019.

Marcus, Abraham. *The Middle East on the Eve of Modernity: Aleppo in the Eighteenth Century*. New York: Columbia University Press, 1989.

Massad, Joseph. *Desiring Arabs*. Chicago: University of Chicago Press, 2007.

——. *Islam in Liberalism*. Chicago: University of Chicago Press, 2015.

Maussi, Farouq. "A Reading into the Biography of Suhayl Idriss." *Rabitat Adaba' al-Sham*, October 22, 2005. http://www.odabasham.net/61469-قراة61469-/نقد-أدبي.

McMahon, Darrin, and Samuel Moyn. *Rethinking Modern European Intellectual History*. Oxford: Oxford University Press, 2014.

Memmi, Albert. *Decolonization and the Decolonized*. Minneapolis: University of Minnesota Press, 2006.

Mermier, Franck, and Firidrīk Ma'tūq, eds. *Al-Faḍā' al-'Arabī: al-Faḍā'Īyāt Wa-Al-Intirnit Wa-Al-I'Lān Wa-Al-Nashr*. Al-Ṭab'ah 1. Dimashq: Qadmus lil-Nashr wa-al-Tawzī', 2003.

Mihini, Mamduh al-. "Hiwar Ma' Tarabishi." *Jasad Al-Thaqafa*, November 19, 2009, n.p.

Murūwah, Ḥusayn. *Al-Naza'āt al-Māddīyah Fī al-Falsafah al-'Arabīyah al-Islāmīyah*. Beirut: Dār al-Farābī, 1978.

Musa, Salama. *Mā Hiya al-Nahḍa*. Cairo: Hindawi Foundation for Education and Culture, 2011.

Nābulusī, Shākir. *Al-Fikr al-'Arabī Fī al-Qarn al-'ishrīn, 1950–2000: Dirāsah Naqdīyah Taḥlīlīyah Fī Thalāthat Ajzā'*. Al-Ṭab'ah 1. Beirut: al-Mu'assasah al-'Arabīyah lil-Dirāsāt wa-al-Nashr, 2001.

Nashar, Karam. "On Yassin Al-Hafiz: The Man and His Revolutionary Time." *Al-Jumhuriya*. Accessed November 1, 2015. http://aljumhuriya.net/32545.

Olsson, Susanne. *Alternative Islamic Discourses and Religious Authority*. Edited by Carool Kersten. New York: Routledge, 2016.

Pace, Eric. "Malcolm Kerr, Expert on the Arabs." *New York Times*, January 19, 1984. https://www.nytimes.com/1984/01/19/obituaries/malcolm-kerr-expert-on-the-arabs.html.

Popper, Karl Raimund, and Mark Amadeus Notturno. *The Myth of the Framework: In Defence of Science and Rationality*. New York: Routledge, 1994.

Rabinovich, Itamar. *Syria Under the Baʿth, 1963–66: The Army Party Symbiosis*. Jerusalem: Israel Universities Press, 1972.

Rayyis, Riyāḍ Najīb. *Ākhir Al-Khawārij: Ashyā' Min Sīrah Ṣiḥāfīyah*. Al-Ṭabʿah 1. Beirut: Riyāḍ al-Rayyis lil-Kutub wa-al-Nashr, 2004.

Reid, Donald M. *Cairo University and the Making of Modern Egypt*. Cambridge: Cambridge University Press, 1990.

Sabaseviciute, Giedre. "Sayyid Qutb and the Crisis of Culture in Late 1940s Egypt." *International Journal of Middle East Studies* 50, no. 1 (2018): 85–101.

Ṣafadī, Muṭāʿ. *Ḥizb Al-Baʿth, Ma'sāt al-Mawlid, Ma'sāt al-Nihāyah*. Al-Ṭabʿah al-Ūlā. Beirut: Dār al-Ādāb, 1964.

Sayyid, Radwan. "Limadha Hamaltu ʿAla al-Qallaniyyin al-ʿArab." *Al-Sharq al-Awsat*, May 3, 2014. https://archive.aawsat.com/leader.asp?section=3&issueno=12939&article=770501#.YbO4rS1h1bU.

Sayyid, Yasīn. *Al-Turath Wa-Taḥadiyyat al-Aṣr Fī al-Waṭan al-ʿArabī*. Beirut: Markiz Dirāsāt al-Waḥdah al-ʿArabīya, 1984.

Schayegh, Cyrus. *The Middle East and the Making of the Modern World*. Cambridge, MA: Harvard University Press, 2017.

Schorske, Carl. *Fin-de-Siècle Vienna: Politics and Culture*. New York: Vintage, 1981.

Schumann, Christoph. "The Generation of Broad Expectations: Nationalism, Education, and Autobiography in Syria and Lebanon, 1930–58." *Die Welt Des Islams* 2, no. 41 (2001): 174–205.

——, ed. *Nationalism and Liberal Thought in the Arab East: Ideology and Practice*. New York: Routledge, 2010.

Scott, David. *Conscripts of Modernity: The Tragedy of Colonial Enlightenment*. Durham, NC: Duke University Press, 2004.

Scott, Joan Wallach. *Sex and Secularism*. Princeton, NJ: Princeton University Press, 2017.

Seale, Patrick, and Maureen McConville. *Asad of Syria: The Struggle for the Middle East*. London: I. B. Taurus, 1988.

Selim, Samah. "Literature and Revolution." *IJMES* 43, no. 3 (August 2011): 385–86.

Shaheen, Stephan. *Foundations of Modern Arab Identity*. Gainesville: University Press of Florida, 2004.

Shakry, Hoda El. "Lessons from the Maghreb." In *Arabic Literature for the Classroom: Teaching Methods, Theories, Themes and Texts*, edited by Muhsin Mussawi, 109–29. New York: Routledge, 2017.

Shamsy, Ahmed El. *Rediscovering the Islamic Classics: How Editors and Print Culture Transformed an Intellectual Tradition*. Princeton, NJ: Princeton University Press, 2020.

Sharabi, Hisham. "Cultural Critics of Contemporary Arab Society." *Arab Studies Quarterly* 9, no. 1 (1987): 1–19.

——. *Neopatriarchy: A Theory of Distorted Change in Arab Society*. New York: Oxford University Press, 1988.

Sharafi, ʿAbd al-Majīd. *Taḥdīth Al-Fikr al-Islāmī*. Munāẓarāt. Casablanca: Nashr al-Fanak, 1998.

Shukri, Ghali. *Al-Turath wal-Thawra*. Beirut: Dār al-Ṭalīʿah, 1979.

Shuwayrī, Nabīl, and Ṣaqr Abū Fakhr. *Sūrīyah Wa-Ḥuṭām al-Marākib al-Muba'tharah: Ḥiwār Ma'a Nabīl al-Shuwayrī: 'Aflaq Wa-al-Ba'th Wa-al-Mu'āmarāt Wa-al-'askar.* Al-Ṭab'ah 1. Ḥiwārāt. Beirut: al-Mu'assasah al-'Arabīyah lil-Dirāsātwa-al-Nashr, 2005.

Sivan, Emmanuel. *Interpretations of Islam: Past and Present.* Princeton, NJ: Darwin, 1985.

——. *Radical Islam: Medieval Theology and Modern Politics.* New Haven, CT: Yale University Press, 1985.

Stenner, David. *Globalizing Morocco: Transnational Activism and the Postcolonial State.* Stanford, CA: Stanford University Press, 2019.

——. "On the Margins of the Arab World?" *International Journal of Middle East Studies* 52, no. 1 (February 2020): 154–60.

Sulayman, Nabil. "Bou Ali Yassin: Ahad Wujuh al-Fikr al-Naqdi." *Alawan*, April 19, 2009, n.p.

Sullivan, Andrew. *The Conservative Soul: Fundamentalism, Freedom, and the Future of the Right.* New York: Harper Perennial, 2007.

Taji-Farouki, Suha, Basheer M. Nafi, and Institute of Ismaili Studies, eds. *Islamic Thought in the Twentieth Century.* London: I. B. Tauris, 2004.

Tamimi, Azzam, and John L. Esposito, eds. *Islam and Secularism in the Middle East.* London: Hurst, 2000.

Ṭarābīshī, Jūrj. *Al-Adab Min al-Dākhil: Dirāsāt Fī Adab Nawāl al-S'adāwī,Samīrah 'Azzām, 'Abd al-Raḥmān Munīf, Najīb Maḥfūẓ, Tawfīq al-Ḥakīm, 'Abd al-Salām al-'Ujaylī, Albirtū Mūrāfīyā.* Al-Ṭab'ah 1. Beirut: Dār al-Ṭalī'ah, 1978.

——. "Bisabab Ismi Fashiltu Ann Akun Munadilan 'Arabiyyan." Accessed July 8, 2015. https://samisalah.wordpress.com/2012/03/16.

——. *Harṭaqāt.* Al-Ṭab'ah 1. Beirut: Dār al-Sāqī, 2006.

——. *Madhbaḥat al-Turath Ffī al-Thaqāfah al-'Arabīyah al-Mu'āṣirah.* Beirut: Dār al-Sāqī, 1993.

——. *Min Al-Nahḍah Ilá al-Riddah: Tamazzuqāt al-Thaqāfah al-'Arabīyah Fī 'aṣr al-'Awlamah.* Al-Ṭab'ah 1. Beirut: Dār al-Sāqī, 2000.

——. *Min Islām Al-Qur'ān Ilá Islām al-Ḥadīth: Al-Nash'ah al-Musta'nafah.* Al-Ṭab'ah 1. Beirut: Dār al-Sāqī; Rābiṭat al-'Aqlānīyīn al-'Arab, 2010.

——. *Al-Mu'jizah, aw, Subāt al-'aql fī al-Islām.* Beirut: Dār al-Sāqī, 2008.

——. "Al-Muthaqaf w-Siqūṭ al-Mārkisiyyah." *Al-Nāqid* 46, no. 46 (1992): 13–15.

——. *Al-Muthaqqafūn al-'Arab Wa-al-Turath: Al-Taḥlīl al-Nafsī Li-'iṣābin Jamā'ī.* London: Riyāḍ al-Rayyis lil-Kutub wa-al-Nashr, 1991.

——. "Qisatī Ma' Al-'Afīf al-Akhdar." Hakaekonline, July 7, 2013. https://www.turess.com/hakaek/20045.

——. *Al-Rujūlah Wa-Aydiyūlūjiyā al-Rujūlah Fī al-Riwāyah al-'Arabīyah.* Al-Ṭab'ah 1. Beirut: Dār al-Ṭalī'ah, 1983.

——. *Sārtar Wa-al-Mārksīyah.* Al-Ṭab'ah 1. Beirut: Dār al-Ṭalī'ah, 1964.

——. *Sharq Wa-Gharb: Rujūlah Wa-Unūthah.* Al-Ṭab'ah 1. Beirut: Dār al-Ṭalī'ah, 1977.

——. "Sitat Mahatat Fi Hayyati." Accessed June 1, 2015. http://www.atheer.om/Article/Index/11257.

——. "Al-Tarjama Bayn al-Khiyāna Wal-Ijtihād." *Al-Awan*, December 17, 2014. https://www.alawan.org/2014/09/17/الترجمة-بين-الخيانة-والاجتهاد/.

——. *Al-Wiḥdah*. Vol. 1. n.p., 1984.

——. *Woman Against Her Sex: A Critique of Nawal El-Saadawi with a Reply by Nawal El-Saadawi*. New York: Saqi, 1988.

Ṭarābulsī, Fawwāz. *Qaḍiyat Lubnān Al-Waṭanīyah Wa-al-Dimuqrāṭīyah*. Beirut: Dār al-Ṭalīʿah, 1978.

Taylor, Charles. *A Secular Age*. Cambridge, MA: Belknap Press of Harvard University Press, 2007.

Tayyīb, Ahmad. *Al-Turāh wal-Tajdīd: Munāqashat wa-Rudūd*. Cairo: Sharikat al-Quds, n.d.

Telhami, Shibley. "Power, Legitimacy, and Peace-Making in the Arab Coalitions: The New Arabism." In *Ethnic Conflicts and International Politics in the Middle East*, edited by Leonard Binder, 61–77. Gainesville: University Press of Florida, 1999.

"The Center for Arab Unity Studies." *Middle East Studies Association Bulletin* 21, no. 1 (1987): 22–24.

Tīzīnī, Ṭayyib. *Min Al-Turath Ilá al-Thawrah: Ḥawla Naẓarīyah Muqtaraḥah Fī Qaḍīyat al-Turath al-ʿArabī*. Mashrūʿ Ru'yah Jadīdah Lil-Fikr al-ʿArabī Mundhu Bidāyatihi Ḥattá al-Marḥalah al-Muʿāṣirah / Ṭayyib Tīzīnī, juz' 1. Beirut: Dār Dimashq.

Tucker, Robert C., Karl Marx, and Friedrich Engels, eds. *The Marx-Engels Reader*. 2nd ed. New York: Norton, 1978.

"U.S. News Releases 2015 Best Arab Region Universities Rankings—U.S. News." U.S. News & World Report, accessed May 29, 2015. http://www.usnews.com/education/arab-region-universities/articles/us-news-ranks-best-arab-region-universities.

Voll, John O. "Renewal and Reform in Islamic History: Tajdid and Islah." In *Voices of Resurgent Islam*, edited by John Esposito, 32–45. Oxford: Oxford University Press, 1983.

Walīd, Mahmud Khāliṣ. *Law kāna Fūltīr ʿArabīyan?* Masqat: Bayt al-Ghashshām lil-Nashr wa-al-Tarjamah, 2015.

Walzer, Michael. *Interpretation and Social Criticism*. Cambridge, MA: Harvard University Press. 1987.

——. *The Company of Critics: Social Criticism and Political Commitment in the Twentieth Century*. Rev. ed. New York: Basic Books, 2002.

Warner, Michael, Jonathan VanAntwerpen, and Craig J. Calhoun, eds. *Varieties of Secularism in a Secular Age*. Cambridge, MA: Harvard University Press, 2010.

Watenpaugh, Keith David. *Being Modern in the Middle East: Revolution, Nationalism, Colonialism, and the Arab Middle Class*. Princeton, NJ: Princeton University Press, 2006.

——. "'Creating Phantoms': Zaki al-Arsuzi, the Alexandretta Crisis, and the Formation of Modern Arab Nationalism in Syria." *International Journal of Middle East Studies* 28, no. 3 (1996): 363–89.

Weiss, Max. "Genealogies of Ba'thism: Michel ʿAflaq Between Personalism and Arabic Nationalism." *Modern Intellectual History* 17, no. 4 (2019): 1–32.

Whitaker, Brian. *Arabs Without God*. CreateSpace Independent Publishing Platform, 2014.

Wilkinson, Michael. "The Transformation of Religion and the Self in the Age of Authenticity." *Pneuma* 40, nos. 1–2 (2014): 91–108.

Worth, Robert F. "The Arab Intellectuals Who Didn't Roar." *New York Times*, October 30, 2011. https://www.nytimes.com/2011/10/30/sunday-review/the-arab-intellectuals-who-didnt-roar.html.

Yahmid, Hadi. "Jurj Tarabishi: Al-'ilmaniyya Matlab Islami." Islam Online, June 2, 2008. http://www.arabphilosophers.com/Arabic/aphilosophers/acontemporary/acontemporary-names/Tarabishi /D_Islamonline.htm.

Zachs, Fruma. "Muḥammad Jamīl Bayhum and the Woman Question." *Die Welt Des Islams* 53, no. 1 (January 1, 2013): 50–75.

Zaki, Najib Mahmud. *Ḥaṣād Al-Sinīn*. Cairo: Dār al-Shurūq, 1991.

Zayd, Nasr Hamid Abu, and Carool Kersten. *Critique of Religious Discourse*. Translated by Jonathan Wright. New Haven, CT: Yale University Press, 2018.

Zaydān, Yūsef. *Al-Turath al-Majhūl: Iṭalālah 'ala 'Alam al-Makhṭūṭāt*. Cairo: Dār al-Amin, 1997.

Ziyād, al-Hafiz. *Markiz Dirasāt al-Wiḥada al-'Arabiyya: Al-Ahdaf Wal-Injazat*. Beirut: Markiz Dirasāt al-Wiḥada al-'Arabiyya, 2013.

INDEX

ʿAbduh, Muhammad, 134, 232*n*47
ʿAbud, Henriette, 164, 177, 240*n*47
Abu Zayd, Nasr Hamid, 119, 194
Adab. *See* Literature
Adab, al- (journal), 68, 175
Adabuna wal Tarjamah (Our Literature and Translation) (Idris), 174
Adeb (old writer), 67–68, 70, 72, 74, 84, 232*n*47
Adonis, 2, 40–41, 55, 73, 232*n*42
Aflaq, Michael, 68, 74, 102, 148, 165, 187
Age of authenticity, 10–14
Ahram Center for Strategic Studies, Al-, 50
Alawites, 155, 167
Aleppo, Syria, 21, 165, 166, 179, 181, 212; Tarabishi in, 27, 144, 149, 153–56, 158, 160–61, 164; University of Aleppo, 157
Alexandretta-Antioch, 161, 166
Alexandria, Egypt, 21, 101, 212
Algeria, 5, 7, 21, 22, 183, 194
Alignment (*intithām*), 83, 136
Alim, Mahmood Amin al-, 61, 88
Amarah, Mohammad, 197
American University of Beirut, 53, 170
Amil, Mahdi, 68
Amin, Ahmad (1886–1954), 12–13, 33
Amin, Qassim, 205, 245*n*45
Amin, Samir, 9, 37–38, 39, 113
Andalusian school, 26, 123, 127–28, 137
Anticolonial nationalists, 25; decolonization and, 14; social critics and, 4, 16, 19, 127, 210; turath and, 41, 42
Antun, Farah, 227*n*42
Aqad, Abbas al-, 38
Aqlām (newspaper), 100, 104
Arab awakening. *See* Nahda
Arab Cold War, The (Kerr), 53
Arab heritage (*Majallat al-Turath al-Arabi*) (journal), 1–2, 3
Arab humanism, 186
Arabia, 78, 175, 178
Arabic-Islamic philosophy, 26, 123, 129–30, 131, 133
Arab intellectuals and turath (*al-Muthaqafūn al-Arab wal-Turath*) (Tarabishi), 149, 187, 188
Arabism, 48, 102, 110, 150, 184
Arab-Israeli War (1948), 178
Arab-Israeli (Six-Day) War (1967), 4–7, 23, 66, 70, 147–49, 151, 187–88
Arab League, 52

Arab Left, 60, 66, 100–1, 121, 181, 218; connected critic and, 57; publishing houses of, 192; secularism and, 63–64; in Syria, 200
Arab Marxism, 170, 171, 172, 230*n*11
Arab Rationalist Association (Rabitat al-ʿAqlaniyin al-ʿArab), 20, 183, 203
Arab Revolutionary Workers Party, 148, 169–70
Arabs: Center for Arab Unity Studies, 25, 47–51, 55, 184, 228*n*52; "The Crisis of Democracy in the Arab World" conference, 50; elites, viii, 8, 54, 133, 143; existentialism, 68; *The Formation of Arab Thought*, 180–81; heritage, ix; intellectual output, 55, 62, 120; *Khitāb al-Arabi al-Musir*, 115; *Majallat al-Turath al-Arabi*, 1–2, 3; middle-class scholars, 72; nationalism, 48, 101–3, 150, 156; "On the Arab Book Market in the 1970s," 42; past, 1, 11, 43, 45, 118, 149; with past traditions, vii; populations, 22, 211–12; *Tajdid al-Fikr al-Arabi*, 31, 33
Arab Spring, 185
Arab Thought in the Liberal Age (Hourani, Albert), 22
Arab Writers Union, 1
Archival breakthrough, 43, 44–47, 55
Arendt, Hannah, 218–19, 245*n*6
Aristocracy, 165, 167
Aristotle, 105
Arkoun, Mohammad, 87, 152, 186, 194–95, 196, 244*n*29
Arnaldez, Roger, 223*n*32
Arsuzi, Zaki al-, 148, 161, 164, 165, 166
Art, 2, 3, 45, 60, 157, 186
Asad, Hafiz al-, 1, 77, 151, 157, 161–62, 228*n*58
Asad, Talal, 12, 230*n*21
Astronomy, 2, 186
Authenticity: age of, 10–14; authority and, 9–10, 229*n*4; contemporaneity vs., 110, 111; Jabiri and, 118; postcolonial era and, 9–10; veil and Arab, 24
Authority: authenticity and, 9–10, 229*n*4; of connected critics, 60, 83; jurisprudence, 44; of old writer, 67; of past, 11, 38, 39, 58, 72, 74, 213; of social critics, 61
Azm, Sadik Jalal al-, 38, 43, 51, 61, 70, 170, 178, 191, 194, 222*n*8

Baath Party, 159, 162; Aflaq and, 102; coup d'état by, 7, 168; factions, 165; founding fathers, 239*n*31; Hafiz and, 169–70; under Hizb Al-Baʿth, 164–69; landowners and, 165, 167; Nasser and, 163, 167–68; rise of, 241*n*57; Tarabishi and, 148, 163, 164–69
Badawi, Abed al-Rahman (1917–2002), 44, 45, 46, 55
Baghdad, Iraq, 175, 212
Balagha (rhetoric), 2
Balqaziz, Abed al-Ilah, 44–45, 46
Bandung Conference (1955), 238*n*12
Barthes, Roland, 106
Baudelaire, Charles, 40–41
Bayati, Al- (b. 1926), 175
Bayhum, Muhammad Jamil, 205, 206, 207
Baʿalbaki, Munir, 175
Baʿalbaki, Zoher, 177
Baʿth, al- (journal), 161, 166
Beards, 23
Beauvoir, Simone de, 6, 34, 164, 176, 179, 180
Beirut, Lebanon, 42, 69, 101; American University of Beirut, 53, 170; Center for Arab Unity Studies, 48; decline of, 51–56, 185; intellectuals in, 16, 21, 27, 51, 52–56, 64, 65, 76, 88, 116, 119, 120, 121, 137, 138, 143, 150, 173, 175, 177–81; Lebanese Civil War and, 53–55; middle class in, 178; publishing houses in, 3, 49, 52, 54, 147, 150, 170, 173, 175; social critics in, 16, 26, 125, 126, 181, 185, 212; Tarabishi in, 177–81; women and education in, 178
Benbarka, Mehdi, 100
Ben Belleh, Ahmed, 5, 7
Ben Slama, Rajaʾ, 183
Between Past and Future (Arendt), 245*n*6

Bilad al-Sham, Syria, 166
Bitar, Salah al-, 148, 165, 167
Bloom, Allan, 95
Books: literary prizes, 87–88; "On the Arab Book Market in the 1970s," 42; production of, 22, 49, 175; translations, 173, 241*n*74. *See also* Publishing houses
Boumedienne, Houari, 7
Boutaleb, Ibrahim, 223*n*32
Brehier, Emile, 148
Bustani, Butrus al- (1819–1883), 38
"Buthūr al-Almaniyya fi al-Islām" (Secular seeds in Islam) (Tarabishi), 198

Cafés, intellectuals and, 5, 102, 178, 179, 180, 190
Cairo, Egypt, 42, 69; intellectuals in, 16, 21, 50, 64, 65, 88, 119, 120, 121, 137, 138, 143, 175, 178; social critics in, 16, 26, 125, 126, 212; women and education in, 178
Cairo University, Egypt, 45
Camus, Albert, 6, 33, 179
Carr, David, 94
Casablanca, Jabiri in, 99–101
Center for Arab Unity Studies, 25, 47–51, 55, 184, 228*n*52
Children, 155, 157–60
Christianity, 156, 158, 198, 230*n*21
Christians, 160, 169, 229*n*65, 230*n*21
Class: consciousness, 169; intellectual, viii, 19, 51, 53, 55, 65, 138; peasants, 77, 150, 155. *See also* Elites; Middle class
Classical Heritage of the Middle Ages, The (Taylor, H.), 33
Collective consciousness, 187
Collective neurosis, 188–89
Colonial humanism, 21
Colonialism: neo-, 8, 92, 93, 127, 153; social critics with, 210–11; turath and, 17
Colonial modernity, 10–11, 12, 101, 125, 213, 214–15
Colossal cultural failure (*fashal ḥaḍḍārī shāmil*), 147
Communists, 63, 159, 161, 163
Communities, 235*n*36
Conferences, cultural war and, 216
Connected critics: ambition of, 57; anticolonial nationalists with social and, 4; Arab Left and, 57; arrival of, 77–84; great cultural war and, 59–67, 77–84; in historiography, 59–62; Jabiri as, 18, 62, 78–80, 81–83, 85; in Maghreb, 63; in Mashreq, 63; modernity and, 81; persona of, 60; secularism and, 62, 63–67; social and, 25, 57–58, 222*n*8; turath and, 57, 62
Consciousness: class, 169; collective, 187
Conscripts of Modernity (Scott, D.), 232*n*36
Conservative, The (Sullivan), 221*n*2
Contemporaneity, 50, 111, 199
Contemporary Arab discourse (*Khitāb al-Arabi al-Musir*) (Jabiri), 115
Continuity and change (*al-Thābit wal-Mutaḥaūil*) (Adonis), 40, 41
Cordoba School, 141
Corm, Georges, 51
Coups d'état: by Baath Party, 7, 168; decolonization and, 7–8; in Iraq, 7–8, 163; in Syria, 7–8, 161–62, 163, 168, 239*n*35, 239*n*37
"Crisis of Democracy in the Arab World, The" conference (1983), 50
Critical realism, 122, 128, 137, 141
Critics, 68–69. *See also* Connected critics; Social critics
Critique, Tarabishi and, 186–87
Critique of Arab reason (*Naqd al-'Aql al-'Arabi*) (Jabiri), 94, 95
Critique of Religious Thought (Azm), 70
Critique of Theology (Azm, Sadiq Jalal al-), 194
Cultural alignment, 136
Cultural attitudes: shift in, 36–40; Tarabishi and, 185, 207
Cultural critics, 68–69
Cultural heritage (turath), 1, 56, 149; accelerated trends toward, 25; anticolonial

Cultural heritage (*continued*)
nationalists and, 41, 42; archival breakthrough and, 43, 44–47, 55; with attitude shift, 36–40; colonialism and, 17; conferences, 50–51; connected critics and, 57, 62; critical reading of, 126; cultural war and, 16, 18; deorientalizing, 133; future and, 2–3; historical otherness and, 218; historiography and, 20; Islam and, 64, 244*n*24; Jabiri and, 12, 17–18, 49, 89–90, 92, 105–8, 109, 114, 122; literature and, 31–32; Mahmud and, 37; modernity and, 16–17, 37, 222*n*4; nahda and, 38, 188–89; negative connotations, 34, 39, 121–22; "Our Ancient Turath," 12; partisans of turath, 119–20, 207; past and, 2–3, 4, 43–44, 121–22, 124; rediscovery of, 35, 43–44; support for, 40–42, 222*n*8; Tarabishi and, 20, 32, 34, 71, 193–200
Cultural heritage (turath), in postcolonial age: Andalusian school and, 123, 127–28, 137; decolonizing reading and, 130–31; deorientalizing Arabic-Islamic philosophy, 26, 123, 129–30, 131; European frameworks and, 124–27, 130, 133; intellectual output and new intelligentsia, 136–40; Islamic philosophy and, 131–33
Cultural renewal, 50, 134, 166
Cultural symbols, 24, 141
Cultural war: conferences, publishing houses, and, 216; historiography and, 20; social critics and, 16–17, 18; turath and, 16, 18. *See also* Great cultural war
Culture, 147; elite, 68; revolutionary, 137. *See also* Great cultural war

Damascus, Syria: social critics and, 212; Tarabishi and politics in, 160–64
Damascus University, Syria, 157; Jabiri and, 101, 103; Tarabishi at, 101, 148, 160–61, 176, 177, 239*n*37, 240*n*40, 240*n*47
Daouk, Bashir al-, 48, 55, 148, 177–78, 181, 185
Dar al-Adab, 49; Idris and, 48, 174, 175, 180; social critics and, 68, 72, 75, 193; Tarabishi and, 150, 177, 180; with translations, 173–74, 177
Dar al-Saqi, 193
Dar al-Taliah, 147; Daouk and, 48, 55, 148, 177–78, 181, 185; Jabiri and, 49; social critics and, 72, 75, 193; Tarabishi and, 55, 143, 150, 175, 177, 180–81, 185; with translations, 173–74, 175, 177
Dar Al-ʿIlm Lilmalayyin, 175
Dar Riyyad al-Rayis, 193
Decolonization, 115, 217; anticolonial nationalists and, 14; coups d'état and, 7–8; goal of, 5–6; history of, 60–61; politics and, 102; reading and, 130–31
Defeat and the defeated ideology, The (*Al-Hazīmah Wa-al-Īdyūlūjiyā al-Mahzūmah*) (Hafiz), 170
Deorientalizing, 26, 123, 129–30, 133
Dependency theory, 9
Derivation (ishtiqaq), 2
Desiring Arabs (Massad), 222*n*4
Dewey, John, 32–33
Dialectics, 2, 199
Dirasat Arabiyya (journal), 68, 150, 178
Dirus fi al-Falsafa (Lessons in philosophy) (Jabiri, Umairi and Sultani), 104–5
Dislocation, 197
Distanced archeology of memory, A (*Hafriyat Fi al-Dhakira Min Baʿid*) (Jabiri), 96–97, 99
Druze, 50, 180, 229*n*65, 239*n*35

Eastern Mediterranean. *See* Mashreq
Education: Islam in, 157–58; social mobility and, 181; student enrollment in Saudi Arabia, 177; for Syrian children, 157–60; women and, 178, 181
Egypt, 77; Alexandria, 21, 101, 212; Arab-Israeli War in 1948, 178; Arab-Israeli War in 1967, 4–7, 23, 66, 70, 147–49, 151, 187–88; with book production, 22; Cairo University, 45;

geography of contestation and, 229*n*7; Israel and, 168; parliament and Nasser speech, 222*n*10; politics in, 16; Syria and, 151; with translation, 174; United Arab Republic and, 70. *See also* Cairo, Egypt
Elites: Arab, viii, 8, 54, 133, 143; aristocratic, 167; cultural, 68; financial, 178; Marxist, 137; political, x, 178
Emigration, urbanization and, 212
Engels, Friedrich, 104
Epistemic rupture, 11
Epistemological break, 38, 132, 137
Ethics, viii, 2, 4, 46, 57, 69, 156, 228*n*46
Europe: frameworks and turath, 124–27, 130, 133; hegemony, 101, 126; rediscovery of, 36
European modernity, 11, 82, 208, 216; Jabiri and, 91, 114, 115–16, 125–26, 134, 144; Tarabishi and, 144, 207
Existentialism, 39, 69, 96, 216; Arab, 68; Idris and, 179, 180; Jabiri and, 102; Tarabishi and, 101, 150, 176, 179, 185

Fajr al-Jadid, al-, 71
Farabi, Abu Nasr al- (870–950), 105, 128
Farabi, al- (872–950), 132
Fashal ḥaḍḍārī shāmil (colossal cultural failure), 147
Fes, Morocco, 212
Financial elite, 178
Formation of Arab Thought, The (Jabiri), 180–81
Foucault, Michel, 6
Frameworks: intellectual, 42, 62, 222*n*2; of reference, 78, 83, 131, 218; turath and European, 124–27, 130, 133
France, 52, 96, 98, 100, 101, 151; French mandate, 154–55, 165–66; in Lebanon, 165; with Multi-National Force headquarters, 180; in Syria, 154–55, 161, 164–66; in World War I, 238*n*4
Freddy Bar, 179
French mandate (1920–1946), 154–55, 165–66
French resistance, in World War II, 238*n*4
Freud, Sigmund, 34, 41, 122, 148, 152, 188, 193
Friedman, Thomas, viii
Fringe movements, in Islam, 195
From Islam of the Qur'an to the Islam of the Hadith (*Min Islām Al-Qur'ān Ilá Islām Al-Ḥadīth*) (Tarabishi), 202
Future, viii, 2–3, 245*n*6. *See also* Past

Garaudy, Roger, 148
Gauchet, Marcel, 230*n*20
Genocide, structural, 11
Geography, 2, 23, 93, 224*n*38, 229*n*7
Ghalyun, Burhan, 204–5
Ghanim, Wahib al-, 165
Ghazali, al-, 45, 46, 128
Global South, 209; with heritage as burden, viii; past and, 60; in social fragmentation, vii
Grammar, 2, 37
Great Britain, 151, 164, 165, 166
Great cultural war: connected critic and, 59–67, 77–84; past and, 14–17; social critic and, 67–76
Gross, David, 218

Hadith literature, 202–3, 204
Hafiz, Yassin al-, 68, 88, 152, 169–72, 179, 226*n*25, 237*n*1
Hafriyat Fi al-Dhakira Min Ba'id (A distanced archeology of memory) (Jabiri), 96–97, 99
Haifa, port in, 178
Haj Saleh, Yasin al-, 170
Haj Salih, Yasin, 200
Hakim, Tawfiq al-, 38
Halabi, Zena, 84
Hallaq, Wael B., 11, 12, 15
Hamadi, Saadun, 48
Hanafi, Hassan (1935–2021), 62, 187, 227*n*34; Arab Left and, 64; as connected critic, 78, 80; secularism and, 63–66
Haqqi, Yahya, 68, 69
Ḥaṣād Al-Sinīn (Years of harvest) (Mahmud), 112–13

Hashimi, Bashir Al-, 42
Hasib, Khair al-Din, 48
Havana café, 179
Ḥayal-Lātīnī, al- (Idris), 174
Hayder, Hayder, 73, 74, 77
Hegel, Georg Wilhelm, 34, 148, 193, 196
Hegemony, 75, 122; European, 101, 126; social critic and intellectual, 70; Tarabishi and end of, 184–89
Heritage, viii, ix. *See also* Cultural heritage
"Heritage and the Challenges of the Age in the Arab Homeland" conference (1984), 50–51
Heritage and us, The (*Naḥnu wal-Turath*) (Jabiri), 18, 20, 89
Heritage thinkers (partisans of turath, turathiyun), 119–20, 207
Hinnawi, Sami al- (1898–1950), 162
Historical anachronism, 132, 170
Historical otherness, turath and, 218
Historiography: connected critic in current, 59–62; past and, 20–24; social critic in current, 60–62
History: of decolonization, 60–61; Muslims with, 15; owning, 127
History and us, The (*Naḥnu wal-Tārīkh*) (Zuriq), 20–21
History of Atheism in Islam, The (Badawi), 45
History of Western Philosophy (Russell), 32
Hitti, Philip, 52
Hizb Al-Baʿth, 164–69. *See also* Baath Party
Hizb al-Shab, 241*n*57
Hizb al-Suri al-Qawmi al-Ijtima'ī, al-, 241*n*57
Hizb al-Watani, Al-, 241*n*57
Homs, Syria, 155
Honor killing, of women, 168–69
Hourani, Akram al-, 159, 165, 167–68
Hourani, Albert, 22, 225*n*5
Humanism, 3, 21, 186
Hume, David, 33
Husari, Sati al-, 102
Hussain, Taha, 21, 33, 38, 45
Hussein, Saddam, 88

Ibn a-Haytham, 217
Ibn Bajjah (824–887), 128, 132–33
Ibn Hazam, 128, 141
Ibn Khaldun, 17, 81, 125, 128, 217
Ibn Rushd (1126–1198), 65, 66, 119, 217, 227*n*42; Cordoba School and, 141; critical realism and, 122, 128, 137, 141; Ibn Bajjah and, 132
Ibn Rushd Prize, 87
Ibn Sina, 128, 217
Ibn Tufil, 128, 217
Idris, Suhayl, 61, 68, 88, 152, 241*n*78, 242*n*79; Dar al-Adab and, 48, 174, 175, 180; existentialism and, 179, 180; Independent Pen Association and, 175; Tarabishi and, 180; translation and, 174–76
'Ilam, al- (newspaper), 100, 101
Immigration, Lebanon with, 229*n*65
Independent (Istiqlal) Party, 99, 100, 104
Independent Pen Association, 175
India, 119
"Intellectual and the Fall of Marxism, The" (Tarabishi), 183
Intellectual framework, 42, 62, 222*n*2
Intellectual output: Arab, 55, 62, 120; Jabiri, 94, 118, 136–40; Tarabishi, 144
Intellectual persona, 56, 67, 126, 140, 152
Intellectuals: banishment of, 178; in Beirut, 16, 21, 27, 51, 52–56, 64, 65, 76, 88, 116, 119, 120, 121, 137, 138, 143, 150, 173, 175, 177–81; cafés and, 5, 102, 178, 179, 180, 190; in Cairo, 16, 21, 50, 64, 65, 88, 119, 120, 121, 137, 138, 143, 175, 178; class, viii, 19, 51, 53, 55, 65, 138; critique of, 119; North Africa, 184; in Palestine, 179; Syrian, 1, 160, 200; with Tarabishi, 215
Intithām (alignment), 83, 136
Introduction to scientific philosophy (*Madkhal ila Falsafat al-ʿUlūm*) (Jabiri), 106

Iran, 23
Iranians, 52
Iraq, 221*n*2; Baghdad, 175, 212; with books, 175; coup d'état in, 7–8, 163; Great Britain in, 165; intellectuals banished in, 178; Sartre and, 242*n*84
Ishtiqaq (derivation), 2
Islah-reform movement, 232*n*47
Islam, 24; Arabism vs., 110; Arab Marxists with, 230*n*11; "Buthūr al-Almaniyya fi al-Islām," 198; Christianity and, 198; in education, 157–58; fringe movements in, 195; *The History of Atheism in Islam*, 45; Jabiri on, 89; laws, 11, 25; *Min Islām Al-Qur'ān Ilá Islām Al-Ḥadīth*, 202; *Al-Muʿjizah, aw, Subāt al-ʿaql fī al-Islām*, 201; political, 57, 64, 66, 116, 119–20, 201, 215; Sunni, 200; *Taḥdīth al-Fikr al-Islamī*, 46; Tarabishi critiquing moderate, 200–204; turath and, 64, 244*n*24
Islamic philosophy, 13, 105–6, 128; Arab-, 26, 123, 129–30, 131, 133; different reading of, 131–33
Islamic Right (political Islam), 57, 64, 66, 116, 119–20, 201, 215
Islamic Salafi movement, 135
Islamic scholars, 43, 58
Islamist Revolution (1979), 23
Islamists, 231*n*26
Islam Levi-Provencal, 241*n*78
Israel, viii, 167; Arab-Israeli War in 1948, 178; Arab-Israeli War in 1967, 4–7, 23, 66, 70, 147–49, 151, 187–88; creation of, 178; Egypt and, 168; port in Haifa, 178
Istiqlal (Independent) Party, 99, 100, 104
Italy, 24

Jabiri, Mohammad Abed al- (1935–2010), 16, 21, 26, 54, 117; Andalusian school and, 127–28; Arab Left and, 64; Arab Nationalism, Mashreq and, 101–3; authenticity and, 118; in Casablanca, 99–101; childhood and early years, 96–98; as connected critic, 18, 62, 78–80, 81–83, 85; critical realism and, 122–23, 128, 137, 141; on cultural renewal, 134; Damascus University and, 101, 103; Dar al-Taliah and, 49; decolonizing reading and, 130–31; deorientalizing Arabic-Islamic philosophy, 129–30; with different reading of Islamic philosophy, 131–33; education in Morocco, 100, 103–5; with European frameworks, 124–27, 130; European modernity and, 91, 114, 115–16, 125–26, 134, 144; existentialism and, 102; historiography and, 20; as humanities scholar, 17; intellectual output, 94, 118, 136–40; investigation approach and method, 94–96; on Islam, 89; on knowledge revitalization, 106–7; legacy, 140; liberal modernity and, 112–15; with literary prizes, 87; Marxism and, 139; modernity and, 91–92, 93, 112–15, 121–23; with new cultural canon, 119–20; past and, 17–18, 122, 125; postcolonial project and, 115–16; with question of nahda, 133–35; on revolutionary culture, 137; with search for new vision, 108–12; secularism and, 63–66; Tarabishi and, 24, 101–2, 143, 144, 180–81, 184, 185, 187, 237*n*4; turath and, 12, 17–18, 49, 89–90, 92, 105–8, 109, 114, 122; why, 91–94
Jews, 166
Jurisprudence, 37, 43, 44, 46, 128, 194

Kalam (jurisprudence) philosophy, 128
Kassab, Elizabeth, 8, 12, 228*n*54
Kassir, Samir, 190
Kerr, Malcolm, 53, 55
Kersten, Carool, 35, 120
Khal, Yusuf al-, 2
Khatibi, Abed al-Kabir al-, 62, 87
Khitāb al-Arabi al-Musir (Contemporary Arab discourse) (Jabiri), 115
Khouri, Ra'if, 175
Knowledge revitalization, 106–7

Landowners: aristocratic elite and, 167; Baath Party and, 165, 167; in Syria, 240*n*44
Land seizure, 166
Laruoi, Abdallah, 87
Laust, Henry, 223*n*32
Law, 2, 35, 37, 112, 192, 201; Islamic, 11, 25; natural, 206
Lebanese Army, 180
Lebanese Civil War (1975–1989), 15–16, 27, 44, 47, 51–55, 76, 150, 180
Lebanon: with book production, 22; with books translated, 173; France in, 165; with immigration, 229*n*65. *See also* Beirut, Lebanon
Lenin, Vladimir, 104
Lessons in philosophy (*Dirus fi al-Falsafa*) (Jabiri, Umairi and Sultani), 104–5
Levant, 40, 229*n*7
Lewis, Bernard, 198, 225*n*47
Liberal modernity, 112–15
Libya, 21
Light That Failed, The (Krastev and Holms), 118–19
Linguistics, 2, 39, 154, 176
Literary prizes, 87–88
Literature (adab): *Adabuna wal Tarjamah*, 174; Hadith, 202–3, 204; Sufi, 2; turath and, 31–32
Logic, 2, 11, 23, 24, 32, 65, 68, 120
Logic (Dewey), 32–33
Lycée Abdel Karim Lahlou, 99

Maalof, Amin, 55
Madawi, Anwar al-, 175
Madhbaḥat al-turath fī al-thaqāfah al-ʿArabīyah al-muʿāṣirah (The massacre over turath) (Tarabishi), 196
Madkhal ila Falsafat al-ʿUlūm (Introduction to scientific philosophy) (Jabiri), 106
Maghreb: with book production, 22; connected critics in, 63; defined, 224*n*38; Mashreq and, 21–22, 93; rise of, 21
Mahmood, Saba, 65
Mahmud, Zaki Najib (1902–1993), 31–33, 37, 88, 112–13
Majallat al-Turath al-Arabi (Arab heritage) (journal), 1–2, 3
Majallat Shiʿr (journal), 68
Makdisi, Anton, 165
Makings of an Intellectual Woman, The (Beauvoir), 34, 164, 176, 180
Maktab al-Tijāri li-Nashir, al-, 177
Malaika, Nazik al- (b. 1923), 175
Manfaluti, Lutfi al-, 174
Manhal, al- (Idris), 180
Mankhul, al- (Ghazali), 46
Maqasid, school of, 127
Marakesh, Morocco, 212
Marcuse, Herbert, 34, 148
Marx, Karl, 104, 148, 193, 196, 217, 243*n*7
Marxism, 39, 69, 96, 149, 192; Arab, 170, 171, 172, 230*n*11; elite, 137; Jabiri and, 139; secularism and, 63; social critics and, 19, 58; Tarabishi and, 172–73, 183
Mar'ah Fī al-Islām Wa-Fī al-Ḥaḍārah al-Gharbīyah, Al- (Women in modernity) (Bayhum, Jamil), 206
Mashreq (Eastern Mediterranean), 78, 154; connected critics in, 63; cultural disengagement with, 137; defined, 224*n*38; Jabiri, Arab Nationalism and, 101–3; Maghreb and, 21–22, 93; with new intelligentsia, 136–40; philosophical traditions of, 128; social critics in, 61, 68, 126
Mashreqi scholars, 21, 22, 81, 137, 140
Masrri, Ibn al-Muqaffaʿ al-, 199
Massacre over turath, The (*Madhbaḥat al-turath fī al-thaqāfah al-ʿArabīyah al-muʿāṣirah*) (Tarabishi), 196
Matarji, ʿAida, 175
Mawāqif (journal), 41, 68
Medicine, 2, 13
Mediterranean, 21, 154, 166, 176
Mediterranean Sea, 6, 166
Memmi, Albert, 14

Middle class, 53, 72, 144, 169, 181, 210; in Beirut, 178; peasants and, 77; social critics, 67, 71, 155, 211, 212; in Syria, 150, 155–56
Mihyar, 232*n*42
Military Academy, Homs, 155
Mind, structure of, 169
Min Islām Al-Qur'ān Ilá Islām Al-Ḥadīth (From Islam of the Qur'an to the Islam of the Hadith) (Tarabishi), 202
Miracle and the eclipse of reason in Islam (*Al-Muʿjizah, aw, Subāt al-ʿaql fī al-Islām*) (Tarabishi), 201
Miṣbaḥal ʿaql (Reason's light) (Masrri), 199
Modernity: Amin, Samir, on, 37–38; in Beirut, 178; colonial, 10–11, 12, 101, 125, 213, 214–15; connected critics and, 81; *Conscripts of Modernity*, 232*n*36; European, 11, 82, 91, 114, 115–16, 125–26, 134, 144, 207, 208, 216; Jabiri and, 91–92, 93, 112–15, 121–23; Jabiri and liberal, 112–15; *Al-Mar'ah Fī al-Islām Wa-Fī al-Ḥaḍārah al-Gharbīyah*, 206; Tarabishi in mid-century Syria with, 150–53; turath and, 16–17, 37, 222*n*4
Morocco, 9, 21, 23, 88, 224*n*41; with book production, 22; Casablanca, 99–101; Fes, 212; Jabiri and education in, 100, 103–5; Marakesh, 212; National Party, 98, 100–101
Mortality rates, children, 155
Muhammad (Prophet), 12, 201–2
Multi-National Force, 180
Muruwah, Husayn, 41, 175
Musa, Salama, 19, 21, 115
Muslim Brotherhood, 159, 239*n*37
Muslims, 12, 35, 43, 119, 195, 201; Christians and, 160, 169; with Hadith literature, 202–3, 204; with history, 15; in Lebanese Army, 180; medieval scholars, 130; past and, 213; students with religious studies, 160; Sunni, 167
Muthaqafūn al-Arab wal-Turath, al- (Arab intellectuals and turath) (Tarabishi), 149, 187, 188
Muʿjizah, aw, Subāt al-ʿaql fī al-Islām, Al- (Miracle and the eclipse of reason in Islam) (Tarabishi), 201
Muʿtazila, al-, 217
Myth of Metaphysics, The (Mahmud), 33

Nadim, Ibn al-, 45
Nahda (Arab awakening), 21, 23, 27; past and, 39; question of, 133–35; Tarabishi and, 189–93, 204–7; turath and, 38, 188–89
Naḥnu wal-Tārīkh (The history and us) (Zuriq), 20–21
Naḥnu wal-Turath (The heritage and us) (Jabiri), 18, 20, 89
Naqd al-Turath (Balqaziz), 44
Naqd al-ʿAql al-ʿArabi (Critique of Arab reason) (Jabiri), 94, 95
Nashid, Said, 183
Nasser, Gamal Abdel al-, 9, 76, 101, 242*n*79; Arabism of, 48; Asad and, 151; Baath Party and, 163, 167–68; legacy, 5, 102; social critics and, 214; speech to Egyptian Parliament, 222*n*10
National Party, Morocco, 98, 100–1
National-secular movement, 23
National Unity for the Popular Forces (UNFP), 104
Neocolonialism, 8, 92, 93, 127, 153
New Arabism, 48
Non-Aligned Movement, 3, 5
North Africa, vii, 3, 49, 84, 87; historiography and, 20; intellectuals, 184; past of, 128; scholars, 22; with traditions, viii; writers, 21
Nuzʿāt Al-Māddīyah Fī Al-Falsafah Al-ʿArabīyah Al-Islāmīyah, *Al-* (Muruwah), 41

Oil, 53, 77
Old writer (Adeb), 67–68, 70, 72, 74, 84, 232*n*47
"On the Life of Solitude and Marginalization" (Adonis), 73

Ottomon Empire, 164
"Our Ancient Turath" (Amin, A.), 12
Our Literature and Translation (*Adabuna wal Tarjamah*) (Idris), 174

Palestine, viii, 74, 165–66, 179
Palestinian-Leftist party, 52
Pan-Arabism, 102, 150, 162–63, 164, 168, 184
Paradise of the Fool, The (Mahmud), 33
partisans of turath (turathiyun, heritage thinkers), 119–20, 207
Past: age of authenticity, 10–14; Arab, 1, 11, 43, 45, 118, 149; authority of, 11, 38, 39, 58, 72, 74, 213; *Between Past and Future*, 245*n*6; disremembering of, 124; future and, viii, 2–3, 245*n*6; Global South and, 60; great cultural war and, 14–17; historiography, 20–24; Jabiri and, 17–18, 122, 125; Muslims and, 213; nahda and, 39; of North Africa, 128; postcolonial era, 4–10; Tarabishi and, 18–20; turath and, 2–3, 4, 35, 43–44, 121–22, 124; Zuriq on, 21
Peasants, 77, 150, 155
Persona, of connected critics, 60
Philosophy, 2, 6, 104; Arabic-Islamic, 26, 123, 129–30, 131, 133; *History of Western Philosophy*, 32; Islamic, 13, 26, 105–6, 123, 128–33; jurisprudence or Kalam, 128; Mashreq traditions, 128; poetry and, 186; *Toward a Scientific Philosophy*, 33
Poetry, 2, 5, 22, 25, 37, 116; Adonis and, 40; free, 75, 93; movements, 21, 51; philosophy and, 186; trends, 104
Poets, 2, 5, 40, 53, 175, 179
Political Islam (Islamic Right), 57, 64, 66, 116, 119–20, 201, 215
Political nostalgia, 80, 233*n*61
Politics, 2; of blame, viii; cultural war and, 16–17; decolonization and, 102; elite, x, 178; radicalism, 162; Tarabishi and, 148, 160–64
Popper, Karl, 222*n*2
Populations: Arab, 22, 211–12; peasants in Syria, 155
Port, in Haifa, 178
Postcolonial era: authenticity and, 9–10; end of, 4–10; Syria, 181; after World War II, 5, 6, 9, 210
Postcolonial project: beginning, viii–ix; failure of, ix, 14–15, 19, 92, 209–10; Jabiri and, 115–16
Postindependence era (1945–1970s), 1–2
Premade patterns (salaf), 131
Printing presses, 22, 46
Progress, theology of, 72
Psychology, 2, 153
Publishing houses, 46; of Arab Left, 192; in Beirut, 3, 49, 52, 54, 147, 150, 170, 173, 175; cultural war and, 216; Dar al-Adab, 48, 49, 68, 72, 75, 150, 173–75, 177, 180, 193; Dar al-Saqi, 193; Dar al-Taliah, 48, 49, 55, 68, 72, 75, 147, 173–74, 177, 180, 181, 185, 193; Dar Al-'Ilm Lilmalayyin, 175; Dar Riyyad al-Rayis, 193; social critics, 68, 72, 75

Qabbani, Nizar, 55, 175–76
Qadafi, Muammar, 77, 88
Qassim, Abed al-Karim, 163
Qawatli, Shukri al- (1891–1967), 162
Qur'an, 201–2, 203

Rabitat al-'Aqlaniyin al-'Arab (Arab Rationalist Association), 20, 183, 203
Radicalism, 70, 162, 182
Rationalist mechanism, 128
Rawdah café, 179
Rayis, Riyad al-, 51, 160
Razi, 46
Raziq, Ali Abed al-, 45
Reading, decolonizing, 130–31
Reformists, viii, 11, 205, 231*n*26
Regression, 170–71, 186
Religion, 65; colonial modernity and, 10; studies with Muslim and Christian students, 160. *See also* Christianity; Islam
Renewal of Arab thought (*Tajdid al-Fikr al-Arabi*) (Mahmud), 31, 33
Revolutionary culture, 137

Revolutionists, 1, 7, 59, 74, 231*n*26, 233*n*58
Rhetoric (balagha), 2
Rights, of women, 149, 205, 206
Risālah, Al- (journal), 12, 33
Roman Empire, 119
Ruhman, Taha Abed al-, 62
Rushdism, 127
Russell, Bertrand, 6, 32

Sabki, 46
Sadat, Anwar, 77
Safa, Ikhwan al-, 128, 217
Safadi, Muta, 51, 167, 170, 239*n*31
Said, Edward, 87
Salaf (premade patterns), 131
Samarkundi, 46
Sārter wal-Mārkissiya (Sartre and Marxism) (Tarabishi), 149
Sartre, Jean-Paul, 6, 33, 149, 177, 179, 193, 217, 242*n*84
Sartre and Marxism (*Sārter wal-Mārkissiya*) (Tarabishi), 149
Saudi Arabia, 37, 77–78, 177
Sayyab, Badr Shakir al- (b. 1926), 175
Sayyid, al-, 200
Sayyid, Jalal al-, 165
Sa'adah, Antun, 164
School of the Mu'tazila, 119
Scott, Joan, 206
Seale, Patrick, 155, 239*n*31
Secular Age, A (Taylor, C.), 10
Secularism, 199–200; Arab Left and, 63–64; connected critic with question of, 62, 63–67
Secular seeds in Islam ("Buthūr al-Almaniyya fi al-Islām") (Tarabishi), 198
Self-Critique After the Defeat (Azm), 70
Seventh day, The (al-*Yaūmal-Sābi'*) (journal), 62
Sharabi, Hisham, 68–69
Sharafi, Abed al-Majid al-, 46
Shararah, Wadah, 170
Sharī'a, 11, 15, 127, 204, 239*n*37, 245*n*47
Sharq al-Awsat, Al-, 242*n*79
Shatibi, al-, 128, 217
Shishikli, Adib al-, 159, 162, 239*n*35, 241*n*57
Shi'r (journal), 40, 71, 75, 124
Shrines, Sufi, 97
Shukri, Ghali, 41
Siba'i, Mutafa al-, 239*n*37
Six-Day (Arab-Israeli) War (1967), 4–7, 23, 66, 70, 147–49, 151, 187–88
Social critics, 20, 78, 85; Adeb and, 67–68, 70, 72, 74, 232*n*47; ambition of, 77; anticolonial nationalists and, 4, 16, 19, 127, 210; in Beirut, 16, 26, 125, 126, 181, 185, 212; in Cairo, 16, 26, 125, 126, 212; with colonialism, 210–11; connected and, 4, 25, 57–58, 222*n*8; cultural war and, 16–17, 18; Dar al-Adab and, 68, 72, 75, 193; Dar al-Taliah and, 72, 75, 193; defined, 69; eclipse of, 75–76; great cultural war and, 67–76; in historiography, 60–62; Marxism and, 19, 58; in Mashreq, 61, 68, 126; middle class, 67, 71, 155, 211, 212; Nasser and, 214; new class of, 212–13; publishing houses, 68, 72, 75; time of, 67–75; with traditionless society, 61; with translation, 176. *See also* Tarabishi, Jurj
Social fragmentation, vii, 163
Socialist critics, 68, 69
Social mobility, 77, 181, 212
Stagnation model, 23–24
Structural genocide, 11
Student enrollment, in Saudi Arabia, 177
Sudan, 178
Sufi: brotherhoods, 11; literature, 2; shrines, 97
Sufism, 45
Sulayman, Nabil, 179
Sultani, Ahmad, 104–5
Sunni: Islam, 200; Muslims in Syria, 167
Sykes-Picot, 164–65
Syria, 22, 52, 167, 228*n*58; Aleppo, 21, 27, 144, 149, 153–58, 160–61, 164, 165, 166, 179, 181, 212; Alexandretta-Antioch and, 166; Baath Party, 148; Bilad al-Sham, 166; coups d'état in, 7–8, 161–62, 163, 168,

Syria (*continued*)
239*n*35, 239*n*37; Damascus, 160–64, 212; Damascus University, 101, 103, 148, 157, 160–61, 176, 177, 239*n*37, 240*n*40, 240*n*47; education for children in, 157–60; Egypt and, 151; France in, 154–55, 161, 164–66; Homs, 155; intellectuals, 1, 160, 200; land ownership in, 240*n*44; middle class in, 150, 155–56; mortality rates of children, 155; Ottomon dominance over, 164; peasants in, 150, 155; postcolonial, 181; Tarabishi with modernity in mid-century, 150–53; United Arab Republic and, 70; University of Aleppo, 157
Syrian Ministry of Foreign Affairs, 175
Syrian Muslim Brotherhood, 239*n*37
Syrian Radio, 168

Taha, Abdalruhman, 87
Taḥarir, al- (newspaper), 103, 104
Taḥdīth al-Fikr al-Islamī (Sharafi), 46
Tahrir (newspaper), 100
Tahtawi, as translator, 241*n*74
Tajdid al-Fikr al-Arabi (Renewal of Arab thought) (Mahmud), 31, 33
Tamer, Zakariyya, 179
Tamhid, al- (Kalwadhani), 46
Tarabishi, Jurj (1939–2016), 17, 21, 145, 232*n*47; in Aleppo, 27, 144, 149, 153–56, 158, 160–61, 164; Arab-Israeli War and, 147, 148–49; Arkoun and, 244*n*29; Baath Party and, 148, 163, 164–69; in Beirut, 177–81; Christianity and, 156, 158; critique and, 186–87; cultural attitudes and, 185, 207; at Damascus University, 101, 148, 160–61, 176, 177, 239*n*37, 240*n*40, 240*n*47; Dar al-Adab and, 150, 177, 180; Dar al-Taliah and, 55, 143, 150, 175, 177, 180–81, 185; early schooling, 157–60; epistemological break and, 38; European modernity and, 144, 207; existentialism and, 101, 150, 176, 179, 185; French surrender in World War II and, 238*n*4; with Hafiz, 169–72; hegemony and, 184–89; under Hizb Al-Baʿth, 164–69; against honor killing, 168–69; Idris and, 180; influences, 152; intellectual output, 144; intellectuals with, 215; Jabiri and, 24, 101–2, 143, 144, 180–81, 184, 185, 187, 237*n*4; Lebanese Civil War and, 55, 150; Marx and, 243*n*7; Marxism and, 19, 172–73, 183; with moderate Islam, 200–4; with modernity in mid-century Syria, 150–53; nahda and, 189–93, 204–7; politics and, 148, 160–64; radicalism and, 182; Sharia and, 245*n*47; as social critic, 18–20, 26–27, 61, 68, 74, 85; with structure of mind, 169; on Syrian coup d'état, 239*n*35, 239*n*37; Syrian Radio and, 168; as translator, 33–34, 148, 149, 172–77, 179; turath and, 20, 32, 34, 71; with turath embraced, 193–95; with turath secularized, 198–200; with turath through contemporary eyes, 196–98
Tarablusi, Amjad, 223*n*32
Taylor, Charles, 10, 60
Thābit wal-Mutaḥaūil, al- (Continuity and change) (Adonis), 40, 41
Thaqāfa, Al- (journal), 33
Theology, 35, 37, 43, 72, 158, 191
Theory of Knowledge (Mahmud), 33
Third World, 13, 139, 185
Third Worldism, 3, 7, 18, 71
Tizini, Tayyib, 41, 51
Toward a Scientific Philosophy (Mahmud), 33
Trablisi, Fawaz, 178
Transference, 197
Transjordan, 165
Translations: *Adabuna wal Tarjamah*, 174; Adonis and, 40–41; books, 173, 241*n*74; cafés and, 178, 179; Dar al-Adab with, 173–74, 177; Dar al-Taliah with, 173–74, 175, 177; Egypt with, 174; Idris and, 174–76; objectives, 174; social critics with, 176; Tahtawi and, 241*n*74; Tarabishi and, 33–34, 148, 149, 172–77, 179; wages, 176, 177
Tunisia, 6, 9, 21, 22, 178, 212
Turath. *See* Cultural heritage

UN (United Nations), 163
UNFP (National Unity for the Popular Forces), 104
United Arab Republic (1958–1961), 70
United Nations (UN), 163
United States (U.S.), 52; Marines, 180; with Multi-National Force headquarters, 180
University of Aleppo, Syria, 157
Urbanization, emigration and, 212
U.S. *See* United States
ʿUthman, Bahij, 175

Veils, 24
Vietnam War, 192

Wages, translation, 176, 177
Walzer, Michael, 67, 73, 76, 83, 222*n*8
West Asia, 3
Western civilization, 2
Wiḥdah, al- (journal), 151, 185
Women, 185; Beirut and Cairo with educated, 178; at Damascus University, 240*n*40; with education and social mobility, 181; honor killing of, 168–69; *The Makings of an Intellectual Woman*, 34, 164, 176, 180; *Al-Mar'ah Fī al-Islām Wa-Fī al-Ḥaḍārah al-Gharbīyah*, 206; rights of, 149, 205, 206; as subordinate, 206; veils, 24
Women in modernity (*Mar'ah Fī al-Islām Wa-Fī al-Ḥaḍārah al-Gharbīyah, Al-*) (Bayhum, Jamil), 206
World War I, 154, 164, 165, 238*n*4
World War II (1943–1947), 149, 165, 166, 171, 215, 231*n*26; French resistance in, 238*n*4; modernity after, 37; social critics after, 61, 67, 68, 71, 74, 78; turath after, 2, 3, 39

Yasin, Abu ʿAli, 179, 192
Yasin, Sayyid, 50
Yaūmal-Sābiʿ, al- (The seventh day) (journal), 62
Years of harvest (*Ḥaṣād Al-Sinīn*) (Mahmud), 112–13

Zaid, Naser Hamid Abu, 42
Zaʿim, Husni al- (1897–1949), 161–62
Zayat, Ahmad Hassan al-, 33
Zayyat, Ahmad Hassan al-, 174
Zinaz, Hamid, 183
Zuriq, Constantin, 20–21

GPSR Authorized Representative: Easy Access System Europe, Mustamäe tee 50, 10621 Tallinn, Estonia, gpsr.requests@easproject.com

www.ingramcontent.com/pod-product-compliance
Lightning Source LLC
Chambersburg PA
CBHW022041290426
44109CB00014B/941
* 9 7 8 0 2 3 1 2 0 4 9 5 8 *